WALKING THE TIGHTROPE:
ETHICAL ISSUES FOR QUALITATIVE RESEARCHERS

Edited by Will C. van den Hoonaard

In recent years social science research projects have been required to undergo increasingly restrictive ethics testing. But are formal guidelines on ethics in research congruent with the aims and methods of inductive and qualitative research? In this collection of essays, sixteen Canadian, American, and British researchers address this question in a variety of contexts, drawing on their experiences in settings ranging from high schools and maternity homes to the unfolding 'virtual' terrain of cyberspace.

This volume challenges the 'biomedical' basis of policies on reviews of research ethics in the authors' respective countries. Guidelines were created, the authors argue, for quantitative work, and can actually impede or interrupt work that is not hypothesis-driven 'hard science.' Through examination of a number of topics – confidentiality, sensitive settings, questions of 'voice,' and the complex new challenges of internet research – the authors test the appropriateness of current protocols for ethical review.

Scholars and practitioners in social work, education, and sociology will find these essays useful and stimulating, as will teachers and students of qualitative research methods in fields as diverse as medicine, comparative literature, and business studies.

WILL C. VAN DEN HOONAARD is a professor of sociology at the University of New Brunswick.

EDITED BY WILL C. VAN DEN HOONAARD

Walking the Tightrope: Ethical Issues for Qualitative Researchers

UNIVERSITY OF TORONTO PRESS
Toronto Buffalo London

© University of Toronto Press Incorporated 2002
Toronto Buffalo London
Printed in Canada

ISBN 0-8020-3683-X (cloth)
ISBN 0-8020-8523-7 (paper)

Printed on acid-free paper

National Library of Canada Cataloguing in Publication

Main entry under title:

Walking the tightrope : ethical issues for qualitative researchers
/ edited by Will C. van den Hoonaard.

Includes bibliographical references and index.
ISBN 0-8020-3683-X (bound).   ISBN 0-8020-8523-7 (pbk.)

1. Qualitative research – Moral and ethical aspects.   2. Social
sciences – Methodology – Moral and ethical aspects.   I. Van den
Hoonaard, Will. C

H61.W275 2002   174'.93'0072   C2002-901576-6

University of Toronto Press acknowledges the financial assistance to
its publishing program of the Canada Council for the Arts and the
Ontario Arts Council.

University of Toronto Press acknowledges the financial support for
its publishing activities of the Government of Canada through the
Book Publishing Industry Development Program (BPIDP).

University of Toronto Press is grateful for a grant that it has received
from the Qualitative Analysis Conference, held at the University of
New Brunswick and St Thomas University, Fredericton, May 2000.

To Michael G. Rochester
and
Lynn Echevarria

Each friend represents a world in us
– Anaïs Nin

Contents

Acknowledgments

Any trip towards a publication involves many passengers whose participation in the enterprise needs praise and accolades. Since 1990 I have been presenting papers in Ontario and New Brunswick at the Canadian 'Qualitatives,' as they became affectionately known through the community of qualitative researchers, fieldworkers, and symbolic interactionists in North America and beyond, comprising at least two dozen disciplines. These meetings have heightened my moral sense about the ethical conduct of research. My first paper there dealt with the problems of written consent forms. The ideas of many of the sessions' participants have allowed me to explore more fully the meaning of doing work ethically. It was during these particular moments that research agencies began to articulate formal ethical guidelines.

I must admit that I had felt that the end of field research was just around the corner. The participants' enthusiasm about their work, however, coupled with the integrity of their research, led me to revise my initial fears and to do something about my own prediction. Hence I am grateful to all those participants who have contributed to a change of vision on my part.

There is no one to whom I owe more than my spouse and colleague Deborah K. van den Hoonaard. She offered a number of insights and constructive critiques, and her support remained undiminished in strength and fervour. There is no keener mind and heart. To her goes my unbounded gratitude for her help in every way – her struggles with her University Research Ethics Board have made this volume personally more urgent and, I hope, a boon to its readers.

This is also the time to thank the contributors for their timely submissions to this volume. I appreciate the discovery of new friends and colleagues, despite my badgering them about style and references – especially secondary sources.

There has been a considerable interest on the part of publishers in Canada, but it was Virgil D. Duff, executive director at the University of Toronto Press, who was the first to respond to the manuscript proposal. I also appreciate the extent of the work undertaken by the Press's reviewers and by John Parry, copy-editor.

Funding for publication came out of the proceeds of the Qualitative Analysis Conferences for 1999 and 2000, held in Fredericton at the University of New Brunswick and St Thomas University, respectively. I thank Dr Dan O'Brien, president of St Thomas University, for his instant support of these conferences, and Dr John McLaughlin, vice-president of the University of New Brunswick, for his keen interest in qualitative research. The Social Sciences and Humanities Research Council of Canada generously supported the conferences. More personally, I wish to thank Dr Hugh Lautard, my neighbour across the hall, for his enthusiastic and full support for my research and writing projects in general.

Will C. van den Hoonaard
Fredericton, October 2001

Contributors

Patricia A. Adler and Peter Adler received their PhDs in sociology from the University of California – San Diego. He is professor of sociology at the University of Denver, Colorado, which he chaired from 1987 to 1993. She is professor of sociology at the University of Colorado in Boulder. They have written and worked together for nearly thirty years. Their interests include qualitative methods, deviant behaviour, sociology of sport, sociology of children, and work and leisure. They have published numerous articles and a number of books, including *Momentum* (1981), *Wheeling and Dealing* (1985), *Membership Roles in Field Research* (1987), *Backboards and Blackboards* (1991), and *Peer Power* (1998). The Adlers served as editors of the *Journal of Contemporary Ethnography* (1986–94) and as founding editors of *Sociological Studies of Child Development* (1985–92).

David Altheide is Regents' Professor in the School of Justice Studies at Arizona State University. He received his PhD in sociology from the University of California – San Diego in 1974. Much of his work (10 books and 125 articles, and chapters) has focused on the role of mass media and information technology in social control. His most recent theoretical and methodological statements on the relevance of the mass media for sociological analysis are *An Ecology of Communication: Cultural Formats of Control* (1995) and *Qualitative Media Analysis* (1996). He has undertaken qualitative research in the nature and process of educational reform, with particular emphasis on school context and culture. His most recent book, *Creating Fear: News and the Construction of Crisis* (forthcoming), looks as the news media's constructions of a discourse of fear and the social consequences of this.

John M. Johnson received his PhD in sociology at the University of California – San Diego in 1973. He is professor of justice studies and director of graduate studies at Arizona State University. His interests include social theory, philosophy, domestic violence, qualitative methods, and crime. Of his eleven books, his first was *Doing Field Research* (1975), and his most recent, co-edited with Joseph Kotarba, is *Postmodern Existentialism* (2002). He is past president of the Society for the Study of Symbolic Interaction and was editor of the journal *Symbolic Interaction.*

Florence Kellner received her PhD from Rutgers University in New Jersey, having done her graduate research mainly through the Rutgers Center of Alcohol Studies. She is professor of sociology and anthropology at Carleton University in Ottawa, Ontario, and is also a faculty member of the Summer School of Alcohol Studies at Rutgers University. She has published in such journals as the *Canadian Journal of Sociology*, the *Canadian Review of Sociology and Anthropology*, the *Journal of Studies on Alcohol, Substance Use and Misuse*, and *Symbolic Interaction.* Recently she has worked with the Bureau of Statistics and Health and Social Services in the Yukon government and with Health Canada on alcohol and drug-related issues. She currently serves on Carleton University's Ethics Review Board.

Heather Kitchin received her PhD from Carleton University in Ottawa, Ontario. She is assistant professor of sociology at Acadia University in Wolfville, Nova Scotia. Her interests include qualitative methods, addiction studies, women's studies, sociology of deviance, and criminology. Her current research includes examining availability of addiction programs in provincial correctional institutions in Canada and phenomenological analyses of residents' adoption of and/or resistance to such programs.

Erin Mills is a doctoral student in the Department of Sociology at Carleton University in Ottawa, Ontario. Her research interests include women and work and qualitative research methods, particularly narrative accounts and life histories. Her PhD dissertation will explore the social organization of the dental office as a place of work and how dentists, dental workers, and patients experience dental work on a day-to-day basis. While completing her studies, she worked as a dental assistant for several years.

Gillian Nichol has over twenty years of private-sector experience facilitating client-centred and employee-driven programs of organizational change. She received her BSc and MSW from the University of Toronto, where she is a PhD candidate with the Faculty of Social Work. She is a co-ordinator of centre development with the Association of Ontario Health Centres and a part-time health promoter with the Anne Johnston Health Station in Toronto. Her research interests include adoption and child and family policy, the role of social work in organizational change, and health-sector systems of accreditation.

Patrick O'Neill received his PhD from Yale University. He is professor of psychology at Acadia University in Nova Scotia. He has two major areas of scholarship – community psychology, for which he wrote *Community Consultation* (1982) with Edison J. Trickett, and ethical decision making, as represented by *Negotiating Consent in Psychotherapy* (1998). He has been a member of the Committee on Ethics of the Canadian Psychological Association since 1988 and served on the Academic Freedom and Tenure Committee of the Canadian Association of University Teachers for nine years, including three years as chair.

Melanie Pearce is a postgraduate research student in the Institute for the Study of Genetics, Biorisk, and Society at the University of Nottingham in England. She received her MA in 1999 and is due to complete her PhD on genetic counselling in October 2002. She is also a practising counsellor in the private and voluntary sectors, with a particular focus on survivors of rape and sexual abuse. Her interests include medical sociology, genetics and society, genetic counselling, conversation analysis, ethics in health-related research, childhood abuse, and the history, theory, and practice of psychotherapeutic and pastoral counselling.

Linda Snyder has a PhD from Wilfrid Laurier University in Waterloo, Ontario. She is assistant professor of social work at Renison College, University of Waterloo. Her research interests include community organization; poverty issues, especially among women; diversity and its implications for social work practice; and Canadian–Latin American comparative studies. Her dissertation examined women's employment initiatives as a means of addressing poverty in Canada and Chile. She has published in *Canadian Social Work Review* and has a chapter in Anne Westhues's forthcoming edition of *Social Policy in Canada.*

Mary Stratton is a PhD candidate in the Department of Sociology and Anthropology at Carleton University in Ottawa, Ontario. She is research co-ordinator at the Canadian Forum on Civil Justice in Edmonton,

Alberta. Her interests include collaborative approaches to research and community development, adolescents' experiences of the education system, and the role of informal learning in gaining and applying new knowledge. Her collaborative research has led to a recent co-written article in *Interchange* and a chapter in a book (currently under review) of case studies on informal learning.

S. Anthony Thompson is completing his interdisciplinary doctoral studies in the Faculty of Education at the University of British Columbia (UBC) in Vancouver. He trained extensively in behaviour-analytic psychology at St Mary's University in Halifax, Nova Scotia, and worked as a behaviour therapist for people with autism and other developmental disabilities. While in UBC's Educational Psychology and Special Education Department, he took a course on student motivation and was introduced to socio-cultural theory. Now he is keenly interested in queer theory, disability theory, curriculum theory and people with developmental disabilities, feminist epistemologies, and qualitative methods. The 'apparent' paradigmatic clash between 'special education' and socio-cultural theory underpins most of his current work. He has published in the *International Journal of Disability, Development and Education* (an article written with Mary Bryson and Suzanne deCastell), and *JASH* (*Journal of the Association for Persons with Severe Handicaps*).

Michael Ungar received his PhD from Wilfrid Laurier Unversity in Waterloo, Ontario. As both a social worker and a marriage and family therapist, he specializes in child and family mental health. He is an associate professor at the Maritime School of Social Work at Dalhousie University in Halifax, Nova Scotia. His research interests include the social construction of resilience, family therapy interventions, and qualitative research methods. His writing and clinical work have focused on relating research with high-risk populations to case management and treatment of hard-to-reach 'problem' individuals. He has written and spoken on resilience, high-risk youths and families, and non-pathologizing models of intervention in family therapy, contributing to *Adolescence, Child and Youth Care Forum*, and the *Journal of Strategic Therapies*. He is also a member of the Child Welfare League of Canada's National Consultation Centre and provides clinical support to corrections and providers of mental health care throughout the Maritimes.

Will C. van den Hoonaard received his PhD from the University of Manchester in England. He is professor of sociology at the University of

New Brunswick in Fredericton. His interests include qualitative methods, social movements, ethnic relations, gender, Baha'i studies, and the social organization of cartography. He has published or presented some 130 papers. His books include *Silent Ethnicity: The Dutch of New Brunswick* (1991), *Reluctant Pioneers: Constraints and Opportunities in an Icelandic Fishing Community* (1992), *The Origins of the Baha'i Community of Canada, 1898–1948* (1996), and *Working with Sensitizing Concepts: Analytical Field Research* (1997). He serves on an adjudication committee of the Social Sciences and Humanities Research Council of Canada and on the Interagency Panel on Research Ethics.

Barbara Waruszynski in 1990 received an MA in sociology from Concordia University in Montreal, specializing in organizational stress in policing. In 1991 and 1992, she was a management consultant and researcher in Ottawa. She was project manager and researcher for a nation-wide study of pharmacists' interventions in prescriptions and over-the-counter medications. For the past six years she has been a defence scientist with Defence Research and Development Canada.

Merlinda Weinberg is pursuing a PhD in sociology and equity studies in the Education Department of the Ontario Institute for Studies in Education (University of Toronto). Her research interests include qualitative methods, ethics in social work and research methods, gender, feminist postmodern and critical social work theory, and clinical social work practice with young single mothers. She has published in the anthology *Running for Their Lives* (2000), edited by Sherrie Inness, and written for *Resources for Feminist Research*.

WALKING THE TIGHTROPE:
ETHICAL ISSUES FOR QUALITATIVE RESEARCHERS

Introduction:
Ethical Norming and
Qualitative Research

WILL C. VAN DEN HOONAARD

There is a paradoxical process at work today among qualitative research-ers when it comes to formal research ethics. While they largely reject the prevailing, mainly biomedical, approach of the ethics review of research, they are opening up new perspectives and sensibilities about the ethical dimensions of their own work. This collection reflects the tension be-tween the demands of formal ethics review and qualitative research as a counterpoint. The former, qualitative researchers believe, erodes or hampers the thrust and purpose of their research because current ethical research standards are designed in terms of issues relevant to quantitative, hypothesis-driven research.

Ethics review, as a broad-based approach to conducting scientific re-search, emerged from the aftermath of the horrors of the Second World War, when Nazi-sponsored medical experiments furthered macabre so-cial aims (Charbonneau, 1984: 20). The Nuremberg Code tried to fore-stall the use of such experiments by codifying viable, ethical guidelines for medical, scientific, and social research, with particular emphasis on informed consent. While the code remained an ethical hallmark, the history of scientific research would take at least another fifty years to catch up to its principles. Scientific experimentation with human sub-jects ranged from exposing soldiers to atomic blasts (Welsome, 1999), through imposing medical procedures on prisoners or forensic in-patients,[1] to experimentation with drugs, whether LSD, DepoProvera,[2] or drugs near market entry.

When the latent effects of these experiments became manifest – often twenty or thirty years later – and with the subsequent rise of lawsuits, the public and governments became acutely aware of the ethical implica-tions of medical research and, indeed, of all research. First through professional societies and then more vigorously through the state, ethical guidelines became explicit. During the latter years of this evolution of ethical 'norming' in Canada – i.e., in the early 1990s – the Medical Research Council of Canada (MRC), the Natural Science and Engineering Council of Canada (NSERC), and the Social Sciences and Humanities Research Council of Canada (SSHRC) started the process in 1994 of developing the *Tri-Council Policy Statement: Ethical Conduct for Research Involving Humans* (MRC, NSERC, and SSHRC, 1998d). Political authorities in many other Western countries established similar policies. Bolstered by legal enforcement, formal ethics review took on a legitimacy that has spread across the world, including to the Third World, where researchers are more likely to abandon traditional moral principles in favour of the ethics codes in which they were trained in the West (Charbonneau, 1984: 21). Similarly, social research on Canada's north must undergo a process of ethics review that seems more appropriate for the hard sciences than for the social sciences. For the stated purpose of protecting Inuit culture from researchers, northern granting bodies rely on a Western model of ethics review, reinforcing the very research approach that is being rejected as Euro-centric. The setting up of such non-Western review bodies[3] still echoes the Western, deductive template. Structurally, these policies produce a dislocation of the qualitative-research enterprise.

Florence Kellner (chapter 2 in this volume) avers that implementation of an ethics code may 'bring natural science even closer to us than it has been before the new policy came into effect.' The 'gold standard' for ethics review might in fact be tainted because of its blindness to the reality of qualitative research. For example, the word 'subject' is favoured over 'research participant' – a term that finds more resonance among qualitative researchers because 'subject' has a pejorative connotation. For while one may occupy the position of 'researcher,' there is a far greater sense of collaboration with interviewees in qualitative research than is customary in, for example, survey research. The *Tri-Council Policy Statement* extends to judging the adequacy of the research design itself. It speaks of maintaining a 'common standard' of research and scrutinizes applications on the basis of various levels of harm that might be inflicted on research subjects. It refers to research 'protocols' – a term that makes eminent sense to medical researchers, but is quite unfamiliar among qualitative researchers, who see their work in a more collaborative sense.

Patricia A. Adler and Peter Adler (chapter 3) write about the unintended consequences of institutional review boards (IRBs) in the United States, whose original aim was to protect human subjects, but that now 'represent a major bane and obstacle to active researchers.' The inevitability of involving university lawyers and the police in reviewing research ethics is all too clear: the process becomes one about protecting institutions, fearful of lawsuits. If signed forms of consent are used for legal purposes, might not the interviewees guess that such forms are, after all, designed to protect a body awarding research grants or some other institution, rather than them? Would not such an interpretation encourage cynicism among participants and researchers? Melanie Pearce (chapter 4) expresses her discouragement at the loss of precious time in her all too-short PhD program when her ethics committee absorbed so much of that time. It is when we differentiate the spheres of ethics, according to John M. Johnson and David L. Altheide (chapter 5), that we can solve the issues of control and policing. Research ethics is an elephant, but to make the process manageable, Johnson and Atlheide propose five realms – personal, research, intellectual, professional, and corporate ethics.

Universities and research-granting bodies, without considering the diversity of research paradigms, may inadvertently generate a campaign that sustains scholarly outrage about methods on the margins. Quantitative researchers demand that qualitative research issues be rephrased in the language of the former – an unsettling form of colonization. Biomedical and legal authorities assert their dominance and define the shape of the equivalent of a moral panic (Cohen, 1972), in the face of which the community of qualitative researchers must exert more effort to counter the social control exercised by these traditional authorities. Young or novice scholars in qualitative research, however, will feel the most deleterious effects It refers to qualitative research by research ethics boards (REBs) because they are vulnerable and are usually not well placed in the social organization of research to resist ethical norming. The unintended influence of formal ethics review of qualitative research is not a private problem; rather it is the social organization of ethics review itself that needs to be considered.

The consternation that has seized all field researchers has a paralysing effect on the climate of their research. A recent editorial in *ASA Footnotes* (Levine, 2001) bemoans the unintended actions of IRBs when they are interpreting narrowly U.S. federal guidelines for the protection of human subjects. Thus, given the strictures imposed by such boards in Canada, the United States, and England, there is a vital need to 'let our voices be heard' (Levine, 2001: 2) to demonstrate that social scientists in general, and qualitative researchers in particular, are no less concerned about ethics than their colleagues in other fields, but also claim that any judgment of their work in terms of medical and natural-science research is inappropriate and disturbing.

What we therefore need is a collection of papers that not only more clearly articulates the ethics of field research, but describes the problematic nature of formal ethics review based on hypothesis and variable-driven research. The origins of these hitherto-unpublished papers are three conferences – namely, the Qualitative Analysis Conferences (the 'Canadian Qualitatives'), held in May 1999 and May 2000, and the Annual Meetings of the Pacific Sociological Association, in March 2000. The former two gatherings took place in Fredericton at the University of New Brunswick and St Thomas University, respectively, and the latter in San Diego, California. Each year, qualitative researchers have been bringing similarly discouraging stories to the attention of their colleagues. In 1999, the issue became so compelling that they organized an impromptu session at the Canadian Qualitatives. Once word got out that a volume was in preparation, I received, as editor, several more papers. The eagerness of all these researchers to explain their frustrations with REBs, as well as their enthusiasm to set out ethical dilemmas and solutions in qualitative research, convinced me that the volume is long overdue.

The collection is comprehensive because it examines the influence of formal ethics review for research in the context of theory, confidentiality, sensitive settings, and voice. The chapters represent myriad social settings: women's employment initiatives, development of women artisans (6), a maternity home (7), people with developmental disabilities (8), the career of a dental assistant (9), high-school students (10), an alternative academic conference (11), and cyberspace (12, 13). All these settings, however, are but the outer trimmings of the heart of doing inductive or qualitative research with the highest ethical standards in mind.

The title of the volume – *Walking the Tightrope* – can apply to both the painful process of ethical review of qualitative research and to the very process of qualitative research. It reflects the present-day debate about the evolution of ethics among qualitative researchers. It takes little imagination to realize that both external and internal contexts shape this debate. Ethical review of research, so prevalent now in universities and other research settings, constitutes the external context; and the rising awareness and the moral deliberations among qualitative researchers set the parameters for the internal context. Veteran researchers generally spearhead debates about the external context, while novices are plunging into the internal dimensions, focusing on increasing the ethical dimensions of their work.

Fortunately, qualitative researchers do not stand alone in this regard. Michael Ungar and Gillian Nichol (chapter 11 in this volume), talk about the sense of community and its relationship to ethics and research and about how the interests of all researchers at a given conference also weave a seamless web among all participants, allowing for ethical reflection about research. They refer explicitly to another, wider community – the wider world of researchers themselves. They discuss other social workers as researchers who 'can account for the aspirations of practitioners while authenticating the knowledge claims of those with whom they work.' They speak graphically of consummating 'a relationship with an emancipatory consciousness.' To that end, they believe that research that 'disregards its consumers must be judged ethically suspect.'

For qualitative researchers, the external context raises the issues of anonymity and confidentiality, the use of (signed) consent forms, and the tendency of REBs to exaggerate risk and harm. The internal context speaks more specifically to the nature of the research question in qualitative research, the potentially heterogeneous (and sometimes vulnerable) populations researched, and the intermeshing of the biographies of the researched and of the researcher (the issue of 'voice').

The External Context

That veteran scholars are taking to task the very foundation of the ethics review of research reflects in part the social organization of the world of scholars. Having proven themselves in battle, so to speak, having the benefit of the long perspective, and, not least, having received tenured positions, they can afford to take a critical stance. In doing so, they also define anew what qualitative research is supposed to do, in counterpoint to formal ethics review.

Ensuring Anonymity and Confidentiality

Given reliance on the biomedical model of research, aided by legal advice, the *Tri-Council Policy Statement* (MRC et al., 1998d) emphasizes anonymity and confidentiality. Legal enactments in Canada and the United States give the right of maintaining confidentiality (and anonymity) generally only to physicians, lawyers, priests, ministers, rabbis, and one's spouse. Social researchers in the United States, however, cannot invoke promises of confidentiality as a 'scholar's privilege,' as attested in 1993 in a court case involving a doctoral student at Washington University, whom the courts asked to surrender his field data in connection with his research on a radical animal-rights group (Comarow, 1993: A44). Some, like Murray Comarow (1993), a lawyer and former federal official in the United States, suggest that sociologists ought to be prepared to spend time in prison if they wish to follow through on their promises of anonymity to their sources and of the confidentiality of their research data when faced with subpoenas or court orders – hardly an inducement to conduct field research!

There has so far been only one such case in Canada. A court in 1994 asked a graduate student, Russel Ogden, in criminology at Simon Fraser University, who was researching assisted suicides in cases of people with HIV, to divulge confidential information in a matter involving a death (Lowman and Palys, 1998: 6).[4] The student defended his refusal, succeeding only after a long struggle without the aid of the university[5] REB. By intertwining ethical and legal issues that emphasize institutional liability over ethics, an REB leaves researchers 'to twist and turn in the wind when they take seriously the responsibility to protect research participants from harm ... [by which the university] abrogates its obligation to create an environment in which researchers can collect and publicly disseminate information about all aspects of society' (Lowman and Palys, 1998: 7).

In other ways, too, emerging ethics guidelines reaffirm the quantitative model of research. While Heather MacDonald, a PhD candidate in nursing at the University of Manchester, was permitted to use a consent form that she, rather than the research participants, signed, she struggled with a move in the United Kingdom to store qualitative data for future review or for secondary analysis (MacDonald, 1999): 'To gain access in one area I had to agree to have my data – and I mean transcripts – available for review for ten years. I had great difficulty with this since I am interviewing a vulnerable group and have taken great pains to provide anonymity.'

A number of the contributors to this volume express an ethical awareness of their work, raising it to a new moral height. Using Mary Poppins's often-cited quote about 'pie-crust promises,' several authors suggest that promises of confidentiality are easier to make than to keep. For Linda Snyder (chapter 6), the need to be open with data – an eminently sensible objective for researchers – may violate the promise of confidentiality. It is easy for quantitative researchers to ensure anonymity and confidentiality – after all, their data are quite remote from the people whom they have studied – but Snyder points to the pitfalls when confidentiality and closeness to the research setting are inherently conflictual.

Merlinda Weinberg begins her chapter (7) by claiming that 'no research proceeds without ethical dilemmas.' This is a given. What the researcher must do, according to her, is to prioritize these dilemmas. Which ethical obligations carry the most weight? The answer is not easy. A research project is the fulcrum of the interests of many 'participants,' from (in her case) members of REBs, through administrators of a maternity home, to pregnant teenagers.

The final essays in this volume ask whether anonymity can be an issue in cyberspace. Barbara Waruszynski (chapter 12) addresses the dilemmas of a specific research design on the internet: what critical, ethical issues do we face when we solicit information or data from specific research participants on the internet? She sketches the ethical challenges that every researcher must face. Heather A. Kitchin (chapter 13) offers a perspective about research in cyberspace that seems to challenge our ethical sensibilities. On reflection, we see that she has a point: we should treat the texts in cyberspace just as we would derive research data from such sources as magazines and newspapers. People who have submitted texts to Usenet newsgroups, including listservs, chatrooms, newsgroups, and similar cyber forms of communication, know and expect that their material, however intimate sometimes and however self-blemishing, is now publicly available and as such, according to the *Tri-Council Policy Statement* (MRC et al., 1998d), exempt from formal REB approval. Naturally, data sought from specific individuals for a research project should not be considered to be in the same public domain.

Using (Signed) Forms of Consent

Research ethics, as it currently stands, is developed and used in the context of a liberal democratic tradition that emphasizes individual rights and freedoms. The tradition of individualism has become a problem in sociological research for several reasons. It may be quite foreign to other cultures where collectivism prevails and where individual rights are defined by the collectivity. In such cases, the seeking of individual consent may be an affront to the larger group. The idea of informed consent of the individual – described by Charbonneau (1984: 20) as the '*cornerstone of all Western ethical codes*' – is extremely difficult to implement vis-à-vis groups living on the margins of society. Aside from problems of illiteracy, the difficulties multiply as one investigates not only those whose lives are touched by social problems, but also areas of secrecy, whether of marginal or even elite groups. It is ironic that just as society is devoting more resources to 'applied' research to solve problems, the legal emphasis on signed consent undermines the study of these problems.

The use of signed consent forms is one of the most highly contested areas for qualitative researchers. It might be easy for REBs to insist on use of the signed form of consent in all research involving interviewees, but the situation is complex and requires detailed understanding of ethnographic field research. Patrick O'Neill (chapter 1) writes about the 'gatekeeping' functions of REBs in the light of the problematic nature of signed informed consent in qualitative research.

An insistence on using such forms may sometimes destroy natural anonymity. Whereas it would have been possible in the past to retain the full anonymity of those being interviewed, it is now necessary to acquire a name and signature. One can imagine many instances where the insistence on signed consent may be unwise or tactless. Using consent forms in studies of street-corner people, poachers, hookers, fishers, drug users, professional thieves, and the homeless would simply elicit an angry response. The difficulty persists even vis-à-vis those who occupy positions of power and prestige.

Ethnographic research, in the light of its purpose, is conducted by 'participant observation.' A researcher of this methodological tradition endeavours to understand the whole subculture that surrounds the 'subjects.' To do so, he or she endeavours to leave the culture intact. This involves a process whereby the researcher respects that culture and effects the least possible intrusion. He or she must be careful not to aggressively assert his or her rights or views. The introduction of a signed consent form violates the very essence of ethnographic research, because human 'subjects' would regard the requirement of such a form as *coercive*. Shulamit Reinharz (1993: 78) writes eloquently about the problematic nature of using coercive formal statements, on official university letterhead, about the 'importance' of doing the research. Its inappropriateness is further highlighted by the fact that ethnographic research does not entail experimentation. Such experimentation could, for example, involve the placement of 'surface electrodes,'[5] or, not infrequently, hidden tapes, whereby subjects are told one thing – but not the desired research plans. This approach to research is quite alien to ethnographic research. In the case of interviews, the datum rests within those interviews, consistent with the purpose of the research's being made clear to interviewees.[6]

In the experience of qualitative researchers, requiring signed consent may prevent some individuals from participating in research. A colleague of a researcher in one of Fredericton's universities, though eager to take part in a research project, could not do so because she refused to sign such a form (Anonymous A, 2000). A nurse and sociologist who is interviewing people in home-care situations reports:

> I gave each of them [caregiver and the older person] a copy of the consent form and asked them to review it and then I would answer whatever questions they had. Both Mrs. McK [caregiver] and George [older person] read it carefully (took time). George says that he has a question for me about the form ... He looks at me rather thoughtfully and asks, 'What difference will it make whether I sign it or not?' Thinking he might be having second thoughts about my being there for the study, I reminded him that he could ask me to leave his home if he didn't want to participate. 'No, you don't understand my question,' he replies. 'Will you do anything differently here this morning if I sign the form than if I don't sign it?' I can see that he is not concerned about my being there but seems to be questioning the need for his signature. I've just driven for 45–50 minutes to be at this home. If he's not objecting to my being there and knows why I am there, would I actually have to leave if he doesn't sign? These thoughts are racing through my head. While I'm thinking about this, George leans over and signs the consent. I still have another form for George to sign, the consent for the follow-up interview with the family caregiver. (Anonymous B, 2000)

Even if no signed form is needed (as in a participant-observation study) some of the solutions to this 'dilemma' proposed by ethics committees are just plain silly. For example, a member of a departmental ethics committee told a graduate student to turn her face the other way when she was doing participant observation in a group that had any human subjects who did not explicitly consent to the research. Such circumspect behaviour would create problems and cast doubt among the subjects about their own behaviour and beliefs. Use of signed consent could break a personal, friendly bond. Other interviewees will regard it as disloyal on the part of the researcher.

This dilemma may occur even though participants know that one is a researcher in advance of any project. A graduate student doing fieldwork in Nunavut had obtained ethics approval from her department, and her proposal was passed by the Nunavut Council on Research. Both groups insisted that she use consent forms, which 'seemed to ferment the stereotype of a researcher from outside as self-centered' (Anonymous C, 1999). In addition to having a signed consent form and a mission statement, the student had to repeat the process for the interpreter, who also had to receive an 'Interpreter Confidentiality' form. Each sheet was not only drawn up in two languages, but copies were made for all parties involved, including research agencies – a total of twenty-two sheets of paper had to be available and signed before the interview could begin. In the words of the researcher: 'The woman looked at all of the papers, looked at the consent form, and refused to sign it, stating that her daughter had told her not to sign anything. I had to respect that ... I wondered just how different the interview might have gone had I not felt the need to be so formal with her. When I left she refused to even keep the (unsigned) participant consent form ... Every other interview started with a confusing first five minutes and the interviewees would say, 'whatever,' whenever she would explain why she had all of these forms. The researcher concluded that the 'consent forms were obtrusive and established an atmosphere of formality and mistrust' (Anonymous C, 1999).

Signed consent forms become particularly problematic in research on sensitive topics. Some researchers show ingenuity. Gracy Getty, who researches men who have sex with men, reports a method of allowing interviewees to sign the form with a code that they had made up. 'Few of them would have been willing to have their name attached even to a consent form that was kept separate from the tapes, etc.' (Getty, 1999).

Exaggerating Harm and Risk

REBs can overstate risks. In my university, the first topic that appears after one gives a summary of one's research in an ethics-review application form is risk in research. In fact, about one-third of the questions are directed towards risk in the research setting. Yet in a study of teenaged girls, for example, where the research topic invited disclosure of experiences 'that require[d] professional follow-up or intervention,' the researchers found that 'the adolescent girls appreciated the opportunity to discuss their experiences and concerns with interested adults who inhabit a world outside their everyday realm of parents and school' (Anonymous D, 2000: 6). Social researchers such as these, delving into emotive topics, have not found interviews cascading into the sort of troubled waters that require work by therapists. It would be helpful to have phone numbers or people available, but professional interviews are usually quite trouble-free.

Many researchers are painfully aware that research may generate unintended results, but they also know that one cannot always predict those outcomes. While there is no perfect vision in that regard, some unintended results have proven beneficial, despite the perceived risks. I refer the reader to a mapping expedition among the Aboriginals in Australia in the 1930s, organized by Adelaide's Board for Anthropological Research in the Warburton Range. The survey involved measuring and photographing individuals, eliciting their genealogies, drawing blood and hair samples, and even making plaster casts of part or of their whole bodies. As Woodward and Lewis point out (1998: 389), even though politicians and ethicists criticized the survey, the work was 'done systematically and with care,' later allowing Aboriginals to find out 'more about their family histories, their ancestry, and their land-based affiliations' (389).

While the external context is important in ethical research, qualitative researchers have a sanguine and more nuanced view of these ethical matters. There are also ethical dimensions that define the internal context of qualitative research but are hardly recognized as such by REBs.

The Internal Context

The features that are salient for qualitative researchers and relate to ethics involve developing the research question, the likely heterogeneity (and sometime vulnerability) of the researched population, and 'voice.'

Developing the Research Question

Every research project must be guided by a relevant or appropriate research question. While for many types of research such a question will emerge from a review of the literature or from some practical issue, ethnographic research may adopt a different position. Qualitative researchers find REBs' insistence on knowing the exact questions being put to interviewees impossible to fulfil. The nature and direction of questions in in-depth interviews tend to be dictated by the interviewee, not by the researcher, who instead defines the broader research dimensions.

Usually, the specific research question emerges only *after* a series of in-depth interviews. Typically, a review of the literature comes at the end of the research process. According to Anselm Strauss, 'The analysis of these [ethnographic] data begins (in our style of research) with the very first, second, or third interview or after the first day or two of fieldwork ... It follows also that the next interviews and observations become informed by analytic questions and hypotheses about categories and their relationships. This guidance becomes increasingly explicit as the analysis of new data continues' (Strauss, 1987: 27).

Alternatively, what may have seemed important during the initial stages becomes marginal in the course of the research, and other areas open up for study. Scientists who are used to stating formal hypotheses and practising deductive reasoning may be appalled at such an approach. Nevertheless, ethnographic research has yielded significant insights, because of its open, inductive approach.

Heterogeneity (and Vulnerability) of the Researched Population

The researcher needs to be open to the fact that a setting may have a heterogeneity of research participants that will defy a common ethical template. In her study of the sex trade, Hancock (1999), like others, urges the recognition of such heterogeneity. Even though she studied one social setting – namely, the health and safety experiences of women living in the sex-trade subculture – her method included both observation of and interviews with street prostitutes, exotic dancers, body-rub attendants, and escorts. Research ethics has differing implications for each group, requiring sensitivity on the part of the researcher.

S. Anthony Thompson, a contributor to this volume, has gained a solid reputation for working with people with developmental disabilities and writes from that experience in chapter 8. The ethical dimensions in his research do not conform to the expectations of normative ethics review. Such populations are 'vulnerable' (although in some cases such a judgment cannot stand the test of reality), but sometimes research does not fulfil participants' expectations of friendship, and they share 'too much' with the researcher. The waters get muddier (from an outsider's perspective) when the researcher deals with 'voluntariness' and institutionalization.

'Voice'

As qualitative researchers may immerse themselves in the setting that they are studying, the boundaries between them and the community can become 'blurred' (Pollack, 1999). Pollack notes in her study on women in prisons that the 'notion of the self as a research influence is an important aspect of qualitative research that deserves further exploration.' For her, the ethical issues of research centre around 'the responsibility of the researcher to her/his subjects when one disturbs the equilibrium of a community.' Increasingly, social researchers have come to understand the unmitigated nature of deductive approaches, because in recording their findings, deductive researchers amplify their own voice rather than that of the research participants. Qualitative researchers are increasingly recognizing the struggle to find the right balance between the autobiography of the researcher and the biography of the participants (Chahal, 2000).

The chapters in this volume by Erin Mills (9), Mary Stratton (10), and Michael Ungar and Gillian Nichol (11) reinforce the current debate among qualitative researchers about the issue of 'voice' – a debate about which members of some REBs are painfully unaware. Is it ethical to replace the interviewee's voice with the researcher's voice? Is it more honest to reproduce, *ad verbatim,* the whole transcribed text in a publication, even without commentary? Or, is that carrying things too far? Erin Mills (chapter 9), realizes her dilemma when Hazel the dental assistant just does not come forth with a narrative that conforms to the researcher's expectations. Hazel's voice is not about exploitation and 'internal political battles and feuds,' but about a 'social bit and fun night' during the executive meetings. Was Hazel politically naïve? Or was Mills, the researcher, ideologically naïve?

Mary Stratton(chapter 10) echoes the experiences of naïveté. Participatory action research (PAR) embodies the noble idea of engaging everyone in social action and social change. But this idea assumes a democracy of sorts in the researched social setting that allows for full participation. What Stratton found instead was the 'trap of pseudo democracy.' Were her ethical obligations to the PAR model of research compromised? Did she promise too much to her research participants? She avers that such a situation is no reason 'to abandon any attempt to give such [total] communities a research voice.' Who will break the barriers surrounding total institutions to 'release the voices of the captive populations,' if not qualitative researchers?

All the essays constitute an expression of the two processes that both haunt and edify qualitative researchers: the often-inappropriate application of codes of ethics designed for other types of research and the search for a higher level of ethical sensitivity by qualitative researchers. Gnashing teeth and grasping the ethical dimensions of research are difficult to do at the same time.

However, this volume has, I believe, a number of strengths. First, it casts the ethical parameters of qualitative research in a larger, theoretical perspective. Second, each author brings to bear his or her experience in the domain. Third, the volume offers a practical guide to committees and agencies making decisions about the ethics of qualitative research.

The contributors to the volume come from the United Kingdom, Canada, and the United States and are generally quite new to the field and offer a more 'cutting edge' view of ethics in field research than is usual in textbooks on method. The range of topics and illustrations is broad enough to be applicable to most other instances of ethics in field research. The varied disciplines of the authors are an added bonus – education, psychology, social work, and sociology.

The principal users of this volume, I venture to claim, would be graduate students and faculty members, as well as the increasing number of policy makers who engage in qualitative research and members of REBs who wish to take better stock of the ethical potential of qualitative research. The volume should attract the attention of university and research libraries, course instructors, and, in particular, the many students (and members of faculty) who must, through thesis and grant proposals, implore REBs to reconsider the needs of qualitative researchers.

I invite the reader to consult the concluding chapter if he or she is interested in knowing how REBs can consider proposals for qualitative research more fairly.

Notes

Elements of this essay appeared in van den Hoonaard (2001). I owe a number of these observations to several readers of a draft of this Introduction, especially Mary Stratton, Deborah K. van den Hoonaard, Heather Kitchin, and Barbara Waruszynski.

1 Regehr, Edward, and Bradford 2000 cite the case of a forensic in-patient who was the subject of research without consent. The research resulted in a scale that was later used to deny his release.
2 Depo-Provera is a three-month injection for birth control, used since 1967 on 2 million women in 80 countries, but the drug had not yet been approved by the FDA (Charbonneau, 1984: 20).
3 The United Nations Conference on Science and Technology, held in Vienna in 1979, recommended such medical councils, followed by a similar suggestion from the World Health Organization (Charbonneau, 1984: 21).
4 The case was brought against a graduate student; there are striking parallels with other cases brought against less powerful members of professional groups.
5 'Consent Form – Digital Myoelectric Controls Study,' provided to the author by the Ethics Review Committee of the University of New Brunswick, 30 October 1989.
6 One researcher (Anonymous A) in a Florida retirement community just could not visualize pulling out a consent form from her bathing suit as she was chatting with community residents while standing around in the pool.

1

Good Intentions and Awkward Outcomes: Ethical Gatekeeping in Field Research

PATRICK O'NEILL

Researchers in the biological, medical, and social sciences have done controversial research that offends ethical sensibilities. The most extreme cases have been well publicized, such as the Tuskegee study on syphilis (United States Public Health Service, 1973) and other research that put patients at risk (Barber, 1976); psychologists may think of Milgram's obedience study (Baumrind, 1964; Milgram, 1963), while sociologists may think of studies of homosexual encounters in public places (Humphreys, 1970; Von Hoffman, 1970).

In the light of the publicity generated by such work, it is not surprising that funding agencies and other regulators have demanded that the public be safeguarded. Nevertheless the constraints that some have imposed are sometimes misguided and may limit socially important research (O'Neill, 1998). Qualitative researchers may be particularly vulnerable.

This essay focuses on research in socially sensitive areas. I consider a number of related issues that, taken together, pose a problem for such research: informed consent; guarantees of confidentiality; inability to predict pressure to break confidentiality and the researcher's response to such pressure; and the protocols of ethics gatekeepers, which may make research impossible. The resulting dilemmas involve researchers, research ethics boards, universities, and the legal system. The first part of this chapter looks at three cases of research complicated by a requirement of knowing in advance. The second part offers possible solution for researchers, for REBs, and for universities.

Knowing in Advance

Ethics rules, such as those embodied in the *Tri-Council Policy Statement: Ethical Conduct for Research Involving Humans* (MRC, NSERC, and SSHRC,

1998d) require that both the researcher and the participant know in advance what may happen both during the research and as a consequence of it. According to the *Tri-Council Policy Statement*, 2.1(a): 'Research governed by this policy may begin only if (1) prospective subjects, or authorized third parties, have been given the opportunity to give free and informed consent about participation (2) their free and informed consent has been given and is maintained throughout their participation in the research.' If the researcher does not know what will happen in the research, he or she cannot tell the participants. If the participants are not told, they cannot be said to have given informed consent before participating. The researcher also has to know the research question in advance in order to provide full disclosure to a research ethics board (REB) in order to get approval before starting.

This requirement that the project be fully known in advance is troublesome in qualitative research, where the notion of discovery during inquiry is usually considered to be a strength – not a weakness – of the approach. It is a particular problem for inquiry into socially sensitive issues. The aspect of this problem that I discuss in this chapter is the question of confidential information. Often, studies cannot be conducted unless the informant's identity and/or other details are kept secret. That secrecy must be assured in advance. But REBs require that participants give informed consent before they are involved in a research project. To be 'informed,' the participant must know the risks involved in participation. One such risk is that a guarantee of confidentiality will be challenged in the legal system, and a researcher may be required to give information that was supposed to be confidential. To inform the participants of this risk in advance is to invite them not to participate. This would put some important areas of research beyond the scope of social science inquiry.

Three Cases

The following three sketches illustrate the problem. In Quebec, a prestigious research team surveyed a large sample of parents about child-rearing practices. Five years later they wanted to do a follow-up, interviewing a random sample. They could not predict in advance what frustrations, fears, and conduct parents might talk about – potentially including material that might be reportable to some social agency. The ethics committee of Santé Québec (Quebec's Health Department) said that the team must warn parents that the researchers had a legal obligation to report anything that 'gives reason to believe that the security or development of a child is compromised.' The research team did not know what might be covered by this rather general wording; neither did the lawyers whom they consulted, nor (it turned out) did the ethics committee. The ethics gatekeepers told the researchers: when in doubt, report. At the informed-consent phase they could hardly explain something to parents that they did not understand themselves. The researchers believed that the warning was likely to be so worrisome that many parents would refuse to participate from an excess of caution. After months of stalemate, the government vetoed the study because these problems could not be resolved (Bouchard, 1998).

A dissertation research project at the University of California at Berkeley provides the second illustration. Richard Leo did participant-observation in the Criminal Investigation Division of an urban police department. The study focused on police questioning of suspects, and the police allowed him to sit in on many interrogations. His dissertation committee had insisted that he maintain strict confidentiality and that he convey that assurance to the detectives involved. In one interrogation, a suspect confessed to a serious crime. Later, the suspect recanted and said that he confessed only because detectives had threatened him. The office of the public defender learned that Leo had been present and subpoenaed him to testify. The office threatened him with both criminal and civil proceedings if he refused. He asked the university for legal help, but the university administration questioned whether the issue was important enough to justify the expense. Leo went over his research notes and decided that they supported the detectives' interpretation; on the basis of that assessment, he reluctantly agreed to testify. But the public defender was able to use the notes to raise doubt, and the suspect was found not guilty of three of the four charges against him (Leo, 1995).

A thesis project at Simon Fraser University in Burnaby, British Columbia, serves as a third illustration. A social worker, Russell Ogden, studied assisted suicide of persons with AIDS. He attempted to gather anonymous data, but if anonymity broke down he guaranteed absolute confidentiality, since assisted suicide is against the law. After he had completed his thesis, local newspapers reported aspects of his work. A coroner read some of the material and decided that one case was probably a 'person unknown,' whose identity he had been trying to establish for more than a year. The coroner subpoenaed Ogden and his records. Ogden destroyed any records that would identify participants and refused to break confidentiality. At a contempt hearing, he managed to convince the coroner that he should be permitted to withhold the information. In the aftermath of the case, however, the university's ethics committee prohibited any further research in which any researcher proposed to guarantee absolute confidentiality. This decision seriously delayed proposals from social workers, criminologists, and psychologists who needed to guarantee confidentiality to study delicate topics ranging from assisted suicide to drug use to underage sex trade workers.

These three cases exemplify situations in which crucial social topics cannot be studied if the investigator and the participant must know in advance exactly what will happen in the research context. The Quebec researchers did not know what information would be revealed by participants, and a sweeping declaration about disclosure would have removed so many nervous parents from the study that its conclusions probably would not be valid. Leo at Berkeley did not know that he would be subpoenaed, and he could not anticipate that the university would not support him. As well, he did not know that his research notes would affect a trial outcome. Ogden could not predict that publicity about details of one of his cases would interest a coroner or that he would be able to talk his way out of a contempt citation.

Possible Solutions

The remainder of this chapter focuses on possible solutions to the problems of confidentiality and informed consent. It deals with these first as issues that researchers must solve, then as problems for REBs, and finally as challenges for universities.

The starting point is a situation that prevents proper study of some social problem unless there can be a guarantee of complete confidentiality. In qualitative research, methods usually do not lend themselves to collection of anonymous data. Researchers must rely on making promises of confidentiality, but REBs may pre-empt the research by not granting approval. If they do grant approval, legal requirements may put pressure on the researcher to surrender confidentiality.

For Researchers: The Wigmore Criteria

How is this situation to be resolved? Russell Ogden was successful in convincing a coroner, who very much wanted the information, to allow him to maintain confidentiality. The legal argument that he used is based on the Wigmore criteria, named for American jurist John Henry Wigmore, who outlined them in 1909 (Wigmore, 1983). These are the criteria that may enable a researcher to maintain confidentiality in the sort of situation that I have been describing:

1 'The communication must originate in a confidence that they will not be disclosed.' This is the bedrock criterion. It sounds simple, but, as we see below, it can complicate matters for the researcher and the REB.
2 'The element of confidentiality must be essential to the full and satisfactory relationship between the parties.' Journalists can argue that sources will dry up unless they are promised confidentiality. Researchers can make a similar argument about interviews on sensitive topics. Note that a thief and a fence could make the same argument, which leads to the next criterion.
3 'The relationship must be one that it is in the community's interest to foster.' It may be in the community's interest to foster the relationships of trust between priest and penitent, journalist and source, and researcher and participant. It is presumably not in its interest to foster the relationship between 'fences' and thieves.
4 'The injury that would be done to the relationship by the disclosure of the communication(s) must be greater than the benefit gained for correct disposal of the litigation.' This criterion gives judges the most headaches. They must weigh the outcome of the matter before them against the social benefit of research that requires collecting confidential information. In the Ogden case, the coroner himself decided that, as much as he wanted to know the identity of the year-old suicide, the benefit of knowing was not as important as the potential damage done to the relationship between researchers and their participants.

In some U.S. jurisdictions the Wigmore criteria have been used to establish a 'class privilege.' With some (rare) exceptions,[1] a class privilege exists in attorney–client communications in both Canada and the United States. In a class privilege, one does not have to argue every case over again. In all but exceptional circumstances, lawyers are supposed to maintain attorney–client privilege, and their clients have a right to this privilege.

Beyond the attorney–client privilege, however, Canadian courts have been unwilling to exempt a whole class of communications from disclosure rules. Instead, cases are judged on their own merits. A social scientist who refuses to disclose confidential information, and who relies on the Wigmore criteria, has to show that the criteria should apply to the particular situation.

An excellent study of the application of the Wigmore criteria in Canada has been done by two law professors, Michael Jackson and Marilyn MacCrimmon (1999). In their opinion,

> The Wigmore criteria, interpreted and applied in accordance with *Charter* [of Rights and Freedoms] values, can be invoked by researchers to establish a case-by-case privilege for confidential communication with their subjects. Whether in any particular case a claim for privilege will be granted for the researcher–subject relationship can only be determined in the context of that case. It will depend on the nature of the confidential information, [and] the interests that protecting the confidentiality of the relationship serve ... this will include the importance of a particular research project, the extent to which this kind of research could not have been carried out without assurances of confidentiality and the impact on future research if this kind of confidentiality is not protected. (66)

For Research Ethics Boards

I have explored some options, mainly by invoking the Wigmore criteria, open to the researcher. Let me turn now to the impact that all this has on the relationship between the researcher and the research ethics board (REB). The researcher goes to the REB with a proposal to undertake an inquiry into a sensitive topic. The board wants to ensure that the researcher will obtain from the participants informed consent. The researcher may attempt to keep sources anonymous, but the identity of the source may well become known to the researcher anyway. With or without an attempt at ensuring anonymity, the researcher will have to deal with confidentiality. The researcher's plan is to guarantee confidentiality.

The REB is concerned that there are circumstances in which the researcher *will* have to disclose information. It suggests (or recommends or requires) that the researcher explain to potential participants that confidentiality is not unconditional – that there may be circumstances in which information provided by the participant (or perhaps the participant's identity) will have to be disclosed.

An ethics board at Simon Fraser University, in the aftermath of the Ogden case, demanded that the consent protocol specify that information would be kept confidential 'to the full extent permitted by law ... However, it is possible that, as a result of legal action, the researcher may be required to divulge information obtained in the course of this research to a court or other legal body.' This is the sort of caveat that psychotherapists routinely give to their clients.

The caveat sounds reasonable; but unfortunately the warning is fatal to the first Wigmore criterion – that 'the communications must originate in a confidence that they will not be disclosed.' Any qualification of that confidentiality invalidates the rest of the legal argument. In a Canadian case, for instance, a clergyman met with a woman who was subsequently accused of murder. She disclosed information to her pastor, then sought to have the information suppressed because it was given in the context of a professional relationship that she *assumed* was confidential. She lost in court and again on appeal to the Supreme Court of Canada (*Regina v. Gruenke*, 1991). The case reinforced the principle that the promise of confidentiality must be explicit and unconditional for the Wigmore criteria to apply.

The REB may ask the researcher, 'Well, what will you do if you are subpoenaed and required by law to disclose confidential information?' The answer might well be, 'I will fight to maintain confidentiality, but if I lose I am prepared to go to jail to protect my sources or the information, or both.' But, reasons the REB, what if the researcher, faced with a contempt citation and jail, or with a civil suit, has a change of heart? The researcher's decision to resist or comply with such a legal order would be beyond the jurisdiction of the REB. The board could hardly insist, for example, that the researcher go to jail to maintain the confidentiality that was guaranteed in the informed-consent process. How is this problem to be solved?

Universities: Certificates and Consent Formulas

There are two potential solutions. The first (and best) is available in some U.S. jurisdictions, but not yet in Canada. Legislation permits a researcher to apply for a certificate that gives advance immunity from having to break confidentiality. With such certification, the researcher can truthfully tell the potential participant that confidentiality is unconditional. Ethics gatekeepers can be reasonably sure that the researcher, armed with a certificate, will maintain the confidentiality that has been promised.

Simon Fraser University adopted another possible solution to solve its impasse between ethics gatekeepers and criminology researchers. The university commissioned the study by Jackson and MacCrimmon that I referred to above. After an exhaustive examination of guarantees in Canada's Charter of Right and Freedoms and legal precedents,[2] they recommended a formula to be used in the consent process. The wording was acceptable to the REB, to the university, and to the researchers whose work was at issue. Here is the Jackson–MacCrimmon (1999) formulation: 'The researchers will do everything possible to maintain the confidentiality of information obtained during this study and the anonymity of its sources. If an order is made by a court that the researchers provide information or reveal the identity of their sources, the university will provide legal representation until all available court processes have been exhausted to assist the researchers to maintain confidentiality of information and sources. Even then, the researchers will not reveal any confidential information and will *never* do so unless they believe it ethically proper, considering the circumstances, to reveal that information' (88–9).

The philosophical importance of the statement is that it does not subjugate ethics to the law. With appropriate substitutions, this wording would protect even the confidentiality of the priest–penitent relationship. Its practical significance is that it commits the university, which has deeper pockets than the researchers or the REB, to pursue defence of the researcher all the way to the Supreme Court of Canada if necessary.

It may be a challenge to get a university to make such a commitment, but it can be done. It takes a vigorous representation on the basis of academic freedom. Unless a university is willing to make such a commitment, researchers who study sensitive topics will not be able to do their work. If such researchers are to have meaningful academic freedom, universities have to protect them when the chips are down.

The courts, by the way, tend to agree. In the Ogden case, the administration at Simon Fraser University at first failed to support the researcher financially. Since the thesis topic was assisted suicide, the administration argued that to provide funds for a legal defence might make it seem that the university condoned or favoured euthanasia. After he won the case, the researcher sued the university for legal fees that he had incurred. In his judgment, Provincial Court Judge Steinberg commented: 'The principles of academic freedom and privilege are fundamental to the operation of any accredited university. There is no question that the research of the claimant [that is, the researcher] was of great social value and very topical in today's society. Research such as is contained in the claimant's thesis is therefore vital to help inform the [euthanasia] debate ... The vague statements of personal support as expressed by the president of the university ... and the Dean of Graduate Studies ... sound hollow and timid when compared with the opportunity they had as leaders of the university to promote the demonstrated value of academic freedom and academic privilege as evidenced in this case' (*Ogden v. Simon Fraser University*, 1998).

Judge Steinberg condemned the university for what he called 'a surprising lack of courage.' When the judge's harsh comments were publicized, the university administration paid the researcher's legal costs without further delay and then agreed to support future research by authorizing the informed consent statement that guaranteed the university's financial support all the way to the Supreme Court of Canada. That court has generally supported the study of controversial topics and has recognized the importance of academic freedom for social inquiry. In three separate cases the court has affirmed and reaffirmed the central role of academic freedom in ensuring that truth, no matter how unpalatable, be discovered.

Notes

I would like to thank Paul Jones, with whom I shared ideas on this topic while we were both associated with the Academic Freedom and Tenure Committee of the Canadian Association of University Teachers (CAUT).

1 *Smith v. Jones*, [1999] 1 SCR 455.
2 They also relied on an excellent paper on confidentiality that staff lawyer Paul Jones of CAUT prepared for the Academic Freedom and Tenure Committee in 1998.

2

Yet Another Coming Crisis? Coping with Guidelines from the Tri-Council

FLORENCE KELLNER

This essay addresses continuing concerns of those of us whose work depends on the field as a primary source of data – those of us who conduct, produce, and analyse observations of social life, interviews, and group discussions. When we consider ethical issues, we are often less than comfortable, for we must grapple with a lack of correspondence between codes of ethics and the conduct of ethnographic methods. Satisfying of research demands may entail some violations of ethics codes, especially when the codes are interpreted literally and without regard for the range of research circumstances that are not informed by the methods of natural science. Nevertheless, if we are careful and thoughtful about our fieldwork and throughout the research process, we can be fairly certain that we can do the right thing, despite the limited 'fit' between ethics codes and research activity.

Through applying Zygmunt Bauman's contrast between ethics and morality (1993), I attempt to distinguish between letter (the ethics code) and spirit (morality). First, I outline the main points of the new ethics code for Canadian research, and then I consider a report on its effectiveness by the Centre on Governance. Second, my discussion section looks at some of the principles of the ethics code of particular interest to qualitative researchers, as well as at its implementation. Third, the final section contains practical suggestions about where and how the code might inform, affect, and apply to our work.

On 17 September 1998, the Medical Research Council (MRC), the Natural Sciences and Engineering Research Council (NSERC), and the Social Sciences and Humanities Research Council (SSHRC) launched the Tri-Council Policy Statement: *Ethical Conduct for Research Involving Humans* (MRC, NSERC, and SSHRC, 1998). The three-council statement is a policy document and replaces the three separate ethics guidelines that were previously in effect for the councils. The introduction makes it clear that it is serious: 'The Councils will consider funding (or continued funding) only to individuals and institutions which certify compliance with the policy regarding research involving human subjects' (i.1). Key phrases are 'consider funding,' which indicates that proposals will not even begin to be adjudicated by the agencies if proper procedures are not followed, and 'certify compliance,' which indicates involvement of third party officials mediating dialogue between the researcher and the funding agency.

One document's replacing three separate ones might seem a good idea, as one document is more efficient than three, and all three councils fund research on humans. Dr Henry Frieson, president of the MRC, hailed the policy as a triumph: 'Canada is the first country to produce a comprehensive ethics policy statement for research involving humans in all academic disciplines' (Centre on Governance, 2000: 2).

We, as social scientists, do not have to scratch the surface of ethics review too deeply to imagine a potential for serious trouble. Regarding social science, worries around ethics codes are not new. Two decades ago, Thorne (1980: 285), responding to a U.S. federal policy statement, observed that, while guidelines for funding research on humans may be appropriate to most situations in biomedical work, they do not address many situations in social science. In particular, ethics policies do not address fieldwork research, because its purpose and direction are likely to change in the course of the work, after the initial proposal has been written and the project has been reviewed. The current Canadian document adds to these concerns, as now we have a code that may bring ethics pertaining to natural science even closer to us than it had been.

The Tri-Council Policy

This section reviews the highlights of the parts of the *Tri-Council Policy Statement* that are most likely to pertain to those of us who do fieldwork and interviewing. The statement institutionalizes a commonly shared ethical framework and, like the common framework, avoids the dominance of particular disciplines over others (MRC et al., 1998a: i.2).[1] The policy recommends flexibility on the part of adjudicators (i.9) and includes a disclaimer of any intention to inhibit reasonable research. The key moral foundation is respect for human dignity (i.5).

Primary issues are those of free and informed consent and privacy/

confidentiality. Researchers should obtain consent from the subjects, preferably in writing (article 2.1a), but the councils recognize that, in some instances, signed releases are not possible or would likely interfere with data-gathering (article 2.1[c]iii). In some cases, as when children or incapacitated people are research subjects, third parties or guardians may provide research permission (article 2.6). The sections on privacy and confidentiality obligate the researcher to state the measures used to safeguard the data, to be explicit about measures used to safeguard the data (article 3.2), and also to be explicit about intended use of the data for purposes of secondary analysis (article 3.3).

The councils have also stated a guiding principle of distributive justice. Research should be fair, and it should be equitable. No sector of the population should be disproportionately burdened with the costs of the research, and no group should be – gratuitously or by custom – excluded from study (articles 5.1 and 5.2). For all these principles, there are disclaimers that emphasize the importance of academic freedom and the denial of intention to restrict any reasonable research. The policy also highlights and repeats statements concerning temperate judgment, including the need to balance the incorporation of principles that may be contradictory. For instance, minimizing of risks of harm from research might contradict maximizing of possible benefits from research results (MRC et al., 1998a: i.6). Research on medical procedures constitutes the more obvious examples. In social science, asking questions that might disturb a respondent or make him or her uncomfortable may be balanced against an impetus to uncover valuable information about the range of social issues important to qualitative researchers: often the best knowledge about alcohol and drug abuse, self-image, divorce, voting preferences, intolerance, and so on, comes from asking people about these things.

The *Tri-Council Policy Statement* describes membership and functions of the REBs, which every academic institution with applicants to the councils must have in place (articles 1.2–1.9). These boards must be free from institutional pressures, and their membership should be familiar with the disciplines whose proposals they review. There are also to be REBs in individual departments, which should adjudicate undergraduate work involving human subjects when this work is part of normal course requirements. Should the institution-level board refuse to approve an application after appeals to do so, an appeal may go to an appeal board, established by the institution. This board is not *ad hoc*; the councils do not hear appeals (article 1.11).

The policy states that some research on humans is exempt from ethics review. Research involving minimal risk to participants need not be reviewed, and publicly available information need not be reviewed (article 1.5). Moreover, 'Naturalistic observation that does not allow for the identification of the subjects, and that is not staged, should normally be regarded as minimal risk' (MRC et al., 1998a: 2.5). As expected, research involving photographs and taping that allow for identification of individuals must be reviewed and would be normally expected to include assurances of informed consent or some release mechanism by the subjects (article 3.2).

Report from the Centre on Governance

Between October 1999 and April 2000, the Centre on Governance at the University of Ottawa examined the governance of the ethics process mandated by the *Tri-Council Policy Statement* (Centre on Governance, 2000). The main content of its report consists of results of interviews with members of the various committees responsible for implementing the Tri-Council Policy, as well as with people from the research community. The report also contained recommendations for reorganizing the structures charged with applying the policy.

The review emphasized that the document is still evolving. Both its content and its application – especially the latter – need refining after initial trials. The recommendation is to concentrate on making governance as smooth as possible in universities and then broadening the policy to include other groups in government and in the private sector. 'We envisage the TCPS (Tri-Council Policy Statement) becoming the "gold standard" for research not only within university, but also within government, non-profit groups and the private sector. But this objective will not be achieved unless we get the implementation right' (Centre on Governance, 2000: 2).

A critique of the current governance structure and discussion of possible different arrangements or models comprise much of the substance of the centre's report. Respondents – the document reported interviewing 'about 60' (Centre on Governance, 2000: 2) – who had worked with or who had experienced the new policy directly, believed that the current process and structure needed change. Particularly at the university level, respondents thought resources for reviewing and administering research ethics insufficient. The report recommends release time for REB members, especially in large institutions.

The report identifies attributes that respondents recommended for application of the Tri-Council Policy: transparency, room for learning and evolution, fairness and inclusiveness, and accountability. Governance should also be 'engaging,' meaning that the principles of ethics in the document should come to be accepted by the researcher and by the boards administering the policy.

Right now, the policy does not satisfy these criteria, as there is an unclear division of labour in its administration. The arrangement of structures that adjudicate and oversee ethics in Canada is quite complex – the three councils, their associated standing committees, a Tri-Council advisory group, the National Council on Ethics in Human Research, and its associated co-ordinating committees. These bodies link with some of each other and with the REBs in the universities. The REBs in turn deal with individual researchers and their project proposals. Both the policy and its review emphasize learning – once a person becomes familiar with the policy content and the process of review, conformity and perhaps commitment to the policy are likely outcomes.

The report found lack of trust in the process of adjudication, which is complex and therefore not well understood, and in the adjudicators themselves, if their disciplines were very different from those of the applicants. The following quotations from interviews conducted with researchers and reviewers illustrate some of these problems: 'If in general we don't trust the researchers or the institutions, can we really expect that we can trust the monitors? Who watches the watchers?' 'The current structure encourages fragmentation and unevenness in the application of ethics' 'How expert are the REBs? Do they have the appropriate research and ethical expertise?' 'What premise do we hold of researchers and institutions? Do we really believe that they are all just trying to get around the rules?' (Centre on Governance, 2000: 50–2).

Discussion

In his examination of current culture, Zygmunt Bauman (1993) contrasted morality with ethics. For Bauman, ethics is an attempt to codify morality or to set forth norms. By necessity and by definition, codification is situation- and culture-bound and therefore relative and limited. According to Bauman, morality is an orientation to the Other that is infinite, in the sense that one's obligation to it is limitless. The truly moral stance involves a caring for the Other and an attending to the welfare and the needs of the Other. The requirement to care knows no bounds in scope and in time. One can never do enough, and one is never through with the Other. One is never without obligation to act on behalf of the Other.

Therefore, universalistic[2] criteria that involve third-party regulation are different from moral criteria, as attention to the needs and welfare and demands of all the different Others is unlikely in real life – not to mention in the research situation – through codified regulations. Codes of behaviour, such as those set forth in law and in ethics codes for research involving human subjects, have to be limited – and perhaps rather superficial – in order to address a wide scope of situations. The mandate to respect human dignity that informs the code of ethics that we are considering falls far short of invoking *caring* about the people being studied. One cannot codify caring and the sense of infinite obligation required by morality.

One of the sources of crisis that we as fieldwork social scientists experience from time to time, when a new and 'improved' code of ethics surfaces, is confusion between ethics and morality. Ethics in the biomedical and natural science disciplines does not demand morality, in Bauman's sense, as almost all these studies address some aspect of people's constitution or physical functioning. They do not usually attempt to address those aspects of human beings that are uniquely human. The human attributes to which we pay attention are the wilful ones, influenced, but not determined, by physical and social environments. We concentrate on the interactions of 'our' Others with other Others, whose words, meanings, and behaviour are likewise influenced, but not determined. In attempting to understand the uniquely human dimensions of the social world – and in order to do the right thing – ethics guidelines, as set forth in codes such as the Tri-Council Policy – constitute minimal criteria for responsible research: most of our fieldwork instruction to our students and ourselves takes ethics for granted. When ethics are not taken for granted – as in introductory courses on methods – we view ethical conduct as a minimum criterion for conduct in the field.

We have very little argument with requirements of privacy and with requirements to avoid inflicting harm. What is probably needed now is an orientation of respect and, particularly, suspension of judgment. These stances involve ethics of course, but their application in the field and during the write-up have more to do with morality than with ethics. They have more to do with an orientation to the welfare of the Other, with taking into account the particular life circumstances, values, beliefs, goals, obstacles, and worldviews of that Other. Codes of ethics, or any codes, do little to inform us about taking these very human aspects into account and doing the right thing with them. It is our morality, our diffuse, unlimited obligation to the welfare of the Other, that must inform these more important aspects of our conduct in the field. And where ethical requirements and moral requirements conflict, the latter must take priority.

Practical Considerations

Despite the publicity, the resources, the negative reaction, and the elaborated governance structure, the *Tri-Council Policy Statement* presents little that is new for field researchers. Parts of the document are explicit in endorsing our continuing to do what we have always done. For instance, always problematic for us has been informed consent, but even this requirement has been covered in flexible ways in a number of places in the ethics code. For example, there are sections that exempt from review certain types of naturalistic observation. There is also the criterion of minimal risk, which absolves some proposals from review in the first place. Some statements about informed consent are somewhat more elaborate in the Canadian Sociological and Anthropological Statement of Professional Ethics (see CSAA, 1994:3), which states that there are conditions under which respondents may be put at risk for harm if they signed consent forms.

In my judgment, where there is any doubt, or where an investigator has doubt that reviewers would have doubt about whether or not a project should have ethics clearance, it should be submitted with some statement about its position in a grey area regarding the necessity for review.

Probably the big difference in the *Tri-Council Policy Statement* is its requirement that studies – funded or not funded – using human subjects and which are not undergraduate course exercises require review by university-level REBs. This means that all independent student research and all graduate student projects must go there. Therefore, much of our behaviour and preparation will have to change, if it has not already. Our projects and those of our students must contain an ethics section that may be more elaborate and explicit than it has been in previous years. Adjusting to the new conditions means taking some time to learn the relevant parts of the policy and how to address them and checking the schedules of ethics meetings in our institutions so that we can meet other project deadlines.

The governance study identified a two-pronged lack of trust in the application process. Researchers did not trust adjudicators to judge submissions fairly and responsibly; administrators of the code had the impression that researchers were cavalier and not as responsible as they should be in protecting their subjects. Given this situation, for a researcher the most useful stance is to communicate good intentions to comply with the code. For the course instructor, the policy and its interpretation should probably now constitute a greater part of the course content.

Finally, it is necessary to be aware of the distinction between ethics and morality as they have to do with research practice. Ethics has its limitations and its limits. Requirements of codes of ethics may be met and monitored from time to time. Morality, which entails care and attention and sympathy and appreciation of the Other, necessitates consistent obligation, whether we are in the field, 'reading' the other, or at the keyboard, 'writing' the Other.

Notes

I thank Anne Burgess of the Faculty of Graduate Studies and Research at Carleton University for an invaluable introduction to the subject-matter of this essay. Much of what the reader finds to be useful is the result of her input.

1 I cite MRC et al. (i.e., MRC, NSERC, and SSHRC) whenever I refer to interpretive text. Otherwise, I designate specific articles in the *Tri-Council Policy Statement* (MRC et al., 1998d).

2 In the Parsonian sense, 'universalism' refers to a set of role expectations that all occupants of the same role have in common, regardless of the occupants' relationship to role partners outside that role. Codes of ethics are universalistic, as they attempt to describe researchers' obligations to those researched. These obligations are limited to the research relationship. Please see Parsons 1951: 102–4.

3

Do University Lawyers and the Police Define Research Values?

PATRICIA A. ADLER AND PETER ADLER

Significant changes during the later twentieth century have profoundly affected the conduct of social scientific research. During this time institutional review boards (IRBs) at major universities all over North America came to regulate scholarly research. Originally called committees for the protection of human subjects, they have revealed themselves to have simultaneously greater and lesser goals, as we argue below.

The directives and judgments of these boards have evolved, becoming considerably more restrictive, and they now represent a major bane and obstacle to active researchers. Although they present themselves as something other than petty, narrow minded, restrictive bureaucratic 'rangers,' it is often hard not to suspect otherwise. Board members assert that they are not making the rules, that they are merely following the dictates of the U.S. federal government. They claim that failure on their part to restrict our research would result in a loss of federal funding for the institution and possibly a halt to all permissible research. Yet it has become increasingly clear that the standards of these committee vary from school to school, not just between our two schools – the University of Colorado and the University of Denver – but among others as well. Some are laxer, and some are tighter. For example, Denver started regulating teaching only in the late 1990s, while Colorado had done so since the late 1980s, and Colorado is much stricter all around, requiring all research – undergraduate, graduate, and faculty, funded or unfunded – to pass through its approval process. To force people to comply, they have the power to withhold students' degrees and to revoke the tenure of faculty members. An Orwellian atmosphere of surveillance and compliance has emerged.

The experiences that we discuss draw on our familiarity with our field, on our own experiences, and on those of the students whom we have mentored and taught. In particular, Patti teaches a two-year graduate ethnography sequence (gathering and analysis of data) that has run un-interrupted for fourteen years, and Peter teaches shorter graduate courses in ethnography as well. We have had ample opportunity to see the work-ings of these boards closely as we have tried to pass our own and our students' projects through.

We have noticed two major changes over time in standards – in permit-ted research practices and in standards for clearance – although commit-tee members deny this. Research practices that used to be allowed are no longer allowed. For example, in the 1980s, a distinction was made if peo-ple gathered their data through a membership role in the field, as we did in the bulk of our research for *Peer Power* (Adler and Adler, 1998). For this project, we often acquired information as we stood informally chat-ting with other parents on the sidelines of athletic fields, at parties, at meetings of parent–teacher associations and back-to-school nights, or conversing with our children and their friends. We could then use this everyday-life knowledge as data for research. Our students were told that if they gathered data through a membership role, as one young woman did as a volunteer with a group before she decided to make it a project of study, that they could then convert the information to usable data.

In the new century, that is no longer allowed. Colorado's IRB adminis-trator told Patti's students in the autumn of 1999 that if they talked with people informally, in a naturally occurring role, they were not free to use that information. If they decided that individuals had said something they wanted to use as data, they would have to go back and retrospectively get written permission to use their remarks. The distinction that used to exist between private life and research life has been obliterated. This sig-nificantly inhibits researchers' spontaneous use of their sociological im-aginations.

As well, standards for clearance have changed (although IRB members deny this as well). Proposals that used to clear through with exempt sta-tus now require expedited review, and formerly expedited proposals now need full committee approval. Many that previously went through with-out consent forms now are being required to use such forms. Others that used to be acceptable with consent forms are now not acceptable in any way, shape, or form. We put forth an interview study with female imper-sonators seven years ago and received exempt status, but, after letting the project lapse and then looking into picking it back up, we learned that it would then require consent forms and full committee review.

Some projects are now just impossible, as the following five stories show. In the mid-1990s Patti had a student who took an extended leave of absence from graduate school because his inability to clear his project through the IRB after three attempts proved fruitless. He was gay and had been working with the Boulder County Health Project, facilitating, with two others, a support group for teenagers who were dealing with coming-out issues related to being gay, bisexual, lesbian, and transgendered. The committee started out by insisting that the teens not only give signed consent to be studied, but obtain parental consent as well. This was an unthinkable requirement for most subjects, who were attending support groups precisely because they could not talk to their parents about their developing thoughts and feelings. They were telling their parents that they were at friends' houses or the grocery store or offering some safe 'cover' story. Obtaining parental consent would have harmed these youths.

The IRB next rejected his role in the setting as a co-facilitator, arguing that this represented a role of potential power among the youths. It insisted that he had to find another group, probably in Denver, an hour's drive away, and do research there. He had made a three-year commitment to the group in which he was working and would have had to attend this group and do research in another. But he could not find another group that would take him as a non-facilitator and a non-teen.

The IRB finally told him that he would have to declare his research interests each time a new person attended the group and that if that person did not feel comfortable with his conducting research he had to leave. He tried to negotiate with the committee and suggested that he could just leave the stories or case examples of the non-consenters out of his fieldnotes and data, but it rejected this idea. He still had to leave the setting. There was no way he could do this project under the IRB regulations. He left the university in frustration.

Another gay student wanted to study public sexual activity to learn about at-risk behaviour. Again, the IRB made untenable demands. Every time it told him what it would require from his subjects, he went back to his gay friends in the field to ask them if they or others would agree to the stipulations, and each time they told him, 'No.' He was never able to find a middle ground between what his subjects and the committee would accept.

A female student who was studying sexually transmitted diseases planned to initiate a support group for women who had been diagnosed with one. With a strong background as a peer educator, she had led support groups for women with eating disorders and thought that this project would be a good way to gather data while helping women. The university's student health service was highly supportive and offered to refer newly diagnosed women to her group, but the IRB placed too many obstacles in her path. Again, it did not like her prospective position of power over the group members. It worried about individuals who did not want to be studied. She offered to screen people before they came into the group, advising them that she was collecting dissertation data on the topic. But the IRB said that she could not deny people access to the support group because of their refusal to be researched. If even one person refused consent, she would lose her permission to study the whole group. The IRB told her that she would have to run another group, a non-research group, and offer that to people. But she was unable to recruit enough individuals for two groups in order to guarantee a non-research group, even if no one asked for it. So it said, 'No.'

Another young woman wanted to do research on incarcerated women in the state penitentiary. She hoped to find out about their lives, relationships, social environment, and criminal careers. After several unsuccessful rounds through the IRB, she and Patti were sent to meet with the university lawyer to discuss consent issues. She was told that she had to warn women at the outset of each interview that if they said anything about illegal behaviour in which they had ever engaged she would not be able to keep it confidential. It might be subject to subpoena, which might increase their prison terms. These obstacles were so daunting that she abandoned her project and also left graduate school.

Finally, Patti had a student who wanted to study women arrested for domestic violence. That became a hot topic around 1990, when mandatory arrest policies began to be enforced. The police would arrive on the scene, see which party was more badly beaten, and arrest the other. For the first time, women were arrested for domestic violence in more substantial numbers and placed in treatment groups for violence prevention. Although these women all had histories of chronic battering, and most had resorted, in desperation, to violence as a way of protecting themselves, the committee insisted on mandating her to report on her subjects. If women hit their husbands, they might hit their children, board members argued. She was thus required to inform women prior to the interview that if she observed or heard of any violence she had to report it to the authorities. She had to go into the research telling these women that she could not hold what they said in confidence and that she would be forced to turn them in.

These requirements fly in the face of everything that we learned in graduate school, in books and classes on field research ethics – our loyalty lay with our subjects, whom we protected. If we found others needing protection, we tried to help them too. We certainly did not turn them in to the police. John Van Maanen (1983) published a now-classic piece on ethics in field research about getting caught in a situation where the police with whom he was riding were charged with using excessive violence to suppress a Black subject. He was subpoenaed to testify against his subjects, yet he felt an ethical imperative to hold their confidentiality and managed to keep his fieldnotes out of court. Others and we have written about the practice of self-censorship (Adler and Adler, 1993) precisely because sociologists use discretion about what they report. We do not advance our careers at the expense of our subjects.

But the new Code of Ethics of the American Sociological Association (ASA) supports the rights of the police over the subjects' claim for loyalty. In the 1980s and 1990s the ASA filed *amicus cura* (friend of the court) briefs in two fieldwork cases. Mario Brajuha was studying a restaurant when a fire of suspicious origin burned it down (see Brajuha and Hallowell, 1986), and Rik Scarce was studying animal rights groups when an animal research laboratory was 'liberated' (see Scarce, 1994). Both men were graduate students whom the police approached to subpoena their field notes, and both resisted. Scarce went to jail for almost six months. The ASA backed his stance. But now the ASA would not support him. Its new ethics code is that the law of the land is the ethics code of the ASA. Is that right? Do we have a moral obligation to our subjects to protect them?

The new code is grounded in litigious U.S. society. Lawsuits have become pervasive there, and people use them as a way of creating and enforcing morality as well as gaining riches. American universities have influential legal departments that advise administrators at every step on protecting themselves from lawsuits. They do not want to house any research that the police or the courts will not support. Applicants for certificates of confidentiality from the department of health and human subjects must now meet with university lawyers prior to applying for a certificate (to further protect their subjects) to see if these lawyers would be willing to support them. Publishers are taking the same precautions, and our U.S. publisher asked us after we wrote our last book if we had collected the appropriate informed consent forms. The editorial board cared not about the ethics of our research, but about its exposure to lawsuit. Similarly, in Patti's class on the sociology of deviance, for a norm-violation assignment, students have to sign a contract (required by the IRB) stating clearly what they are going to do. This has to be approved, under restrictive guidelines, by Patti. If they do something else and get in trouble, the university has the contracts and can show that the students are out on their own. In fact, in our increasingly bureaucratic society, documentation is now required of everything.

But the ASA has totally capitulated. Its code means that whatever the IRB demands becomes its ethics stance as well. The police, the lawyers, the U.S. government, and the universities are ethics guardians now. And at what price? We, the researchers, are to protect our subjects from ourselves. We are to protect them from telling us anything that we cannot hold safe, because we are not allowed to hold anything safe. We are 'rollover' stooges. We are the children of Tuskegee (see James H. Jones, 1993), of Milgram (1965), of medical researchers and experimentalists who abused their positions of authority. We in fact have never heard of any field researchers undercutting their own subjects. We ethnographers are too deeply involved with our subjects to do these kind of heartless and unethical things to them. We spend the longest time of any researchers with them and forge the deepest relationships with them. We write about things such as self-censorship (Adler and Adler, 1993), precisely because we use discretion in what we report. Becker (1967) asked us bluntly to answer the question, 'Whose side are we on?,' by telling us to side with the underdog. But the new regulations drive a wedge between our subjects and ourselves by requiring us to become the 'stoolies' of law enforcement.

What types of research are hardest hit by the new changes in the ASA code? First, illegal activity has become extremely difficult to study. The warnings that we give people against ourselves and the lack of support that we get from the government in shielding our subjects expose both them and us to danger. We risk going to jail or sending our subjects to jail if we uncover anything illegal. Second, we are constrained from looking too closely into powerless or vulnerable groups. Studying children, mental patients, prisoners, foreigners, or people with psychological stress, or dealing with sensitive topics necessitates jumping through all sorts of extra hoops, which makes these groups and subjects sometimes unresearchable. Third, it is hard to get information on publicly accountable individuals, those who do things that affect the public, because they are now off-limits. These people or corporations can now 'SLAPP' (see

Pring and Canan, 1996) researchers or concerned individuals who try to reveal information to advance the public good with a public-interest lawsuit if they are challenged in any way. Fourth, powerful elite or semi-elite groups can deny research access by refusing consent. Fifth, all aspects of investigative and covert research have been banned. Many classic pieces of research, including Humphreys's (1970) *Tearoom Trade* and *Wheeling and Dealing* (Patricia Adler, 1985), could not be done today. Like the outcomes of many other moral entrepreneurial campaigns, the 'protection of human subjects' movement has favoured the dominant classes over the weaker. Powerful, elite groups can now better hide their mechanisms of control, while weak and powerless groups have lost the ability to tell their stories from their own perspective.

Is ethnographic research hit the hardest by these changes in the ASA's code? There are five reasons why we believe this to be the case. First, acquiring informed consent is delicate in participant observation. Participant observation has a fuzziness about what is research and what is not, as ethnographers are observers of everyday life and may be generating insights and gathering data from people in all kinds of situations (a waitress at a restaurant, a fellow passenger on an airplane, a person whose child is the same age as one's own). They may not know in advance what information will drift their way that may prove explicitly useful, either currently or in the future. And it is often not exactly clear when, where, and how research begins. To push for informed consent when people have not determined if a particular setting is viable, if they can forge a role in it, and if they can generate relationships with setting members may be premature, damage relationships and status, and doom the research. To wait too long leaves previously collected insights potentially unusable later if subjects leave or become unavailable.

Explaining the purpose and interests of research may be harder in ethnography than it is in other methods of approach, especially because it is still emerging. For example, in studying hotel employees in Hawai'i, we began by obtaining the official permission of the hotel that we studied first. We conducted interviews with the management and did 'chat swings' with employees as we wandered around the property, chatting with people while they were at work. We had maybe five minutes to strike up a casual conversation with these strangers and ask them such questions as, What department do you work in? Do people from your department stay at work here year-round? Do they hold multiple jobs? Are they mostly transient or stable? What is your living situation – do you live with your nuclear or extended family? And then we had to move on, before their supervisors looked over and they thought that they had better return to work or they could be in trouble. We could spend the whole five minutes explaining that we were researchers wanting to study their working situations and way of life. But then we would be doing all the talking. Anyone we talked to a few times we tried to inform of our research interests, or if they asked us, we told them. But we did not blurt this out to everyone; it could not be the first thing that we mentioned. If we made our research interests the first subject of our conversation with people, many of them would think that we were spies for the management.

Second, ethnographers have a more difficult time than survey and experimental researchers anticipating what will happen in their research. As Van Maanen found out, his subjects behaved in ways that put his position in jeopardy and made protecting them difficult. What would he have done had the beating that they administered to their recalcitrant subject led to his death? Or, new issues may arise during the course of research that were not anticipated, leading researchers into sensitive and problematic topics. For example, one of our students researching pregnant teenagers found that these young women were often the victims of physically and sexually abusive parents.

Third, the power differentials between researchers and their subjects are not the same for ethnographers as they are for quantitative researchers. Experimental and survey researchers take more of a command position, while ethnographers are more often learners in the field, there at the good graces of their subjects. As Murray Wax (1983) noted, we are relatively more powerless compared to researchers using other approaches.

Fourth, researchers' roles throughout the data-gathering process vary between these methods. Survey and experimental researchers more clearly play the role of 'researchers' at all times, while ethnographers cannot do so. It is unnatural. Punch (1994) noted that it jeopardizes their role as participants. This makes it harder for ethnographers to do research in a formal way, i.e., by using the legalistic consent forms that are scary and alienating.

Fifth, ethnographers cannot use anonymity in gathering data as survey and experimental researchers can, where they do not know the identities of their subjects, since ethnographers gather data face to face from people whom they know. It is often harder to offer confidentiality as well, disguising the identities of their subjects, although they try, because the populations that they study are small and personal. Members of such groups may be more easily recognizable. These characteristics of ethnographic research make it harder to pass the IRB criteria.

What are the goals, then, of regulating research, and how can these best be attained? Clearly, if we are being told that we cannot protect our own subjects from official investigation short of our or their going to jail, which not everyone is willing to do, some changes are necessary. Is the new system the best way? If you fundamentally shut down research there is no risk to subjects because researchers will not know anything. But should we be willing to pay the price of losing knowledge about huge chunks of society, because people with the most to lose are the most likely to see the consent forms as barriers? What are we really being driven by here – an ethical imperative to protect the rights of people or an unethical imperative designed to keep universities, publishers, and sponsoring agencies from being sued? We are called to question the motives of these regulations when standards governing research on the same behaviour differ in private and in public settings. Researchers can study something if it is done in public, where people presumably have less right to expect privacy, that you cannot in private, where they can be sued. This applies to crack dealing occurring in crackhouses versus on the street. It makes one think that the regulators do not care about the subjects getting hurt as long as they cannot sue. The fundamental issue in reformulating the ASA code should be trust and professional ethics, not further protecting the elites.

No matter how much ethnographic research is regulated, no matter how tight the stipulations, unanticipated situations will always arise that are not covered in a research plan or proposal. Researchers will always have to make situational decisions and interpretations about the ethical and safe thing to do. We argue that not alienating researchers and their subjects increases the chances for a proper decision. We advocate a joint, reciprocally respectful relationship, more attuned to legal nuances, that looks ahead to anticipate potential problems while still respecting the fundamental bond of obligation and trust between researchers and those whom they study.

4

Challenging the System: Rethinking Ethics Review of Social Research in Britain's National Health Service

MELANIE PEARCE

There is growing awareness among researchers about the problems of working with ethics review committees in medicine and health in the United Kingdom. Although Sorenson (1978) noted such obstacles as far back as the 1970s, there has been a steady chorus of protest over the past five years (see, for example, Alberti, 1995 and 2000; Jenkins, 1995; Nicholl, 2000; Oddens and De Wied, 1995; and While, 1995). Ethics review bodies of the National Health Service (NHS) have remained surprisingly untouched by the shift towards primary care and the growing interest in the perspective and voice of patients. A culture of hospital-based medical and experimental research still prevails.

Much of this essay looks at the difficulties that I faced as a PhD student seeking ethics review for a qualitative research project in a quantitatively based system. The process not only undermined the qualitative tenets of my research but delayed an already-tight working schedule. While I would not disagree that the maintenance of ethical standards is of central importance, when the review process becomes a hindrance to research, then problems exist that need revision.

Local research ethics committees (LRECs) in the United Kingdom undertake the ethical review of all proposed research that is to take place within their region. Although they are accountable via health authorities to the NHS, they are often based in the hospitals where they originated. Both in operational terms and in principle, they remain oriented primarily to medical research, and hospital-based research in particular. Clinical or experimental studies make up the bulk of their applications, and the quantitative paradigm continues to predominate. For the increasing number of social researchers undertaking research under NHS auspices, this poses something of a problem: can they and should they frame their proposals in the terms of clinical trials and other experimental research, which are the *raison d'être* of the LRECs?

Beginning with a more detailed overview of LRECs, I move on to present an account of my attempt to submit my proposal for review and of the ensuing frustrations and compromises, along with analysis of areas of difficulty and impediments to research. This leads to a discussion of the issues raised and of whether modifications in procedures and principles are necessary to provide effective ethical review of health-related social research.

Local Research Ethics Committee (LRECs)

In the early 1960s the birth of babies seriously damaged by thalidomide resulted in a statement in the annual report for 1962–3 of the United Kingdom Medical Research Council about 'Responsibility in investigations on human subjects' (quoted in Evans and Evans, 1996: 4). This document was followed by the World Medical Association's Declaration of Helsinki in 1964 and by the (British) Royal College of Physicians' recommendations in 1967 and 1973 that ethics review committees be set up in institutions involved in clinical research. Britain's Department of Health formally endorsed these recommendations in 1975 and produced guidelines for their implementation. Revised guidelines published in 1991 instructed district health authorities to create committees to 'consider the ethical implications of all research proposals which involve human subjects' (Department of Health, 1991: 11). This oversight was to cover both 'therapeutic' research, of direct benefit to the participant, and 'non-therapeutic' research, which is unlikely of direct benefit but contributes to the general state of knowledge. The committees might cover one or more institutions. They are generally known as local research ethics committees (LRECs).

Unlike the institutional review boards (IRBs) set up in the United States, the LRECs are currently not subject to statutory control. British universities do not have individual university ethics review committees governing university research. Research on schoolchildren, for example, is not formally regulated but supervised by local education authorities or by management in schools. The LRECs effectively act as 'gatekeepers,' guarding access to NHS clinical populations, but Department of Health instructions and guidelines, not legal obligation, control them. LRECs based in university-affiliated hospitals will usually include some university members with research experience, but in a non-university hospital this expertise may be absent. This may significantly affect the level of committee experience.

LRECs should consist of eight to twelve members from both sexes and a range of age groups and include members of the hospital's medical staff, nurses, general practitioners, and two or more lay persons (Department of Health, 1991: 7). An LREC that covers what I call a general hospital consists of thirteen people and holds monthly review meetings. In recent years complaints have been made of divergent practices between area LRECs (for example, Alberti, 1995). This has caused particular difficulties for multi-centre studies. In an attempt to rectify this situation, regional multi-centre research ethics committees (MRECs) have been created throughout the United Kingdom. Multi-centre studies still have to apply to relevant LRECs for ethical review, but the LREC addresses only local factors, not the scientific merits or method of the study, where these already have the MREC's approval. MRECs are usually more influenced by individuals with research expertise than are LRECs.

Problems continue with the time taken for review of proposals, and complaints are still being aired (for instance, Nicholl, 2000). However, such proposals rarely give sufficient detail to enable the reader to consider what ethical issues the proposed studies may have entailed. I intend the in-depth description of my research to make explicit some of the details of the review process.

The report of the Royal College of Physicians (1990) states, 'The objectives of Research Ethics Committees are to maintain ethical standards of practice in research, to protect subjects of research from harm, to preserve the subjects' rights and to provide reassurance to the public that this is being done' (3). Within these broad objectives, the Department of Health specifies that ethical practice should cover areas such as the provision of adequate procedures and information to ensure informed consent, voluntary participation, the preservation of confidentiality, scientific merit, sufficient qualified supervision of researchers, and consideration of hazards to health (Department of Health, 1991). Safety procedures and financial considerations should also be monitored.

The Royal College of Physicians (1990) adds the recommendation that committees should ensure that the research objectives are 'directed to a justifiable advancement in biomedical knowledge that is consonant with prevailing community interests and priorities' (3). However, research is performed for the benefit of society, and care should be taken not to hinder or impede 'good medical research ... without good cause' (3).

The experience of some qualitative researchers may at times appear to contradict this desideratum, although the many letters of complaint in the *British Medical Journal* in the last few years indicate that excessive delay is not restricted to qualitative studies alone (for example, While, 1995). Although few would dispute the need for practices that ensure the protection of research subjects, the letter heading 'Ethics Committees: Impediments to Research or Guardians of Ethical Standards?' (While, 1995) may raise a valid question.

My Story

I now turn to a description of the difficulties that I faced in steering a qualitative proposal through the LREC application system. The process was to take five months from initial submission to confirmation of approval, and at times it was very frustrating. This is not intended as criticism of the general hospital's LREC. There are many pressures on LRECS, and the resources are often limited. They are seen as protection against litigation but may have only general guidance.

The General, which is not the main research hospital in the area, is less immersed in the research culture and has less experience on which to draw. Its LREC has dealt with very few qualitative projects, and so its system will be less flexible and able to cope better with quantitative studies. I see the difficulties that I experienced not as intentionally obstructive but rather as reflecting the problems facing a local committee in finding its way under challenging circumstances. The dilemmas raised are not about individual liability or about an LREC organizational bias against qualitative research, but about elements of an overall system of research review that would benefit from discussion.

The objective of my research was to provide a qualitative assessment of the impact and effect of genetic counselling on a group of clients receiving counselling for a common genetic disorder. I was conducting the study with the co-operation of the genetic counselling department at the local general hospital. The work was to form the basis of my PhD thesis but was also responding to a specific request from a clinical team for a feedback on services provided for this disorder. I was hoping to conduct and tape-record pre- and post-counselling interviews with about twenty new clients to establish, first, their hopes, needs, and expectations of the counselling consultation and, second, their feelings on what has been achieved, how satisfied they are, and the impact of the counselling. To compare clients' perceptions with those of the counsellors, I planned similar interviews with counsellors. I would then analyse conversations from the tape-recorded genetic-counselling consultation to see how pre-counselling expectations and post-counselling perceptions relate to what happens in the actual interaction.

Both in terms of gaps identified in existing research and in methodological fit, a qualitative method is best for this research. Much of the existing research has been conducted from a social psychological standpoint and has concentrated on outcomes. This has led to a divorce between process and results (Kessler, 1997) and has produced little knowledge about what occurs within actual genetic counselling sessions (Michie and Marteau, 1996). As a consequence, there is a lack of information on the practice of non-directiveness and agenda setting within the consultation – areas where counsellors' and clients' hopes and expectations are purported to differ. Little is known also about clients' expectations and satisfaction, about the inter-relationship between counsellor and client, and about the relationship between expectations, perceptions, satisfaction, and behaviour. Finally not much research has considered genetic counselling as a two-way communication, or interactional process – a significant omission when 'genetic counselling is defined as a communication process' (Lindhout, Frets, and Niermeijer, 1991) and can be fully understood only 'when considered as such' (Pilnick et al., 2000).

The major innovation of my research is its potential to link the expectations and perceptions of the participants with the actual features of the interaction. As well as filling the acknowledged gap in research on the process, the conversation analysis should show how these expectations affect behaviour in the consultation. It may also provide insight into areas such as non-directiveness or the giving and receiving of advice, initiation of topics and agendas, interactional asymmetry, and communication of information. The information on clients' expectations, satisfaction, and understanding gained from the interviews will be of use for service development and refinement. This may permit greater fulfilment of clients' expectations or, as Michie, Marteau, and Bobrow (1997) suggest, appropriate *modification* of their expectations. Comparison with counsellors' perceptions and expectations may shed further light on the reported mismatch between counsellors' and clients' 'agendas.' I will also be gathering data on the impact of genetic counselling on psychosocial aspects such as mood and emotion. All these areas will have relevance for training and the provision of an effective service.

The combination of methods will also allow me to explore how what is discussed in interview is reflected in what is actually done. This will avoid the criticisms made of ethnographic research that only subjective opinions can be gained and of conversation analysis that it is reluctant to move beyond the details of the interaction. The selection of informal or semi-structured interviews will allow the study to be open and responsive to clients' and counsellors' concepts of efficacy, impact, and expectation rather than focusing on what researchers or genetic-policy professionals expect to find. This approach is consistent with the qualitative method, which sees theory and ideas as coming out of the data rather than using the research to refute or confirm pre-existing assumptions.

Both ethnography and conversation analysis operate primarily inductively, allowing the research material to be searched for regularities, themes, and patterns that recur in the data and that the participants clearly see as having meaning. Using this approach, I hope to identify the organization of any interactional structures that the participants are employing to construct the 'institution' of genetic counselling and to discover how their subjective expectations and interpretations affect their responses, feelings, and behaviour.

This method contrasts with the quantitative process of establishing a hypothesis in advance and setting out to prove or disprove it to provide explanation and prediction. *There* one selects the variables to manipulate or measure before the research begins – for example, the measure of information recalled. As 'knowledge' is only that which can be externally and objectively observed, and internally held roles, norms, perceptions, and motives do not count as data, the quantitative method would exclude the *process* of genetic counselling from study and ignore internal perceptions of what it means to be a counsellor or client. This limitation would significantly restrict the ability of this research to answer the questions at hand and would limit what it could achieve.

Nevertheless, as I have indicated above, this is still the dominant approach within medical research, and many of the review procedures are geared towards it.

This quantitative predominance is reflected in the ethics application process at the general hospital, and it is to this that I now turn. Table 4.1 presents a timetable of events as they occurred. As is clear, this was a prolonged procedure. Although my delays in returning amendments because of illness or attending conferences accounts for perhaps three weeks, this still leaves a waiting period of about four months during a limited research period. I used up a further two weeks prior to submission com-

Table 4.1
Ethics application: Timetable of events

Week	Date	Action
0	June 2000	The process begins with my requesting the application form from the selected hospital. I must apply for this directly, as copies of the application form for LREC approval of research projects are not permitted to be held at the university.
4	End of July	Form completed, photocopied fifteen times, and taken to the Research Ethics Committee Office at the end of July – three weeks before the August meeting, as required
6	21 Aug.	Application heard at the General Ethics Committee
10	11 Sept.	First set of requested amendments received, just prior to fortnight of conferences for me
12	28 Sept.	Amendments sent to genetics counsellors for comments after review by supervisor
13	5 Oct.	Amendments returned to committee by me
18	11 Nov.	Second set of amendments received from committee after my absence, letter dated 1 November
19	15 Nov.	Amendments sent to genetics counsellors for comments after review by supervisor
20	21 Nov.	Second set of amendments returned to committee by me
24	19 Dec.	Approval confirmed in telephone call by me to ethics office
26	4 Jan. 2001	Confirmation letter received in internal mail

pleting a complex application form. This total represents a substantial chunk of my three-year PhD schedule.[1]

It has been a frustrating period, in which I have lost potential time for field research and related work. I used the time as productively as possible, preparing potential thesis chapters – a function that would have been best performed *after* I had collected the fieldwork data. The content of the eventual data may necessitate significant amendments. As I discuss in more detail below, the difficulty in defining a qualitative proposal according to quantitative-type parameters and the resulting requests for difficult-to-provide amendments may well have contributed to the delay.

The procedure as a whole entailed a considerable amount of work not only for me but also for a number of other people. This is no doubt true of the committee members involved as well. At each stage, whatever work I prepared needed to be checked by my supervisors at the university and, if it was information to go out to clients, by the genetic counsellors. I did not have to seek the approval of the latter, but it seemed desirable, in the interests of good practice and co-operation. In addition, the structure of

the form and the type of information required were not easily compatible with the nature of my research. Thus I faced a number of difficulties
in fulfilling the committee's requirements, and the nature of what I was
requested to do may cause problems later in my research.

Although the consideration of ethical issues is an important priority
and something on which I would expect to spend time and effort, I feel
that it was at times more challenging than necessary. In the following
sections I detail the specific areas in which difficulties arose and where,
as a result, there may be impediments to the research itself.

Areas of Difficulty

The first area of difficulty that I encountered lay in the form itself and
relate to the predominance in medical research of clinical or experimental projects; the second concerns the related downplaying of qualitative
research. Part of the header on the front page reads 'Application for
Ethical Approval of Clinical Research Project.' The organization of the
form is complex, and many of the sections are irrelevant for a qualitative
piece of social research such as my own. These sections do not need to be
completed, but they do need to be worked through and understood to
ascertain this fact, and they do make the forms appear daunting. As I was
unfamiliar with some of the hospital terms and departmental systems,
some other necessary sections were also difficult to complete.

There were also a number of sections on finance for which I had to go
to some trouble to make contact with or attain signatures from NHS department heads. As my research is funded entirely by the Economic and
Social Research Council (ESRC) and I did not need NHS support, this
seemed somewhat extraneous. This observation may support Alberti's
(1995) suggestion that financial questions should not be the responsibility of LRECs but should be clarified before submission.

My second difficulty lay in the application's clinical emphasis and in
the incompatibility between some quantitative and qualitative parameters.
It was difficult to define my research with the precision required by some
of the criteria. Terms such as hypothesis, rationale, investigator, and scientific background are more typical of an experimental model than of a
qualitative one, and I found myself confused as to what information was
required and about where or how to arrange my information to fit. It
would have required less work to structure my proposal using the more
familiar format of research question, methodology, method, researcher,
and so on (although the form did give the alternatives of research question or hypothesis). It would also have been less restrictive to the practi-

calities of my final research plan. The most significant difficulty of this quantitative bias, however, lay in the modifications or amendments requested to the original proposal. These were to lengthen the process, and I was to find it hard to give the level of detail asked for in some areas.

The most obvious example was the repeated request for a list of clearly defined questions or themes for the interviews. Burgess (1984) describes interview styles as running along a continuum from structured interviews to 'semi-structured' or 'interviews-as-conversation.' He defined a structured interview as one in which 'the interviewer poses questions and records answers in a set pattern' (101) and a semi-structured interview as one that 'employs a set of themes and topics to form questions in the course of conversation' (102). The informal or semi-structured interview itself is conducted along a continuum from mostly pre-set questions to totally unplanned time, and I had decided that its greater flexibility made it more appropriate for my needs.

I had anticipated constructing an interview guide of the type described by Maykut and Morehouse (1994), which would involve using a number of planned themes while leaving some elasticity for the interviewee. This approach is compatible with my overall qualitative method and with the inductive nature of my research. Coffey and Atkinson (1996) describe the process of qualitative data analysis as cyclical – a 'reflexive activity' that should inform all stages of research. So the reading on the issues present in genetic counselling should guide the initial questions and themes, and the findings concealed and revealed in the data should prompt further questions, research, and theory. The same process might be said to be applicable to the informal interview schedule. As the information from all sources in the research program comes in, the themes to be explored in interview will be partially dictated not only by the individual session, but also by the findings emerging from the data as a whole.

This factor makes it impossible to produce a precisely defined set of interview questions in the research proposal – a factor that was to cause me problems. The first set of amendments requested me to provide details of the format of the semi-structured interview. I took this to mean some idea of the composition of the interview and of the general areas to be dealt with, and so, for example, I included the following on the precounselling interviews: 'Client interviews will take place in their homes unless an alternative location is preferred. They are expected to be between 30 and sixty minutes in length. Themes for discussion will include the expectations, needs and wants that the clients have of their counselling session in terms of content, information, advice and any other areas the client might introduce, and their understanding of what genetic counselling involves. Counsellor interviews will include their understanding of the structure of the consultation and of what they expect to cover within the session. They will also involve their ideas of what the *clients* are expecting and wanting in terms of content, agenda and also advice.'

As the research protocol discussed the interviews, I enclosed an amended version of it along with the other amendments requested on the information and consent sheets. This development summarized progress to date, and I felt that it would cover the LREC review's requirements. However, the second response included the same request. I then created, on a separate sheet, a more detailed list of questions, including the following: 'What do you expect is going to happen when the genetic counsellor comes to your home?' 'What do you want to happen?' 'What do you expect will be talked about?' 'What kinds of things would you *like* to be discussed?' I also included a brief description of the inductive nature of informal or semi-structured interviews to allow myself some latitude to include other areas.

This version was accepted, and approval was given. However, the precision required seems excessive. The LREC transformed my method from an informal, semi-structured interview to a closely structured interview that approximates a questionnaire. If rigidly held to, the questions will be restrictive, and if ignored, they hold limited purpose. In addition, at what point could I be held accountable for changing the conditions of my approval?

Returning to the recommendations of the Royal College of Physicians, I also believe that this precision exceeds the scope of the LREC's remit. This is *methodological* material, not ethical, and to a level of detail not realistically compatible with my research ethos.

Amendments with Implications for Progress of Research

The LREC made two sets of amendments, however, that both were very specific in detail *and* may harm the research; as I show below, they also slowed the progress and affected morale. The amendments related mostly to patients' information and consent. Informed consent is essential and is a vital part of the LREC's recommendations. When the level of involvement may hinder progress, however, does this equate with While's 'impediments to research' (While, 1995: 661)? The Department of Health and the Royal College's recommendations for committees include ensuring the voluntary nature of participation, with clear indication to participants that no difference to treatment will ensue from refusal or withdrawal at any stage, adequate information, written consent, and assurance of confidentiality about a patient's identity. Patients should also be told if the trial is non-therapeutic. The general hospital has assembled its own comprehensive guidelines, which detail under headings how information should be displayed.

I had constructed a patient information sheet in the form of a one-page letter covering most of the above recommendations – although I had omitted a specific statement on the study's involving no direct benefit. I designed it to be easy to read, friendly, and not too long, and it was to go out with the initial appointment arrangements sent by the counsellors. I also included an 'opt-in' form for the client to return to me if he or she were willing to take part.

Both documents had been checked, commented on, and altered, where it felt necessary, by the genetic counselling team.

The first amendments made the important point that I must state that the study is of no direct benefit to patients. They also requested that I change the structure of the letter to include all the section headings contained within the hospital's guidelines. I was to mention details about storage and destruction of tapes and include more on confidentiality.

These changes transformed the sheet. Including all the sections extended the letter to nearly two full pages, and writing under headings resulted in a much more formal presentation than I originally intended. Instead of getting an informal and friendly 'invitation,' patients will receive a complex set of formal, explanatory guidelines. In addition, the second amendments required a covering letter from the counsellors. Along with their appointment notice, the patients will now receive a detailed two-page letter, an opt-in sheet, and another 'covering,' or explanatory, letter from the counsellors. These changes may intimidate patients by the formality of the presentation and/or put them off by the excessive amount to read. This result could hamper recruitment to the study. It could reduce the numbers responding or, alternatively, bias the sample population. The highlighting of the taping of material may also be off-putting. The intention to tape had been declared in the original letter but not emphasized, and even this had been questioned by the genetic counsellors.

The second amendment letter also asked for provision of counsellor information sheets and consent forms. Although it included an apology for not having mentioned these before, it still necessitated more work. As the counsellors had been consulted and involved from the start, the information sheet, at least, seemed unnecessary. It might also cause irritation at yet more material to read. The call for inclusion of specific input on taping also reveals another difficulty – at times the committee's requests were in conflict with the views expressed by the genetic counsellors. This may not only unsettle the professional research participants on whose co-operation I depend, but also challenge the views of those who are better informed to comment on particular patients' needs. Similarly, the level of explicit information that I needed to provide, both in the information sheet and in the interview schedule, has given the hospital detailed data on the specifics of my research questions. Potentially this might influence the counsellors' interviews or the consultation material. The genetic counsellors will be aware that they are being studied, and, as Sorenson comments on the institutional review board's review of his observational research, it 'seem(s) likely that their behaviour would be modified less if they did not know exactly what we were observing and why we were observing it' (1978: 2). I am not advocating covert research, but a fine balance exists between ethically sufficient and over-influential informing.

These direct and specific influences on the research material again raise some of the questions mentioned above. Is this level of methodological detail part of a committee's review role, and is it appropriate for qualitative, as opposed to quantitative-type, research? Are all the areas included relevant, and how far, however unintentionally, does the committee's review impede the process and the progress of research? Again I do not intend to cite the general hospital's work as individually liable for criticism, but significant questions do merit general discussion.

All the areas mentioned above lengthen the application process. The long gaps between sending of material and response, the production of two sets of amendments, and the amount of work and detail required resulted in a five-month procedure. If attention had focused on purely ethical issues, only one set of amendments would have been necessary, and the wait could have been shorter. The delay has seriously affected my research timetable and put back the potential start of my fieldwork by a number of months. Given a financial time limit and Economic and Social Research Council (ESRC) departmental quotas and deadlines for research completion, this could harm my – and the university's – research career (see note 15).

This application procedure also brought out a more personal difficulty, but one, I imagine, not unique to me. The long periods of waiting, the disappointment at a second set of amendments, and the feeling of wasting time when useful activity became a limited option all contributed to an overall sense of frustration on my part as time went by. Lack of motivation became a problem, as I wanted to be getting to a point where fieldwork was a possibility, and anxiety crept in as I could see my schedule being eroded. I felt that I had little control and that some things that I was required to do were either unprofitable or detrimental to my research. Overall it was a procedure that, although I recognize it as essential on an ethical level, I would not look forward to repeating.

Issues Raised

The difficulties that I encountered in this application pose, I believe, a number of practical and ideological questions for the ethical review of qualitative social research within the NHS. I briefly discuss these questions and show the areas that need to be addressed if the review procedure is to fulfil its functions of maintaining ethical standards of practice, protecting subjects' rights, and encouraging, rather than hindering, 'good medical research.'

Perhaps the most significant practical question relates to the need for reducing the delay. As well as being frustrating, delay has additional consequences beyond the disruption to research schedules. The time taken, says Nicholl (2000: 1217), 'has become a barrier to our research' and also adds up 'to the impossibility of doing practical research in the NHS to help decisions which must be made promptly.' It may discourage some research altogether, may prevent some kinds of potentially informative student projects (Jenkins, 1995), and dissipates resources.

For qualitative social research, should there be a separate system and/or application form? As my experience has shown, the difficulty of fitting qualitative research into a quantitative-type format and satisfying the subsequent demands can add to the time taken. Alberti (1995: 639) suggests that social protocols – methods involving questionnaires and/or interviews, rather than 'physically invasive procedures' – 'seem to create the biggest uncertainty for ethics committees,' and he then describes 'sociological studies' as a 'difficult area' for them to deal with. One solution that he proposes is more consistent central guidance for LRECs.

Oddens and De Wied (1995) observe that many of the problems associated with 'social medical research' relate to the absence of clear guidelines about ethical aspects of this type of study. Sociological studies will often have different priorities for ethics review – less emphasis, for example, on the protection of patients from physical harm – and may require different information. Patients may need, for example, more details on how and why their data will be used. From their position on the board of trustees of the International Health Foundation in Brussels, Oddens and De Wied also advise research ethics committees to design special application forms for social medical studies – a sensible proposition, given the disparity between clinical and social research parameters.

Other suggestions on dealing with forms of research unusual to committees have included the extended use of expert help, particularly peer review by external experts (Anonymous E, 2000). All these ideas might speed the review process by reducing the need for local committees to 'reinvent the wheel' each time they deal with non-clinical research and give them confidence to approve applications without excessive interference. They might also shift the emphasis from the clinical scenario to rethinking what might be significant principles relevant to the more social forms of medical research.

An additional, though closely associated, question concerns the overall scope and purpose of ethics committees. Nicholl (2000) comments that in his department's experience the frustration at delay and interference is made worse by committees' concentration on 'scientific, legal, and confidentiality issues instead of ethical issues.' My own experience supports this observation, although in my case much of the material requested by the committee concerned *method* rather than ethical detail. Committees need greater certainty about what counts as 'ethics review' in sociological studies and should perhaps restrict their involvement to that area. Again this relates to the lack of existing guidelines for social research. The report quoted above seeks clarification of 'the roles and accountabilities of the different bodies involved in research and its management' (Anonymous E, 2000: 21) and again emphasizes external peer review by experts. It points out that most funding bodies will have carried out rigorous checking before allocating funds.

Since it was funded by the ESRC, my research had already been subject to thorough review. ESRC studentships are very competitive and require submission of comprehensive detail on research questions, purpose, method, and methodology, with an increasing focus on ethical issues. The ESRC is skilled at assessing social research. Is full LREC review of the whole protocol necessary after prior peer review by experts? Are LRECs qualified to challenge such review by requiring multiple (and often 'nitpicking' (Alberti, 2000) changes? It may be that 'in order to avoid overwhelming bureaucratic obstruction to legitimate medical research different levels of research activity need to be subjected to a greater or lesser degree of control' (Anonymous E, 2000: 21). This might include more limited review – or even the delegation of review – of projects already passed as methodologically and legally sound by other expert social research bodies.

Conclusion

Britain's system of LRECs fulfils an important role in maintaining ethical standards and protecting the rights and interests of NHS patients involved in research. However, its current organization and the principles on which it is based may not be appropriate for all types of research. For some kinds of social research, it may be, as I have found, potentially detrimental to the research process. There is a mismatch between the ethical review that is needed and the system in place to supply it. As the amount of health-related social research is increasing there is a definite need for change. Clearer guidelines and more suitable parameters are required, and consideration of alternative forms of review might be beneficial. The scope of LREC review in social research needs to be clarified.

There are some overall developments already under way in the ethical review of medical research in Britain. These include the introduction of a Central Office for Ethical Review and operational changes announced in November 1999 that transfer consideration of many large-scale studies of non-therapeutic research to MRECs alone. Perhaps alongside these developments, a rethinking of the principles and procedures that underlie the ethical review of social medical research in the NHS might be constructive.

Notes

I would like to note the contribution of my fellow student Helen Busby to an earlier draft of this essay.

1 In the United Kingdom the performance of public bodies such as the Economic and Social Research Council (ESRC) is subject to regular assessment by government audit. One of the measures on which the ESRC is assessed is the number of students who submit their PhD theses within four years. Attaining a lower rate than other research councils may affect an ESRC's ability to provide funding. This requirement is passed on to universities in the form of submission quotas and sanctions. If a university fails to meet the 60% submission rate within four years it may be precluded from holding ESRC research studentships for a two-year period. As these studentships are

given only to students who are to pursue their degree within ESRC-rated institutions, this removes a major source of funding and therefore potential PhD students. In addition, the ESRC funds PhD studentships for three years only; the fourth year, for writing up, is not funded. For the student this strictly limits the time for research, in terms both of personal finance and of pressure from the university to submit a thesis on time. Delays to the research schedule are therefore too critical to ignore.

5

Reflections on Professional Ethics

JOHN M. JOHNSON AND DAVID L. ALTHEIDE

Professional and research ethics among social scientists have gained more attention and concern as state agencies, public universities, and professional associations have come to influence the nature and process of research and intellectual inquiry. The experiments on human subjects in Nazi Germany and the Tuskegee experiments on Black men with syphilis in the United States were among the first to draw attention to the dangers of state-sanctioned science. Infamous cases such as these led to establishment of institutional review boards (IRBs) in the United States in the 1970s, which promised greater protection and informed consent to human subjects who participate in research. The IRBs have not been unproblematically successful, however, and in 1996 the U.S. government admitted responsibility and financial culpability in killing and injuring hundreds of private citizens in a series of radiation and plutonium medical experiments.

In this essay we explore some of the complexities of professional ethics. After a preliminary overview, we offer some conceptual distinctions to discern five realms, or 'spheres,' of professional ethics. We then propose some further observations and reflections about ethics based on our combined sixty-five years of professional practice as university-based researchers and scholars.

Overview

The last two decades has seen an increase in control and regulation of research in the medical and social sciences. This was arguably stimulated by the horrors of the Nazi experimentation on human subjects during the Second World War, and perhaps by knowledge of the U.S. experi-

ments on Black men with syphilis in Tuskegee, Alabama. Another cause was the psychological experiment conducted by Stanley Milgram (1963) at Yale University in New Haven, Connecticut, where research subjects gave high-voltage 'shocks' to other people whom they thought were other research subjects, but who were in fact confederates in the research process who simulated their responses to the 'shocks.' And in yet another highly controversial piece of research, Leon Festinger, Henry Riecken, and Stanley Schachter (1956) pretended to belong to a cult whose members believed in a prophecy that predicted the end of the world, for the purposes of studying the group. Using deception in experiments and in field studies was common during the 1950s, 1960s, and 1970s. Morton Hunt (1982: 66) estimates that one-third of all psychological and social psychological research done during the 1960s and 1970s involved deception.

Deceiving human subjects is hardly the sole or exclusive issue in the realm of professional or research ethics. Another highly questionable form of research in this mid-century period was 'Project Camelot,' an applied project in social science research in Chile, conducted by U.S. social science researchers, where the research questions and the funding stemmed from the U.S. Central Intelligence Agency (Horowitz, 1970, 1974). When educated people learned about this misappropriation of social science research for the crass political purposes of the CIA, the ethical sensitivities of nearly everyone were offended.

Research and professional 'ethics' in the social sciences form part of a larger picture – the desires of social scientists for access to power and political legitimacy. Arthur Vidich and Stanford Lyman (1985: 300) observe: 'Some sociologists seek to resolve current problems by moving the discipline into an even more intimate professional association with its hitherto most generous patron, government; others seek to justify continued federal and foundational support by pointing to the virtues entailed in its failures. To them the science is worthy because it has not fulfilled the positivist dream of absolutist prediction, by not taking over the awesome powers of the Protestant God, by not wanting more than a service role and an advisory capacity in the American commonwealth.'

The social sciences have a long history of saddling up to government and its institutions for money, power, prestige, control, and more money. They are now pillars of the welfare state and its scientistic legitimacy. They have legitimated legal and criminal-justice control over increasing numbers of citizens and have extended control far beyond the legal institutions of the welfare state. The expansion of surveillance throughout the social order looks at much more than crime. The tools and perspectives of policing have been extended as a format to control society more generally. Richard Erikson and Kevin Haggerty (1997) refer to this as 'policing the risk society,' because post-industrial society has expanded knowledge about a wide range of social and political risks, and public-policy makers routinely use social sciences' knowledge about these risks to try to manage and control these actual or potential situations. Ironically, it is that knowledge that is now being used as a foundation for extending more control, regulation, and surveillance over more and more aspects of life. The recent concerns with regulating medical and social research through IRBs represent only one aspect of this larger situation.

The contemporary focus on 'research ethics' is really about issues other than research ethics. 'Ethics' has been folded into or collapsed into discourses of institutional control. Injunctions to 'voluntarily control' ourselves are not really voluntary, as these are tied into funding sources, symbolic legitimacy control, and the increasing litigiousness of society. The inspiration for the U.S. IRBs, after all, was the federal government, in 1971 – specifically the Department of Health, Education, and Welfare. Its published 'guidelines' for research became binding for research funded by the federal agencies. It sometimes loosened these guidelines in the 1970s to permit continued psychological research using deception, but this is a separate story. IRBs' control over research ethics is now so firm, for example, that our recent search of the NEXIS information base shows that topics related to ethics in the social sciences are rarely mentioned apart from IRBs. The IRBs essentially own, operate, and control the discourse on social science and research ethics. Indeed, what we now think of as 'ethics' has been modified and transformed by its associations with institutional control. University-based researchers and scholars no longer plausibly claim independence from their state patrons and sponsors.

This trend was noted as early as the late 1960s by Alvin Gouldner (1968), in his well-known article 'The Sociologist as Partisan: Sociology and the Welfare State.' In 1970, Gouldner (1970: 260) commented on why functionalists were so enamoured of religion: 'It derives, I would suggest, from the technological weakness of sociology now and from the inability of sociologists to achieve the high places they seek in society through the practical contributions they make. The religious impulse of sociology, that is, arises and is sustained when sociologists and sociology lack the very power that they attribute to society. It betokens a great gap between the ambitions of sociologists and the means they have to realize them as scientists and technicians; piety, in short, becomes a substitute for power.'

Institutionalizing IRBs and the control of social research has transformed what we think of as ethics. The major institutions shaping ethics in our society involve the realms of power, control, surveillance, and legitimation. Universities are becoming more intertwined and interdependent with the corporate world, marketing students with alcohol, cell phones, safe sex, music, and material 'necessities.' Universities are becoming more protective of their stature, prestige, growth, reputations, costs, benefactors, audiences, and political connections. The market and corporate perspective rule in calculations of risks and in elimination of culpability and of potential legal 'exposure.'

Human resource departments now 'handle' or 'manage' faculty members and social researchers. Faculty problems are to be dealt with, but above all they must be separated from those of the institution. When one of us was called to serve on our local IRB, at the first meeting we were instructed to obtain a separate insurance policy to cover our IRB service, since the institution could not guarantee legal coverage. This is the major sociological contribution of IRBs – to account for the process of legitimation and authorization, for all practical bureaucratic (and legal) institutional purposes. If it can be shown that the 'rules' of appropriate research are not followed, then it can be claimed that it is no longer the university's (legal liability) problem. Bureaucratic decision-making and logic now shape our practices and our language. This is the present context, and ignoring it may lead to potentially serious (personal, legal, professional) consequences.

It is a mistake to think that all concerns with ethics are coterminous with IRBs, corporate logic, and legal liability. It is important to discern appropriate differences in the realms or 'spheres,' of ethics, to appreciate the locus of control and other differences that flow from these.

Five Ethical Spheres

For scholars, intellectuals, and social researchers who work in corporate (commonly university) settings, there are five major spheres of ethics – personal, research, intellectual, professional, and corporate. Some of these are partly independent of the patronage or corporate setting; others overlap with it. Understanding these differences allows one to contextualize 'research ethics' and to discern the implications and consequences of these spheres.

Personal Ethics

Personal ethics relates to all those types of behaviour or action that people commonsensically associate with this field, which just might include almost anything or everything to which individuals attach a normative expectation. Among what are commonly regarded as the eight major or world religions, there is loose consensus in four areas (killing of group members, telling lies after taking an oath of honesty before a tribunal or court, stealing property from prohibited people or places, and sexually abusing others), but there are literally scores of iterations on these themes, and even more countless adumbrations, exclusions, and exemptions. And then there are hundreds of other religions, ethical systems, and secular perspectives that have different morals, norms, and ethical obligations. Since specialized training in social science research commonly occurs in adulthood, virtually all those who eventually practise research in the social sciences bring these ethical perspectives, sentiments, and sensibilities with them and commonly retain these after the lengthy training and apprenticeship are over.

Personal ethics is broader and more general than the other spheres of ethics and arguably subsumes all other ethical distinctions. Since it actually or potentially includes about all of life, it is broader and more inclusive than the other areas. Professional organizations generally do not presume to dictate canons or normative rules at this level, and the usual assumption is that most such bodies tend to represent about the same wide swath of people that one finds in the larger culture.

Actual situations in field research surely do confront individuals with ethical decisions that have little or no relation to the research. Are we really so naïve as to believe that scientific obligations are what led Festinger, Riecken, and Schachter (1956) to promote enthusiastically the group that they claimed to study? Or W.H. Whyte (1996) to engage in 'repeat voting' during elections or in 'retrospective falsifications' and self-admitted violations of professional ethics? Or Dalton (1959; 1964) to bribe secretaries for information on their managers and bosses? Or Rosalie Wax (1971: 168) to engage in certain professional 'misdemeanors' while conducting research in Japanese relocation camps, or Malinowski (1967) to hit a recalcitrant informant on the jaw, or John Johnson (1975: 166) to acquiesce in the seductions of a beautiful woman, or Gans (1962: 46) to 'be dishonest in order to get honest data'?

Rather than taking the moral high ground by second-guessing these personal and contextual decisions, perhaps it is more useful at this juncture to suggest that our larger intellectual and research community knows about and is able to debate and discuss such issues only because of the relatively lesser forms of institutional control over research during earlier decades. Are we more or less free today, knowing that we need our local IRBs to approve our future research proposals or those of our students?

Over three decades ago Ned Polsky (1969) wrote a brilliant essay about the ethics of studying crime and other forms of deviant behaviour, arguing in essence the importance for those who elect such investigations of making personal, ethical commitments of loyalty to the settings and their members. Klockars (1979) and Douglas (1976, 1979) have advanced variations of this position. It is fair to say that all the advocates of this ethical stance, however, would insist that it involves a personal ethical decision to attempt such studies and that not all individuals will make such a high-risk, uncertain choice. Fieldwork can be risky, and the consequences serious: Powdermaker (1966) was confronted by a lynch mob while in the field in the U.S. south; Schwartz (1964) was physically attacked by the people at the mental hospital that he studied; Thompson (1967) was beaten up by the Hell's Angels; sociological fieldworkers Vidich and Bensman (1968) were burned in effigy; Wallis (1977) was followed and harassed by members of the Scientology group that he studied; Rosalie Wax (1971) was denounced as a 'communist agitator'; and Yablonsky (1968) was threatened with violence during his field observations of gang members.

Research Ethics

Research ethics includes those forms of behaviour or those actions that have normative expectations for researchers in their role as researchers. Historically and traditionally, this sphere has commonly focused on the following issues: (1) whether studying a particular problem requires overt or covert research, (2) if overt research is elected, then what actions the researcher should take to adequately inform or communicate the purposes of the research, (3) how to gain access to a setting and what is obligated, owed, or required of the 'research bargain' in negotiation of this access, (4) how to gain and maintain the trust of the members of the setting, (5) how to ensure the privacy or confidentiality of the information collected during the research, and (6) what and what not to report formally as part of the final research reports.

There exists a voluminous literature on the above issues, and it is not our present intention to summarize it. IRBs concern themselves with these issues and demand strong compliance on informed consent, confidentiality of research information, strict responsibility over the chain of control of research information and data at all stages of the research process, and scrupulous reporting. Many of today's corporate scholars find these issues unproblematic, and some even advocate strict compliance even in research settings that are outside IRB authority or control (Schensul et al., 1999: 181–9). Those who find these matters the most problematic are those who study the police or other official control agencies (Marx, 1980, Punch, 1986, 1989), criminal or deviant behaviour (Douglas, 1979, Adler, 1985, Adler and Adler, 1999), or covert political or other secretive groups (Brajuha and Hallowell 1986; Scarce 1994, 1995, 1999).

Intellectual Ethics

Intellectual ethics concerns those normative expectations applicable to scholars, intellectuals, and researchers about how to select problems or issues for investigation, how to sponsor and pursue such inquiries, and how to discern and report the truth(s). Problem selection is not a matter of methodological technique and raises critical issues of research funding, patronage, and the politics of corporate affiliation. Many unreflective partisans of the current welfare state rarely see problems in this sphere and prefer to adopt a laissez-faire attitude towards those who choose 'to play the grant-getting games' of various public or private corporate patrons.

Relations between professional organizations and state funding have grown much closer in recent decades, and for most social science professionals this is a matter of pride, not shame. The reigning ethic in the academy is: Going along to get along. Peace in our time!

Professional Ethics

Professional ethics concerns normative expectations and obligations to and for those who belong to professional organizations, associations, or communities, as professionals. Professional membership in such bodies often entails codes of ethics as promulgated by groups of scholars and academics, and these are commonly much broader than the research or even intellectual ethics noted above and may include normative rules about plagiarism; authorship; giving appropriate credit to those who participate in research, writing, or other professional projects; job applications and acceptance; and treatment of minorities. The ethical domain of professional ethics inexorably grows like a bamboo shoot in a rain forest, but inevitably without a corresponding growth in resources for enforcement, so few people seem to take much notice, except those caught in the bureaucratic mesogasters of its committee structure.

Corporate Ethics

Corporate ethics deals with those normative (and usually legal) obligations promulgated by the organizations that employ a scholar, researcher, or intellectual – most commonly, a college or university. It tends to vary significantly between types of organizations, states, provinces, regions, and nation states. In Arizona, for example, there is a formal code for all university employees. While in most jurisdictions there is commonly some overlap between these corporate codes and the professional codes of scholarly associations, the local codes commonly include more focused and concrete areas of interest, which may be related to specific events that have occurred in this community.

With the above distinctions in mind about the five spheres of ethics, we offer our opinion that, based on our own experience of working in American universities for over three decades, the sphere of research ethics is arguably the least problematic of all. In reflecting on research ethics and the violations about which we knew or had heard trustworthy accounts, the worst case of unethical conduct by a researcher of which we could think involved a young man who was studying drug dealing for his dissertation research, while it was widely suspected that he was using his dissertation as a front for dealing. When he was caught for drug dealing, there was absolutely no faculty or administrative support for this unethical conduct. All the other examples seemed quite minor by comparison. Veteran field researcher John F. Lofland (1971) may feel that researchers 'report only the second worst things which happen,' but the first-worst, whatever those might be, pale in comparison with what occurs frequently within 'departmental politics' among corporate actors in most universities.

Further Observations and Reflections

All ethical decisions involve highly complicated responses to and deliberations about complex interactions, usually among and between several individuals, parties, and interests, where there are many unknown aspects of the interactions between one's intentions and one's 'guesstimates' of taking one course of action over another. This choice always involves linguistic and paralinguistic information that is indexically tied to the immediate context. This situation is inevitable, unavoidable, and irremediable. It is preposterous to think that it could be controlled by professional organizations, and it is impossible for such bodies to enforce ethical conduct in a just manner at this level of interaction. Therefore the best ethical decisions in research settings take place at the lowest or most concrete levels of interaction, made by actors who have access to the most immediate, most concrete, most contextualized information. If one understands and accepts this reality, then it is difficult to imagine what a realistic ethical code might look like. This is our best effort: (1) try not to hurt anyone, and (2) when you do hurt someone, try your best to make amends. But we concede that key terms such as 'try,' 'best,' 'hurt,' and 'amends' are problematic, so even this relatively simple code is unenforceable.

Our feeling is that, over the last forty years, the worst case of unethical conduct was probably 'Project Camelot' in Chile, but it was unethical not because of violations of research ethics but because of the initial sacrifice ('selling out') of the intellectual integrity of the project to the official, corporate sponsor. This was an issue of intellectual ethics, not research ethics.

The most outrageously unethical conduct occurs in academic departments by professional actors who are formally recognized as competent by the organizations that sanction, employ, and fund them. Our own direct and indirect university experiences have involved the following eight incidents:

- a member of faculty who went to trial for the rape of another faculty member's wife
- a faculty member who ran an escort service as a front for prostitution, employing some of his own graduate students as prostitutes
- a faculty member who hired a former CIA operative to break into the office of a colleague for the purposes of stealing property
- destruction of personal property of faculty members by other members of faculty
- threatening and harassing of a faculty member's family by colleagues
- theft and destruction of mail by faculty members (which explains why our own unit is the only one of seventy-five on campus to have secured mail boxes)
- a faculty member who ran a separate full-time business while being employed 'full time' by the university
- faculty members selling drugs to students

In addition, perversions of the hiring process for political purposes are legion: lying on personnel records is institutionalized, lying on grant proposals is legendary, and use of state money to reward friends and political allies is too common even to note. For all the behaviour noted here – admittedly but a list of 'second-worst things to happen,' partly because we could not agree about what and what not to report – negative sanctions occurred only in the case of the professor who ran the whore-house in downtown Phoenix; he was allowed to resign in order to protect his pension.

Ethical provocateurs, ethical entrepreneurs, and other claims makers often involve themselves after the fact of some conduct or behaviour in order to pursue some political purpose independent of the initial act or acts. Such persons often use others and commonly hurt others in order to advance their own moral or ethical agendas. This is probably inevitable. Professional organizations, insofar as they become engaged in ethical disputes or controversies at all, do so retrospectively. This was the case in the research controversy involving Mario Brajuha (Brajuha and Hallowell 1986) – a graduate student who was studying a restaurant that was apparently 'torched' by the Mob. It was similarly true for the controversy surrounding the research of Rik Scarce (1994, 1995, 1999), an ethnographer studying ecoterrorists. And it was also what happened at San Diego State University, when President Tom Day tried to fire six tenured sociologists. Some good and some damage control can occur retrospectively, so in making this observation we do not mean to deprecate such actions just because they take place after the fact.

Ethnographic and other forms of qualitative research have proven very valuable in studying crime and deviant behaviour. This is an area where scientists have debated their ethics for a long time, and there is now a robust literature discussing and debating these issues. The arguments of Becker (1967), Gouldner (1968), Polsky (1969), Douglas (1976, 1979), Klockars (1979), Bulmer (1982), and Punch (1986) remain seminal. Researchers such as these have shown much greater ethical awareness and sensitivity than those in other, 'legal' areas of research, and arguably more than most departmental actors who hurt others for political motives. It is ironic that research topics such as these become the easiest targets for IRB moral entrepreneurs. Such trends lead sociologists Patricia Adler and Peter Adler to ask if researchers will allow research and intellectual agendas to be so greatly influenced by lawyers and their corporate police (see chapter 3, above).

In the United States, the first amendment of the constitution protects journalists by guaranteeing free speech and a free press. Social scientists lack such protection regarding confidentiality of sources, however, and we surmise that this is best seen as a political issue, rather than a moral one. If social scientists had such protection, we speculate that we might be addressing a different set of ethical issues – perhaps ones such as how social scientists abuse their constitutional protection. In the absence of such safeguards, we have little choice but to continue our discussions about ethics, to act reflexively, to foster intellectual and research creativity and autonomy, and to avoid policing and legalistic solutions to ethical problems. We must continue to study and reflect on the dominant bureaucratic formats and processes that surround more and more of our lives. We must understand these forms and processes in order to resist them effectively, and to create our own greater freedoms.

Notes

I presented an earlier version of this essay at the Annual Meetings of the Pacific Sociological Association in San Diego in April 1999.

6

Confidentiality and Anonymity: Promises and Practices

LINDA SNYDER

This essay addresses the challenges that researchers face in ensuring the anonymity of research participants when they are working with qualitative data. Codes of ethics prescribe respect for confidentiality, while research strategies to promote trustworthiness require openness with the data. The objective of the chapter is to uncover some of the underlying assumptions of these two, oft-conflicting principles and to provide some suggestions for respecting both.

Because we use qualitative methods in studies involving humans, we have a more difficult challenge than do quantitative researchers in ensuring the anonymity of participants and the confidentiality of their data. The divergent perspectives on protection of privacy held by constructivist researchers gathering qualitative data and by positivist practitioners collecting quantitative data have been the subject of lively debate since the 1960s (Mitchell, 1993). Despite the practical differences and philosophical arguments, ethical integrity demands that we seek better ways to reconcile our promises and our practices.

First, I review the ethical obligations to protect privacy that underpin the promises that we make to participants. Second, I discuss research objectives that may enhance the trustworthiness of the data, analysis, and findings and that are consistent with qualitative methods and work. I focus there on credibility and on transferability as prime examples of objectives that require practices that may conflict with our promises. Third, I illustrate the challenge of honouring ethical obligations and research objectives using as an example qualitative research in Canada and in Chile involving humans – my own multiple case study of women's employment initiatives (Snyder, 1999). Fourth and finally, I offer some suggestions, for researchers doing case studies of identified programs, in hopes of both protecting privacy and ensuring trustworthy research.

Ethical Obligations Regarding Privacy

As Canadian researchers, our ethical obligations to protect privacy are enshrined in the *Tri-Council Policy Statement: Ethical Conduct for Research Involving Humans* composed jointly by the Canadian Institutes of Health Research (formerly the Medical Research Council), the Natural Sciences and Engineering Research Council, and the Social Sciences and Humanities Research Council (MRC, NSERC, and SSHRC, 1998d). For Canadian social workers, the *Social Work Code of Ethics* (Canadian Association of Social Workers, or CASW, 1994) applies as well. The *Tri-Council Policy Statement* speaks to, among other things, the context of an ethics framework, the requirement for free and informed consent, and respect for privacy and confidentiality. Throughout, it acknowledges the complexity and continually evolving nature of these considerations.

In addressing the context of an ethics framework, the statement emphasizes the need for research, with its moral premise of advancing human welfare through such potential benefits as alleviating human suffering and producing better social policy. The document affirms the moral imperatives and ethical principles related to conduct of this research, including the imperative to respect human dignity. The Tri-Council's *Context of an Ethical Framework* (MRC et al., 1998a: 5) recognizes, however, that diversity in research and in fundamental values may generate conflicting principles in specific research cases that 'properly demand probing ethical reflection and difficult value choices.'

Two guiding principles are most relevant to protection of human dignity. First, the Tri-Council's *Requirement for Free and Informed Consent* (MRC et al., 1998c) stipulates that prospective subjects must be provided the opportunity to give free and informed consent about participation, prior to and throughout the study. This means that researchers must share information about their research purpose and process, that subjects may make their own decisions about participation – usually indicating in writing the terms of their agreement to participate – and that participants have a right to withdraw at any time.

Second, the Tri-Council's *Privacy and Confidentiality* (MRC et al., 1998b) obliges researchers conducting interviews to maintain confidential any personal information confided by participants unless they have provided free and informed consent or a compelling public interest such as protection of life is at stake. Researchers should ensure that their research subjects are aware of 'the extent of confidentiality that can be promised' (2). In addition, the document suggests anonymity as the best means of protecting confidentiality.

These guiding principles are not unfamiliar to social workers, who are accustomed to operating within the CASW's (1994) *Social Work Code of Ethics.* This code articulates similar core values regarding the 'intrinsic worth and dignity of every human being' (1). One of the primary ethical duties and obligations is as follows: 'A social worker shall protect the confidentiality of all information acquired from the client or others regarding the client and the client's family during the professional relationship unless: (a) the client authorizes in writing the release of specific information; (b) the information is released under the authority of a statute or an order of a court of competent jurisdiction; or (c) otherwise authorized by this Code' (2).

Clearly, our responsibility as researchers, and for some of us as social workers, to protect the privacy of human subjects in our research is paramount. The complexity increases when we add further principles and objectives.

Research Objectives for Trustworthiness

Many of us carrying out research using qualitative methods are working within the constructivist paradigm. Lincoln and Guba have delineated two criteria for research rigour in this paradigm. First, credibility parallels the criterion of 'internal validity / the ability to make causal claims' in the conventional paradigm. Second, transferability parallels that of 'external validity / the ability to generalize' (Lincoln and Guba, 1985: 290–1).

The objective of the credibility criterion is the adequate representation of truth – which the constructivist paradigm conceptualizes as 'multiple realities' (Lincoln and Guba, 1985: 314). Researchers undertake a number of research strategies or activities to enhance the credibility of research in this paradigm. The two with implications for 'protection of privacy' are member checking and triangulation.

The member-checking process involves sharing preliminary impressions with research participants and seeking their feedback with respect to the accuracy of the researcher's understanding of their data. In Lincoln and Guba's (1985: 301) words, it is 'the direct test of findings and interpretations with the human sources from which they have come.' The triangulation process recommended by Denzin (1978: 21) 'forces the observer to combine multiple data sources.' Diesing (1972: 147) calls this same process 'contextual validation,' wherein 'the validity of a piece of evidence can be assessed by comparing it with other kinds of evidence on the same point.'

The objective of the criterion of transferability, in lieu of ensuring the generalizability of findings to the larger population, is 'providing suffi- cient descriptive data to make such similarity judgments possible' (Lin- coln and Guba, 1985: 316). Hence reports of constructivist research endeavour to include 'thick description,' providing a wide range of relevant information and direct quotes.

The Challenge Illustrated: Canadian and Chilean Employment Initiatives

For illustrative purposes, I describe a research project wherein I encoun- tered several challenges in honouring simultaneously promises of pri- vacy and practices of enhancing the trustworthiness of the research.

My research was a multiple case study looking at women's employment initiatives as a means of addressing poverty (Snyder, 1999). In both Canada and Chile, I examined a governmental and a non-governmental program. In Canada, the government program was the Employment Resource Pro- gram for Single Parents – a municipal program in Ontario's Waterloo Region supporting single parents receiving social assistance. The non- governmental example involved training offered by the Community Opportunities Development Association (CODA) in Cambridge, On- tario, for women wanting to start their own businesses. In Chile, the governmental program was a micro-enterprise training program for women, directed by the National Women's Ministry (SERNAM), in one of the large southern regions. The non-governmental endeavour was Prisma, which developed female artisans in Santiago.

The purpose of my research was to gain insight into the potential of women's employment initiatives to address poverty in terms of both (a) individual and family outcomes related to economic and psycho- social well-being and (b) collective results and social mobilization chal- lenging broader social structures. I conducted the study using qualitative methods of observation, participant-observation, interviews, focus groups, and examination of program materials. I look now at both the promises that I made and at the realities of practice.

Promises: The Consent Form

The protection of privacy that I offered was at the individual level. The consent form included the usual provisos: 'I understand that notes in- cluding my comments will be kept confidential and that I will not be identified in any publication or discussion ... Quotations will be limited to those that do not disclose my identity, unless Linda [Snyder, the researcher] obtains my consent to use quotes that may disclose my identity' (Snyder, 1999: 406–7).

I sought approval to study the programs through their senior administrations and offered them formative evaluations of their programs in return for their co-operation and the opportunity for them to review the preliminary findings prior to my completion of the final reports. From the beginning, there was no intention to disguise the identity of the organizations.

Yin (1994: 143) identifies the two levels at which the issue of anonymity rises in case studies – 'that of the entire case (or cases) and that of an individual person within a case (or cases).' He does not consider anonymity desirable, and he makes a strong case for being able to 'integrate a new case study with prior research' (143). In situations where he does consider anonymity justifiable ... in suggests compromises such as providing anonymity to the individuals, but leaving the case(s) to be identified accurately (144). This latter position is reflected in the protection of privacy promised in my study. However, it is arguable how well that promise can be ensured at even the individual level.

Practices: The Realities of Confidentiality and Anonymity

It was my experience, working in a research modality employing thick description and triangulation, that I could not provide anonymity to the programs' directors. In their own communities, to varying degrees, they are public figures. Particularly, in the case of Prisma, the director, Valentina Bone, is a figure of considerable historical importance and is widely known.

Prior publications offer valuable historical and contextual material for understanding the case studies. Hence I have referenced them and quoted from them. One includes testimony from Valentina Bone:

> After the military coup I was out of a job like so many others, in a short time the Pro-Paz committee asked me to develop some craft work projects with the women. The first group assigned to me were women of the families of the detained-disappeared ... Everything I had been thinking of doing with these women was useless, since the future work we would undertake together ought to serve as a catharsis. Every woman began to translate her story into images and the images into embroidery, but the embroidery was very slow

and their nerves weren't up to that. Without knowing how to continue I walked, looked and thought and finally my attention was attracted by a Panamanian *mola*, a type of indigenous tapestry. I remembered also a foreign fashion very much in vogue at that time: 'patchwork.' Very happy with my solution the very next day we began collecting pieces of fabric, new and used, thread and yarn, and with all the material together we very quickly assembled our themes and the tapestries, the histories remained like a true testimony in one or various pieces of fabric. It was dramatic to see how the women wept as they sewed their stories, but also it was very enriching to see how in some ways the work afforded happiness, provided relief, happiness to see that they were capable of creating their own testimony, relief simply from the fact of being together with others, talking together, sewing, being able to show that by means of this visual record others would know their story. (Agosin, 1987: 94–5)

The directors' contributions to and impact on the programs are central in the participants' comments and the research findings. For example, the best means of illustrating my finding of the threads of positive role modelling throughout the organization was the listing of the following identifying interview quotes:

Valentina [the director] always believed in my ability; this was very important to me – because it was the first time anyone believed in me and in what I could do ... It [my accomplishment] is a good example for my students; I can motivate them to grow, and show them my strength and that we can succeed. (Comment from an instructor who is a graduate of the program)

[The instructor] places a great investment in her students ... She is very understanding and gives a lot of herself ... In reality, they all have a great capacity for the purpose here. (Comment from a student in the training centre)

Now, [my] need to work here is not so great; now it's for personal rewards ... I have grown children, who are professionals and who help me economically. And they ask me why I'm still involved. It's because the women matter immensely to me. (Comment from an artisan workshop leader)

Further compromises to promises of anonymity occur during the member-checking process. When the researcher shares preliminary findings, members can recognize each other. Checking with participants individually was practical only in a very few situations. So I limited this time-consuming exercise to a handful of highly recognizable and sensitive situations.

The Waterloo Region's Employment Resource Program for Single Parents (the governmental example in Canada) had one primary agency sending referrals to it (the social assistance office) and one key agency to which it referred many clients (the local community college's Focus for Change course). In each instance, members of the program's staff knew the collateral agency's contact person whom I had interviewed for the study. Because I was still in close geographical proximity to the program after I had prepared my preliminary findings, I was able to meet with each of them again individually to check their the material that was identifiably from them:

> Mention was made of interest in follow-up, by both a participant and the Focus for Change teacher. The participant was interested in follow-up to the group work. The Focus teacher's interest was of an evaluative nature regarding the outcomes of the action plans developed by students in her classes. (Snyder, 1999: 206)

> A work placement opportunity was suggested by a referral source as a means of increasing confidence and experience. This idea was highly supported during the sharing of preliminary findings. A participant emphasized the distinction between on-the-job learning opportunities (which she would welcome) and mandatory workfare placements (which she sees as slave labour). Another participant, similarly, stressed the importance of focusing on placements providing training and experience, not just 'dead-end' jobs. (207)

I also felt it necessary in Chile to share my preliminary findings individually with the director of the Prisma program, because she was highly identifiable and because she had shared very personal information with me that I doubted she had discussed with staff and program participants. Since I had returned to Canada, I mailed the preliminary findings to her with a covering letter asking if there were any errors in my understanding of what she had told me and if there was any commentary that she would prefer I remove or present differently. In a follow-up conversation, she confirmed her wish that I remove the 'very personal' information before sending copies for staff and program participants but reported that, in terms of accuracy, she had found reading the findings to be like 'watching a film about the program.'

The remaining member checking occurred on a non-individualized basis. For each of the Canadian programs, I held group follow-up meetings with staff members and with program participants. For the Chilean programs, I mailed copies of the preliminary findings to all research subjects simultaneously and asked them to reply on enclosed prepaid aerograms. However, I was very conscious that, although I was giving research subjects the opportunity to remove any identifying information from the final publication, their colleagues were able to see all the information in the preliminary document. As Punch (1994: 92) noted as well, simply refraining from naming commentators does not protect their privacy: 'The cloak of anonymity may not work with insiders who can easily locate the individuals concerned.'

This practice of simultaneous sharing is not uncommon. Lincoln and Guba (1985: 315) suggest arranging a session to which representatives of the source groups are invited. They also suggest providing copies of the report to the 'member-check panel in advance for study and written commentary.' Clearly, some of our necessary practices do not seem to be consistent with our promises.

Finding the Balance

Qualitative researchers, as my study (Snyder, 1999) has shown, enter an ethical grey zone. On one hand, the various ethical codes require us to promise confidentiality; on the other hand, some of the strategies of our research, such as member checking, necessitate our going back to our interviewees and research setting. These conflicts can hamstring both the ethical and the practical elements of our research. There are, however, ways to find the balance. The remainder of this chapter discusses them.

Can we enhance our practices so that we provide a higher level of confidentiality and anonymity? In the multiple case study described, to have met with each participant to carry out the member checking individually would have doubled the cost of the research and might have annoyed some participants.

Should we constrain our promises? Kimmel (1988: 103) recommends that researchers mention routinely, during discussions on informed consent, the potential sharing of research information for such purposes as long-term follow-up. It would follow logically that we attempt to be aware from the beginning how our data will be analysed, reported, and otherwise used and as a result make only very reasoned promises that we can honour. But when working in the constructivist paradigm, we are not always aware from the beginning of how the research design will unfold.

Thus to honour the principles behind both ethics-based promises and trustworthy constructivist research practices, I offer the following four suggestions for informed consent in case studies of identified programs:

First, we should clarify, with each research participant, the distinct nature of work within the constructivist paradigm, with its inherent limitations in ensuring the anonymity of research participants and the confidentiality of their comments, particularly in studies of identified programs.

Second, we should offer participants an opportunity to review the preliminary findings simultaneously with other participants for the purposes of providing feedback regarding accuracy and of indicating if any identifying comments should be removed prior to final publication.

Third, we should seek to understand the degree of anonymity, confidentiality, and / or identification desired by each participant.

Fourth, we should individualize consent forms to reflect the wishes of specific participants.

These suggestions, I believe, will allow us the necessary scope of action to conduct trustworthy research and at the same time ensure that we have been forthright with our research participants and make only promises that we can fully honour.

7

Biting the Hand That Feeds You, and Other Feminist Dilemmas in Fieldwork

MERLINDA WEINBERG

This essay considers three ethical dilemmas inherent in a research project that sought to understand, from the standpoint of the residents, how one administrative document was used in a maternity home. The solution to these dilemmas is the focus of this essay. First, as a feminist, I found that my responsibility to challenge hegemonic ideology clashed with the realities of recognizing the need for some social control in an institutional setting. By analysing power relationships in fieldwork, I decided that while social work contains elements of social control, in this instance the 'relations of ruling' (Smith, 1996) went beyond what was required to maintain a functioning residence. Second, the data that I elicited raised issues that reflected negatively on an agency that I respected. I explore the dilemmas of maintaining a relationship of trust while being truthful to uncomplimentary material. By the development of a dialectical relationship with the director, I was able to resolve this issue. Third, when conducting fieldwork in hierarchical settings, while maintaining confidentiality I found conflicting ethical demands of causing no harm and crediting respondents. The dictum of causing no harm took precedence in one situation, but not in another. In hierarchical field settings, one's responsibility to maintain confidentiality is complex. I was able to ensure confidentiality for only some of the players. Through this inquiry I came to realize that a research project is a 'lived dilemma rather than simply the neat achievement presented in [a] published report' (Yates, 1995: 23), with the researcher accountable to various actors with multiple perspectives. Which obligations are pre-eminent can be determined only situationally.

The following sections explore the relevant theoretical framework, consider the research assignment, take stock of the ethical dilemmas of the research, and present a resolution to those dilemmas.

Theoretical Framework

Standpoint theory (for example, Smith, 1987; Harding, 1991) begins with the premise that all knowledge is socially situated and that individuals from different social locations will have differing perceptions of the world. One needs to change the relationship between researcher and research 'objects' from one of a view from above to that of a view from below (Mies, 1983). This orientation attempts to correct the imbalance of the dominant ideology in the social sciences, which has reflected the values, interests, and needs of the primarily white middle-class Euro-American masculinist social sciences. The research goal is to privilege the knowledge of those who are marginalized as an antidote to the view of the dominant group. As a result of their position, marginal members of society are understood to experience a different reality from those in dominant positions. These less privileged individuals are said to bring a fuller awareness of social reality because they must comprehend both the dominant and the marginal views.

While the knowledge based on standpoint theory is said by some to be 'preferable since it is more complete and less distorted' (Stanley and Wise, 1990: 27), more recent critiques have suggested that every system of knowledge creates systematic knowledge and systematic ignorance (for example, Epstein and Stewart, 1990; Harding, 1997). Because knowledge claims are always socially situated, I do not think that it is possible to obtain value-neutrality. Harding (1992) would say that strong objectivity *demands* recognition of subjectivity. Despite the scholarly critique of standpoint theory, this was the theoretical framework that I was required to apply in a doctoral course taught by Dorothy Smith, one of the theory's originators.

Institutional ethnography is a method developed by Smith, among others, which 'emphasizes that the inquiry is one of discovering how things work ... how they are actually put together' (Smith, 1987: 160). Smith's concern is the day-to-day real operations of social organizations and the relationships that are organized by extra-local replicable means such as text and electronic technologies. Because she believes that 'texts are the primary medium ... of power' (17), the assignment in her seminar was for the researcher, through an interview with those who used a document, to examine how that organization used that text to organize power and knowledge.

My position as a researcher was not 'neutral' in the maternity home in which I intended to fulfil the assignment. I had worked there for about four months as acting associate director during a staff member's maternity leave. My identification varied with different women in the diverse levels of the organizational setting. My previous administrative involvement made me both an 'insider' to other members of staff and an 'outsider' to the residents and to employees who had not known me previously. Consequently, I was 'in' the society, but not 'of' it.

The Research Assignment

This section briefly outlines the research setting, specifies the particular document for analysis, explains the research method, and summarizes a pivotal problem arising out of this research activity.

The Setting

The setting that I chose was a licensed maternity home in Ontario (Child and Family Services Act , 1996).[1] It was a non-sectarian, non-profit charitable residential agency that provided residential care for young single women and their babies, as well as community support to pregnant and parenting teens. The average age of the home's residents was seventeen years. They were all single young women, usually with few material and emotional resources to help them through their pregnancies. While admission was almost always voluntary and not mandated by the courts, many of these young women had few, if any other options for housing.

The Text Chosen

According to the home's executive director, the primary document used to manage the work in the maternity home was the resident stay plan (RSP). This document, according to its developers, was designed to ensure compliance with licensing requirements of the act. Section 105(2) stipulated that each resident be present and included in their own plan of care. Furthermore, there was to be a plan of care between home's personnel and the resident within thirty days of admission, to be reviewed monthly by staff and the 'client.' The province required licensing reviews of the home every year. According to the executive director, an important component of those agencies' evaluations was an examination of the RSP by the provincial Ministry of Community and Social Services to determine if residents had signed the document to demonstrate their involvement. The document, as designed by the administrators, required that a signature be inscribed each time a resident participated in any activity while she was in residence. The executive director saw this document as an active regulator of the work in the residence.

The Method

I interviewed single pregnant teens to understand their perspective about the use of the RSP in the maternity home. I chose a focus group as the most suitable avenue to gain data from the residents within a one-semester course. Being both an outsider and an adult, I assumed that adolescents would talk more if they were with other youths. One individual's ideas might spark thoughts from others in the group. The interaction might also prompt increased openness, since when they hear others declare similar comments people may express thoughts that they might not otherwise wish to share. The focus group allowed for a source of comparison, highlighting areas of agreement or disagreement among the residents (Morgan and Spanish, 1984).

The associate director elicited volunteers for the project. I requested that the group be as diverse as possible in terms of resident's length of stay, their age, their race and ethnicity, and the delivery of their babies. I interviewed four young women, ranging in age from fourteen years to nineteen years, who had been in the home for between 2 and 9½ months. Three had delivered their babies, whom they brought to the focus group. The other was due to deliver that week. One young woman was Afro-Canadian, one was francophone French Canadian, and two were Anglo-Canadian whites.

A small-group discussion transpired over about two hours, which I audiotaped. I led the participants through the discussion, guiding the content in a semi-structured way, but venturing into unplanned areas when a resident suggested a topic that seemed fruitful.

A Pivotal Problem

I was in for a major surprise when I showed the RSP to the residents. My plan had been to determine from the residents' perspectives how this document acted as a 'third party' to the 'conversation' between them and the staff. Despite the executive director's stance that this was the primary document used with residents, not one of the four interviewees was familiar with the RSP in its entirety. Nor were they sure if they had ever seen, used, or signed aspects of it. After obtaining their permission to obtain the actual RSPs, I discovered that on all four of their RSPs only the first one or two pages of a seventeen-page document had been filled in, and by only one staff person. On the remaining fifteen pages, there were no signatures of staff members or of residents.

The residents were disturbed about this new information, especially given my explanation of the RSP's importance. The lack of transparency of the process was also worrisome to them. Furthermore, according to the respondents, they had not been involved on any regular basis in a formalized review conference, with or without the document. Front-line workers had totally by-passed the legislative and licensing requirements that led to the development of the RSP. Consequently, the young women wanted to see exactly what their files contained. They marched out of our meeting and demanded to review their files, only to be told by an administrator that they would have to make an appointment with the associate director to examine the material. While the front-line staff, at that point in time, was not using the RSP regularly, the residents identified another document that regulated their day-to-day life. Staff persons had replaced the RSP with their own textual material, against agency policy.

Three Dilemmas

Three dilemmas emerged in the research process.

*Dilemma 1: Countering Hegemony versus Recognizing the
          Need for Some Social Control*

My plan to elicit concerns about the subordination of residents by demonstrating the social control and regulation that they encountered clashed with my awareness of the staff's need for some management and restrictions to have the home function. Believing that the standpoint of the residents should be unearthed and articulated, I thought that the results would offer a picture of the agency's work different from the perceptions of administration. I wished to expose the residents' perspectives and give, in some very small measure, voice to a component of their reality. Aware that my understanding of injustice towards the young women was artefactual, incomplete, and limited by my very brief and restricted involvement with them, I had to be careful in speaking for them.

Yet as a social worker and a feminist researcher, I saw it as my responsibility to examine critically and depict existing relations of power. Consequently, inwardly I cheered when the residents went storming out of the room demanding to see their files. I was delighted that they understood their omission from their own RSP and supported their action to take more control of the situation. After all, involvement of the 'clients' is a critical component of social change and liberatory activity in social work.

It is easy to valourize the struggle of residents and to see their potential victimization, especially when basic protections have not been ensured. Working to dismantle hegemony is such a 'motherhood' concept in feminist research that it often goes unquestioned and unexamined. Privileging the standpoint of these young women whom I perceived as marginalized, as one component of that dismantling, may be important, but it is not the whole story. While I applauded their raised awareness, I experienced anxiety. I found myself at times struggling with a portrayal of staff members as agents of social control who unwittingly and/or intentionally maintained the status quo. While the findings exposed a negative critique, I respected and empathized with the difficulty and skill required by workers in providing services to this population. Social control is a necessary evil in our society. The residence represented a quasi–'total institution' (Goffman, 1961) that by its very nature exercises a high degree of social control over its residents. And total institutions require a large dollop of that control in order to function. The tensions implicit in trying to manage thirty lives on a daily basis necessitate a certain amount of regulation and co-ordination. When many lives are being managed by only a few, there is a need for group conformity to prevent chaos.

I worried that the staff and the executive director might see me as 'stirring up trouble,' making it harder for them to control their wards. Although sometimes guidelines or legislation, if followed, protect the most marginalized, in some instances a staff member has no means to redress the marginalization of residents. It is not just the residents who are controlled and regulated by the social structure in which they find themselves. There is no such thing as an autonomous agency that is free from external controls. It is too strong to say that members of staff are also victimized, but they are often casualties in an unresponsive system that does not value their work, provides insufficient resources, makes unreasonable demands, and requires compliance with legislative expectations that can further restrain those who already are subordinated in a system. Of course, the powerlessness of the staff is not of the same degree as that of residents. But social service workers must walk a fine line between meeting the demands of an unresponsive system and supporting the individual choice and freedom of those whom they serve.

With all its flaws, this home did provide a valuable service, without which these young women would have been additionally impoverished. But were there opportunities for staff members to alter the work, being more open to the standpoint of the young women, without making the work environment impossible to manage? What would those modifications entail? Social service workers are agents of control but also are advocates for the self-emancipation of residents. The challenge remained: how to sustain a living arrangement with that number of people, in a structure that demanded a certain amount of conformity and regulation, while preserving individuality and a recognition of residents as people outside the institutional 'relations of ruling' (Smith, 1996).

It was my judgment, when I considered the legislative requirements of the home and the inadequacy of residents' involvement in their own plans of care, that the standard of what was acceptable had been compromised. In addition, social work, as a profession, strongly values ethical principles such as informed consent and self-determination (National Association of Social Workers, 1999). I perceived that the practitioners trespassed on these values. Ironically, but also substantiating Smith's contention of the power of text, it was institutional textual documents that became relevant for my research: the legislation and social work's code of ethics provided the rationale for my evaluation. More important, Smith suggests that the 'forms of social knowledge that have made the work processes underpinning them invisible must be remade' (1987: 153). This is a key consideration in the use of standpoint theory and institutional ethnography. It was also a significant factor in the resolution of the ethical dilemma for me. The textual material had subsumed actual experiences of the 'situated subject' (Smith, 1987: 153), and I wished to reinstate their importance.

These rationales led to my decision to present the results of the focus group to the executive director. In this way, I was allowing the particularities of the young women's lives to transcend the abstractions of institutional processes by submitting their words to the director, thus supporting a subversion of the politics of the institution (Smith, 1987) by emphasizing the actualities of these specific individuals' experiences. However, this decision led to the next dilemma: how to maintain a relationship of trust with those people whose work one is critiquing.

*Dilemma 2: Maintaining Relationships of Trust and Respect
with Those Whose Work a Researcher Critiques*

This dilemma revolved around staying true to the results of the research and to the young women whose involvement in their RSPs was being bypassed by front-line workers, while maintaining the trust of those same members of staff. How was I to ensure that the practitioners understood that I cared about them and respected their work, even while I articulated a critique of their agency? How could I stay truthful to the information revealed without jeopardizing my relationship with the director and staff of the agency? This kind of dilemma is exacerbated in organizations that are nurturing and warm (Stacey, 1991). An agency whose focus was mothering took me under its wing as well, willingly providing me with whatever information I requested, leaving me feeling as if I were betraying it when I could not be totally positive and supportive of its interventions with residents. If as a researcher I showed appreciation and warmth, would that lead staff persons to believe that I agreed with their positions, when in fact I disagreed (Martindale, 1987)? Would my stance be seen as manipulation? This concern left me feeling that I was being deceptive, misrepresenting my interest and support.

My research uncovered the problem that residents were not involved in the RSPs. This omission, if it were revealed to the provincial Ministry of Community and Social Services, could affect the home's licence. It also indicated a discrepancy between the directors' understanding and expectation of staff roles and what was actually implemented by staff. I was aware of the power that was inherent in this knowledge. For the agency to obtain funding, the staff had to demonstrate that it was involving residents in their RSPs. But how could I reveal the results without jeopardizing the ongoing monetary grants? The need for resources for teenaged parents is enormous. I did not wish to do anything that would jeopardize the home's continued funding or longevity.

The worries of being perceived as deceitful and of compromising potential funding were a consequence of my judgment about who should receive the results of my research. A critical element in the research process was deciding to whom I should speak (Martindale, 1987). Feminist research principles support feedback to all participants as one way to equalize power relationships and for participants to obtain benefits from the research process, leading me to believe that I had to share my uncomplimentary findings. It was my assessment that both the executive director and the residents should have feedback about my research. I decided that the analysis did not need to be the director's analysis, nor did I require her agreement; but it was necessary for me to grasp her perceptions of my research and for her to understand my findings. The director and I had agreed that after I had submitted the paper to my professor, I would provide her with my findings. I was to report the outcome to her only after all the residents had left the home, to protect respondents from any potential negative consequences from staff members' reaction to my findings.

As a student who needed a research population for my dissertation, I felt very much at the mercy of the executive director, who had the ability to grant or deny subsequent requests for help on my thesis. To obtain needed data, I wished to maintain a positive relationship with her. If I shared the results of my research, would she see my work as a betrayal of trust and not want me to do further research in the agency? While this dilemma might not have been as pronounced if I had not been a student, others have spoken about the dilemmas in fieldwork, in hierarchical settings, of needing to maintain the goodwill of the bosses to have access to those with lesser institutional power (for example, Hsiung, 1996). Whenever funding of a project or access to data is involved, there is the potential of a conflict of interest for the researcher in fulfilling the terms of the project ethically and meeting his or her own professional or personal needs.

When I presented the results to the executive director, I was ambivalent, feeling both anxiety that she might feel angry and betrayed and hope that she would be able to hear me and understand the spirit of support and respect in my report, despite its criticisms. I liked and respected her. I was grateful for the previous opportunity to work with her when I had been acting associate director. I identified with her commitment to social change.

Armed with the material from the residents, I sought a 'dialectical relationship' (Klein, 1983) with the executive director. By 'dialectical,' I mean a new synthesis of personal knowledge that occurs for individuals from conflicting information brought by the other party in the relationship. Knowledge emerges from the self–other dialectic when people bring a critical subjectivity (Lincoln, 1995) to the endeavour. A dialectical relationship consists of the 'mutual and inseparable dependency of facts *and* feelings, figures *and* intuition, the obvious *and* the hidden, doing *and* talking, behaviours *and* attitudes' (Klein, 1983: 98). Intangibles, such as trust and honesty, openness and caring, are all part of the mix in this type of relationship. The process of a dialectical relationship is interactive and exponential, rather than linear, with each person bringing aspects that the other is open to receiving in the resolution of contrasting or difficult information. A dialogue that the executive director and I understood to be ongoing began when I presented the data, comparing my own observations as a researcher with those of the executive director, whose home had been researched and who in turn then added her own perceptions.

My sharing with her the uncomplimentary results of the research pushed the process past simply amassing data to fulfil the requirements of a course without feeling obligation to the people who had opened their agency to me.

Smith (1987) speaks about one's own knowledge of the everyday world being the beginning of an inquiry. It can lead to something akin to consciousness-raising as one takes private experiences, finds the objective correlates, and shares these observations with others. Through my conversations with the executive director, the research, I believe, raised the consciousness of us both. According to Harding (1992), strong objectivity requires strong reflexivity, which would place the subjects of knowledge on the same causal plane as the objects of knowledge. Self-reflexivity involves the researcher's taking into account his or her own consciousness. The self-reflexivity in which I engaged resulted in this paper.

For the executive director, two elements of the research were disturbing. The first was the non-compliance of staff towards administrative expectations vis-à-vis the RSP. I suggested that perhaps the form itself was part of the problem, being too cumbersome and burdensome for overworked staff members to fill out. This problem, however, was not her primary concern. Second and more serious, my research revealed the young women's perceptions of their lack of control as residents. The executive director believed that they did not see the residence as providing a place where they were architects of their own destiny. She requested that the report be given to the employee responsible for all clinical practice in the home. She also asked me to provide a training program for the people on staff. Since an outside expert tends to have more credibility, she felt that they would be more inclined to hear and respond positively to issues identified by someone who was outside the agency, but whom they respected. In this way my 'insider–outsider' status could be a benefit. I agreed to provide this training.

One strategy that facilitated her openness to the results was my attempting to present the data in as respectful a fashion as possible. I acknowledged the pressures and stresses on the agency that contributed to its not meeting the goals of involving the young women in their RSPs. I also included in my report the young women's positive comments about the residence, which aided in ensuring a more balanced picture that recognized the contribution that the home had made to their lives.

The concern about damaging the home's funding emerged as one of the less thorny issues to resolve, although theoretically it could have been very difficult. Because I shared the results with the executive director, she

was able to take steps to correct the problem vis-à-vis licensing requirements. At the time of our meeting, she felt that new personnel coding on
the forms fulfilled licensing provisos more adequately.

Through a positive response from the executive director, the conflict
of interest took care of itself. Had she been angry and refused me further
access to the residence, I would have needed to turn elsewhere for my
dissertation sample. Nevertheless, I based the decision to present my data
on two principles. Being true to the claims of the residents and to
the potential betterment of the agency took priority over my personal
requirements.

Codes of ethics say little about conflict of interest for researchers. The
Canadian Research Institute for the Advancement of Women (CRIAW,
1995) does indirectly address the issue, posing the question, 'Will our
personal/individual needs, as researchers ... be addressed openly through
the whole process of the research?' (6). In the question is buried the
answer: the way to deal with conflicts of interest is to state directly the
personal desires of the researcher.

Dilemma 3: Resolving Conflicting Ethical Principles

While there are many codes of ethics in research, they state little about
how to resolve ethical dilemmas when the research situation invokes more
than one rule and resolution of one precept results in violation of another. The third dilemma arose for me in trying to decide which ethical
principle took precedence when two or more were in conflict. Two separate issues brought this conflict to the fore. First, if providing agreed-
upon credit to respondents causes harm to an agency, which takes
precedence: the researcher's commitment to share perquisites with those
researched or his or her commitment to protect from harm the institution and its representatives, the administrators, that provided the setting
for the research? Second, if sharing agreed-to findings exposes informants, which commitment takes precedence: to give feedback and deliver
the findings or to maintain the confidentiality of informants?

The hierarchy of field research heightened the complexity of these
issues, with participants having differing needs and standpoints and varying access to power. In fieldwork at a maternity home, it is not just the
residents who become the objects of the inquiry, but the staff and the
organization as a whole. When studying hierarchical settings, ethnographers 'face the classic dilemma of not appearing to align themselves with
one group rather than another' (Reinharz, 1992: 70). I kept this consid-

eration in the foreground of my thinking as I attempted to resolve the conflicting ethical principles.

On Giving Credit versus Preventing Harm, or on Revealing versus Not Revealing the Identity of Interviewees

The question of who 'owns' the lives that we use made me sensitive to the desire to share the rewards of privilege, however small. Lincoln (1995: 285) observes that 'we have to come clean about the advantages that accrue to us as knowledge producers; especially the claim that we, and not they, are the genuine producers.' I had no research without the contribution of the respondents and the staff. I understood all too well that 'most of our research is written for ourselves and our own consumption, and it earns us the dignity, respect, prestige, and economic power in our own worlds that those about whom we write frequently do not have' (Lincoln, 1995: 285). As my intention had been to give credit to all the participants in the research, I had asked each of the residents if they would prefer to be anonymous or to be named in the research. All four had requested that their names be included in the report, and I had stated that I would comply.

Not only did I hope to give something back to the residents by acknowledging them by name in the study, I was also aware that the executive director looked forward to the benefits from the research as well. Although it had not been stated prior to undertaking the research, I suspected that she also assumed that I would name the home in my research, thereby furnishing it with more publicity at a time when it was threatened with closure during the push for institutional mergers by the provincial government. 'Visibility' is essential for small social-service agencies in the perpetual struggle for viability in a political climate where government has a harder time justifying the erasure of settings with higher profiles. Wrestling with the idea of revealing the names of the interviewees (which would identify the home) left me feeling caught on the horns of a dilemma. I would give due credit to the interviewees; but I doubted that I would be providing the home with much-needed publicity when my results not only would not enhance its image, but in fact could impede the potential renewal of its licence. The results led me to wonder whether the agency would prefer to remain anonymous rather than to receive negative publicity. How then could I provide credit to the residents?

The differing needs of participants in the research created a dilemma about whose claim took precedence. My agreement to give residents credit and my intention to promote the home came into conflict with another ethical principle – namely non-malfeasance (CRIAW, 1995). In a hierarchy of ethical concerns, potential for harm by revealing the identity of the home outweighed, I believe, the agreement to give credit to respondents. 'Whether I go public with so-called "private" disclosures turns on whom I'm serving at the time' (Martindale, 1987, 49). While I was serving the residents, I also believed that I was serving the home, with the executive director as its representative. Thus in my report, while I acknowledged the young women, I did so only with their first names, and I protected the identity of the home by disguising material that I felt might jeopardize its funding. Equally significant, the existence of the home ultimately supported and protected the very young women whom I was concerned about serving – a benefit that seemed to provide a stronger rationale than providing credit to those same individuals.

There were some minimal benefits to the residents, but not the agreed-to-inclusion of their full names in the research document. The focus-group discussion had raised issues about the by-passing of their rights, leading them to ask directly after our discussion what their files contained. The other benefit was the opportunity for residents to hear about the findings. While only one resident inquired, she stated that she was 'happy' that her observations had contributed to the identification of some important issues in the home.

How Far Does Confidentiality Extend in Fieldwork?

Having been a worker in the maternity home, I had access to information and to relationships in an informal way that could not be covered by signed releases. Confidentiality is a key ethical precept addressed by every code of ethics in research (for example, University of Toronto, 1979; MRC et al., 1998d), but the relevant rules and implications vary within each hierarchical research setting in an ethnographic study. For example, does confidentiality extend to the front-line staff or only to the recipients of service in the home? By waiting for residents to leave, I had been able to protect their anonymity, ensuring that no statement from the focus group would worsen their treatment in the home. But the same was not true for the front-line staff.

While, to protect their confidentiality, I did not interview directly any personnel, they all knew me, and I had good rapport with them. The executive director had instructed the workers to provide all the information that I requested, and they seemed only too happy to comply. For example, after the residents explained that it was another document that governed their lives in the home – and I requested copies – the worker who had developed the alternative form proudly showed it to me and demonstrated its usage. Her openness, however, led to my realization that staff did not comply with administrative expectations. Would that worker's generosity and accommodation to my research requests result in a reprimand by her supervisor? Although I had attempted to protect the confidentiality of the workers, my informal relationship in fact put them at risk. Then by providing the report to the executive director, I exposed the fact that the front line did not inscribe the RSP and had substituted its own, truncated version. In truth, whether or not I had asked about the alternative document, the entire staff's 'resistance' would have been revealed by the residents' focus group, but I had underscored this lapse by describing the alternative documentary process. I had not intended to jeopardize anyone's job. Nor did I wish a staff person to be rebuked.

Given the very supportive and open management style of the executive director, and the sound work of staff in many areas, I did not believe that employees would be let go as a consequence of my research. I decided that the risks of harming staff were not high and that the benefits of potentially improving the functioning of the home outweighed that potential risk. While no staffers were released, the research process had revealed the complexity of protecting confidentiality in fieldwork. In this instance, non-malfeasance was not the highest good, contrary to my decision in the previous dilemma.

Additionally, I began to wonder about the application of confidentiality in field settings. I had not promised confidentiality to workers, only to the residents, although my intention had been to protect the confidentiality of staff as well. In field settings with informants at varying levels of the hierarchy, possessing different perspectives and interests in the organization, comprehensive confidentiality appears difficult, if not impossible. Choosing whom one will protect, and why, becomes an important consideration.

Context is significant in resolving conflict among ethical principles. One orientation to moral reasoning is that of an ethic of care, with its emphasis on connection and its consideration of relationships as primary (Gilligan, 1982). People subscribing to this orientation have a greater propensity to take the standpoint of the 'particular other' rather than that of the 'generalized other' (Benhabib, 1987: 78). According to this orientation, moral problems arise from competing responsibilities. When an ethic of care predominates, moral judgments are more contextual. The researcher sees context and specificity not as signs of weakness in research design, but as manifestations of a conception of ethics that views the self as immersed in a network of relationships. An ethic of care and responsibility both kindled the awareness of a conflict for me as a feminist researcher and allowed me to find the key to their resolution.

Conclusion

Through my research I ran headlong into competing responsibilities to the different actors in the hierarchy of the maternity home, as well as to my profession and to myself. The researcher must attend to many points of view. The paradox is that a multitude of opposing truths, needs, and standpoints, all partial, coexist at the same time. Because of this conundrum, ethnographic research is filled with ethical dilemmas. By analysing contradictions and discrepancies, the ethnographer, I believe, can provide a more subtle understanding of the complexities of differing perceptions of reality and responsibility and of an organization's social construction of knowledge and power. Inclusion of paradoxes may not sit comfortably with the binary world found in much of positivism, but it is very much a component of standpoint theory and field research.

A researcher criticizing the work of staff is potentially naive about their presumed ability to do their work better. However, like Wise (1990: 248), I believe that 'social work *is* about social control and especially the protection of children and other vulnerable people, and this is a morally proper function in feminist terms, because feminism seeks a moral–political stance on questions of power and powerlessness. Once we agree that vulnerable people need protection, we can then begin to address other feminist issues, such as what feminism can tell us about "acceptable standards," who should decide what these are, and how they should be imposed.' While believing in the good intentions of this maternity home, I perceived that those acceptable standards had been compromised and that as the researcher I should reveal this perspective. By making visible the actualities of the lives of the residents, I was attempting to highlight ethical trespasses in the residence.

There is no simple, pat hierarchy of ethical principles that can direct the decisions of the researcher in the field. I learned several lessons in doing such research. On the one hand, in evaluating the conflicting needs of different participants, the researcher should assign very high priority to the needs of the most disadvantaged in determining which route to take. However, doing no harm also maintains prominence as an ethical principle. Additionally, a researcher must weigh potential costs and benefits, which he or she can determine only situationally.

I came away chastened by the interpersonal and ethical complexities of even the simplest piece of research. Whose truths and needs should take precedence? I decided that it was a mistake to focus on one to the exclusion of the others. While I attempted to ensure that the actualities of young women's daily lives were understood and respected, I came to understand the difficulties of dismantling hegemony and to give credit to those who in the real and murky world of practice are attempting, however imperfectly, to meet the needs of less privileged young women. By striving for a dialectical relationship with the executive director, I ensured that she understood in a new way some of the controls felt by residents, pointing the way for valuable ideas for future research and improved functioning of the home. This is a small step towards praxis and change for a more equitable world.

Notes

Two groups of people helped prepare this essay based on research for a doctoral course. First and foremost, I wish to thank the residents and staff of the maternity home, without whom there would have been no research. Also my sincerest appreciation to four scholars who provided feedback on earlier versions of this work: Deena Mandell, Margaret McKinnon, Margrit Eichler, and Will C. van den Hoonaard.

1 I altered some identifying information to protect the anonymity of the maternity home.

8

My Research Friend? My Friend the Researcher? My Friend, My Researcher? Mis/Informed Consent and People with Developmental Disabilities

S. ANTHONY THOMPSON

Research is filled with ethical dilemmas. The first problem that researchers must face is to arrive at a reasoned and reasonable definition of informed consent. Most agree that 'informing-for-consent' is a process (Tymchuk, 1997), rather than a time-limited event. Informing for consent is a responsibility that a researcher must take seriously at every stage of the endeavour, not just at the beginning. What we as researchers understand to be informed consent can change radically as our research moves forward. Researchers must assess a situation to decide the relative priority of many factors so as to create an effective design for consent. Two macro-factors that influence the kinds of safeguards that researchers must employ are research method and the characteristics of selected research participants. This essay discusses issues when the method is engaging, intrusive, and ongoing and/or when participants are particularly vulnerable because of their marginal status and/or life circumstances – specifically here, persons with developmental disabilities.

To this end, I first offer definitions central to informed consent, next look at personal dimensions that affect such consent, later consider relevant contextual factors, and finally suggest how qualititative researchers can adjust informed consent to take account of these various factors. I propose that we use, as a starting point, the indices to assess consent of persons with developmental disabilities in sexual contexts (for example, Ames and Samowitz, 1995) to assess consent in research.

Procedures, guidelines, and models of informed consent might never have emerged had researchers and practitioners not dared to recognize and name the kinds of atrocities practised under the guise of medical research: 'Scientists thought that "madness not medicine was implicated in Nuremberg." But German medicine *was* implicated at Nuremberg, as several recent books have amply shown, and the German experience was relevant to medical research in the United States. The ultimate lesson of the Nazi experience is that protecting the autonomy and well being of each human subject must be the pre-eminent ethical imperative of medical research' (Bonnie, 1997: 106).

Both conceptually and procedurally, informed consent maintains (perhaps even promotes) core assumptions associated with the medical model – the objectivity of researchers and the naïveté of the researched. In social sciences, I argue, medical-consent models are not adequate for certain research protocols, such as those falling loosely under the rubric 'qualitative.' Some observers may say that qualitative methods in special education are 'something a little out of the ordinary' (Ferguson, 1993). Throughout this essay, I hope to show that there is nothing 'ordinary' about informed consent, both conceptually and procedurally – especially for people who have developmental disabilities.

According to the medical model of research, researchers use informed-consent procedures to reduce risk to participants, while factoring in the utility or impact of a project's potential outcomes. To conceive research projects primarily through utilitarian considerations may overlook or minimize the participation of people with disabilities in the informed-consent process. Covert research designs may be the most ethical conduct for certain situations. For example, researchers, historians, and advocates have exposed the subtle (and sometimes not-so-subtle) transgression of human rights vis-à-vis people with developmental disabilities in institutions (see, for example, Bogdan et al., 1974; Ryan and Thomas, 1987). In some of these cases, researchers have not obtained the informed consent of participants. Clearly, the maltreatment of people with disabilities and the immediate need to rectify these abuses warrants a research design that 'uncloaks' these issues in a timely manner.

I do not intend to discredit such *necessary* research projects, but there are implications when we fail to include people with disabilities in the informed-consent processes. Such exclusionary practices may be 'reinscribing' the very disabling regimes that we wish to dismantle in our research work. After all, most researchers are able-bodied, and participants are almost always bearers of a labels (i.e., 'disabled'). In fact, the *way* in which researchers obtain informed consent (if at all) *may be as important* as the research outcome and may speak to how the residue of able-bodied research practices infiltrates our thinking and beliefs about 'people with disabilities.' Even if ethics review boards deem specific research protocols to be of minimal risk for persons with disabilities, there is still a level of risk. I wish to uncover some of the risk factors – both personal and institutional – inherent in qualitative research methods for such people. First, however, I look at the nature of informed consent for them.

Informed Consent Definitions

Characteristics of Participants

Not only must an informed-consent design be tailored to the research method, but, more important, it must respond to the circumstances of potential participants. In research involving people who have developmental disabilities, these circumstances include not only the disability itself, but also the (frequently unjust) social consequences of having such a disability. First, in designing informed consent researchers must take into account participants' intellectual skills, including levels of reading recognition and comprehension, learning-style preferences, sensory impairments, and decision-making skills. Second, many participants are financially dependent, have limited social support, and inhabit institutional settings. Both intellectual and contextual realities affect their levels of vulnerability, and hence the informed-consent design. Advocates and researchers typically espouse a comprehensive account of intellectual dimensions (see Tymchuk, 1997) but tend to downplay contextual realities. Therefore I emphasize the contextual factors that affect the design of informed consent.

Definitions and Conceptions of Informed Consent

Legal definitions of informed consent typically comprise three elements: capacity, voluntariness, and information (see Turnbull et al., 1977). *Capacity* refers to an individual's ability to select and communicate choices through a reasonable or rational decision-making process. *Voluntariness* refers to freedom from coercion, duress, or constraint with respect to the consent process. Finally, an individual must be fully and effectively advised of the procedure or participation in the research; being so advised represents the *information* element. Researchers must make every effort to maximize each of these elements of consent for potential participants. Before researchers design informed consent, however, participants must be deemed legally competent to grant consent. Competence has particular significance for people with developmental disabilities.

Legal Competence

First and foremost, whether informed consent is obtained for medical treatment (Ellis, 1992; Rozovsky, 1997), for admission to a care facility (Lindsey, 1994, 1996), or for research (Turnbull et al., 1977; Bonnie, 1997; Tymchuk, 1997; MRC et al., 1998d), the individual must be legally competent to consent. The label 'developmental disability' (or 'mental retardation') does not immediately mean incompetence in legal terms ('Persons with mental retardation are not, by definition, incompetent: Tymchuk, 1997: 71). 'The law presumes that all patients ... are legally competent' (Rozovsky, 1997: 3; see also Turnbull et al., 1977; Ellis, 1992; Lindsey, 1994, 1996; Robertson, 1994; Bach and Rock, 1996). Competence may be legally removed only through due process, which may include judicial orders and/or a formal assessment process. Typically, this process encompasses appraisals of an individual's ability to function and to make decisions and a physician's evaluation.

The courts are beginning to recognize that competence is not an all-or-nothing phenomenon and that it is possible to be considered competent in some areas and not in others (Turnbull et al., 1977; Ellis, 1992; Bach and Rock, 1996; Rozovsky, 1997). The researcher must consider the ramifications for potential participants who are determined to be incompetent to participate in a research project. For example, a court may schedule a guardianship hearing as a result of a determination of incompetence. Even if a hearing is not convened, however, the process has consequences. Once a person has been deemed incompetent to participate in a research project, questions of competence may arise in other contexts (Bach and Rock, 1996: 5).

Personal Dimensions and Informed Consent

First, qualitative methods, such as participant observation, 'emancipatory' techniques, critical ethnography, and action research often involve relations between researchers and participants that are considerably engaged, ongoing, and therefore complex (Ferguson, 1993, 1995). Second, qualitative strategies in the course of a project 'with a strong commitment to community service or involvement must change if the research is going to be effective and relevant' (Tom, 1996: 347; see also

Tom, 1997; Marshall and Rossman, 1995). Third, these methods tend to have a 'friendly façade' (Tom, 1996; Wolf, 1996), and interviews may occur in a participant's home or over coffee. These three issues – ongoing and engaged researcher–participant relations, flexible research protocols, and the potentially 'pseudo-intimate' nature of research make qualitative techniques quite different from most quantitative methods and point to the inappropriateness of the medical model of obtaining informed consent.

People who are legally competent and non-handicapped who initially grant consent may become confused (or misinformed) about a researcher–participant relationship when an undertaking is prolonged. For people with developmental disabilities, this confusion can become exacerbated. Researchers cannot assume that consent given before a project's commencement is the same as consent given during or after a project's completion. If research is ongoing, as is often the case in qualitative research, so too is the informed-consent process. Individuals must be free to withdraw from participation at any time. Field researchers must take seriously the responsibility of maintaining participants' permission, since usually at least three consent difficulties arise throughout a project.

Expectations of Friendship

The first difficulty with consent is that participants may expect friendship from a researcher (see Stalker, 1998: 10). Extended engagements with participants having developmental disabilities pose very real emotional risks for them (see Booth and Booth, 1996; Swain, Heyman, and Gillman, 1998). Given the often unstable and limited social support systems for persons with developmental disabilities and mental retardation (see Edgerton, 1967, 1993), it is easy to understand why these expectations (or misunderstandings) occur. If the researcher is non-handicapped (as is often the case), the stigma associated with a developmental disability compounds the complexities in these relationships: 'The system expects little of the "clients." As a result, labeled people [persons with developmental disabilities] have internalized this self-image. Just as each individual sees himself/herself as worthless, so he or she tends to see the other people in the workshop/group home as worthless. Because people have such a negative "self-image," the personal relationships that they value are those with so-called "normal" people' (Worrell, 1988: 4).

Booth and Booth (1994) comment that the 'research' relationship is often more significant to the participants with developmental disabilities than is easily surmised by researchers. Accordingly, they suggest that researchers disengage themselves from the lives of the participants at the participants' pace, because to do otherwise would run the risk of exploitation.

Participants' Sharing 'Too Much'

Another consent difficulty has to do with the perceived 'comfortableness' of qualitative methods. Usually, the researcher conducts interviews on the participant's own 'turf.' Consequently, the participant may share more information with the researcher than he or she is ready to and may not even realize the implications of such sharing. For example, given the regrettably high probability that a person with mental retardation or a developmental disability has been sexually abused (see Sobsey et al., 1991; Furey, 1994), such recollections of abuse may appear in the public sphere for the first time during a research interview. Even if a researcher is a trained psychotherapist, a participant needs to process these events in a therapeutic, not a research, milieu (see Anderson and Jack, 1991: 19).

The 'cosiness' of the relation has implications in the informing-for-consent process. The researcher must provide (and keep providing) all information necessary for the participant to decide to continue participating or not. One key piece of information concerns the 'limits' of the research interview; it is not therapy. Therefore, in situations where sexual abuse (or any form of abuse) is disclosed, researchers must make the appropriate professional referrals.

Voluntariness

Compounding the 'cosy' aspects of qualitative strategies is their flexibility, which presents another consent difficulty. The researcher using in-depth unstructured interviews, for example, may find conversations meandering into places where neither participant nor researcher expects or indeed wishes to go (see Swain, Heyman, and Gillman, 1998: 28). This, of course, raises questions regarding the voluntariness of informed consent. The principal researcher in Swain, Heyman, and Gillman 1998, for example, discusses a complicated and unexpected ethical dilemma revealed during an interview with an individual with a developmental disability. The participant was showing signs of anxiety, but the researcher was not sure whether this was the result of general anxiety regarding sensitive topics or of his or her volunteering too much personal information. Researchers must continuously verify consent throughout such interviews; however, most have attempted to determine informed consent only once.

Contextual Factors and Informed Consent

I now present three contextual realities – institutionalization, lack of decision-making opportunities, and 'passing' – that have implications for design of informed consent for many persons with developmental disabilities.

Institutionalization

Instead of creating individualized residential/vocational services, professionals often place persons with developmental disabilities in existing services (see Lindsey, 1994). This situation contributes to external control, as we see below. This locus, coupled with the subtly (and sometimes not-so-subtly) coercive atmospheres in which some persons with developmental disabilities live, has consequences for the informed-consent design. When Bonnie (1997) speaks of 'the ethical significance of institutionalization,' he asks: 'What bearing should the fact of institutionalization have on the validity of consent? It is noteworthy in this connection that the Commission's [(U.S.) National Commission for the Protection of Human Subjects of Biomedical and Behavioral Research] charge defined the vulnerability of this subject population in terms of institutionalization rather than in terms of mental disability *per se*. The reason, of course, is that institutional environments may be thought to be inherently coercive' (107).

While coercion and institutional living may be related, *any* residential setting where persons are subject to surveillance and/or daily monitoring will also influence the design of informed consent. As Ellis (1992: 1793–4) notes, 'Less obvious are placements in group homes and other community residential programs. Although these settings do not involve the 'massive curtailment of liberty' of total institutions, they affect significant liberty interests nonetheless.'

Lack of Decision-Making Opportunities

One of the main issues here is how residential living interferes with decision making. More and more, researchers recognize participants' capabilities in making decisions as related to lack of practice, rather than to lack of 'intelligence.' According to Ellis (1992: 1786): 'Even for individuals whose natural abilities to comprehend and communicate would otherwise allow them to make their own decisions, prolonged and extensive denial of the opportunity to make such decisions in the past may prevent actual effective decision making. It may be that the ability to make such decisions has never been mastered, or that a previous ability has atrophied over time.'

Lindsey (1994: 161), among others, connects deprivation of decision making to learned helplessness in the lives of persons with developmental disabilities. In attempting to account for this lack of opportunity, Jenkinson (1993) cites three clusters of causal influences: environmental, structural, and financial. Although she sees generally an ideological commitment towards positive efforts at self-determination and choice making, in practice, limited residential options, inflexible service-delivery models, and constrained financial resources often reduce occasions for decision making.

Thus persons with developmental disabilities often defer in choices to caregivers and/or other able-bodied persons (Ellis, 1992; Lindsey, 1994, 1996; Bonnie, 1997; Tymchuk, 1997; Weisstub and Arboleda-Florez, 1997; Hickson et al., 1998). Not surprisingly, they feel as though they are not in control of outcomes or choices. They perceive their locus of control as being outward or external. Consider, too, the qualities of choices presented. A choice exists only if at least two competing alternatives have some desirable characteristics or potentials. If, for example, one choice is vastly superior to the other, or if both are undesirable, then the locus of control is perceived as (and indeed may be) external (see Jenkinson, 1993: 366). An individual with only 'less-preferred' choices does not experience any freedom of choice. These situations happen all too frequently to people who have developmental disabilities (Jenkinson, 1993; see also Brown and Thompson, 1997: 698). For the purposes of informed consent, a history of making effective decisions and an internal locus of control provide stronger evidence that the consent was given freely and voluntarily than is the case for an individual without such a history.

Passing

Persons with mental retardation or developmental disabilities who are living independently (or semi-independently) have more autonomy and therefore more opportunities and resources to make choices. As we saw above, institutional or other staff-controlled facilities constrain experiences that require making decisions; however, adults with developmental disabilities living independently present other difficulties with consent. The now-classic study of deinstitutionalization, *The Cloak of Competence* (Edgerton, 1967, 1993), uncovers informal systems of able-bodied 'accessories,' on strategies of coping, on which persons with developmental disabilities rely. Further, such people themselves use strategies of identity management to help in 'passing' as 'normal' in certain contexts.

This desire to pass as normal has implications for informed consent. Persons keen to do so use various tactics to 'hide' the fact that they may not understand research protocols and/or need additional support in making a decision. First, they may tend to avoid asking questions in research situations by simply not objecting or not responding to a researcher's questions (Bonnie, 1997: 108; see also Ellis, 1992; Tymchuk, 1997). Second, they may acquiesce – that is, go along with the wishes, commands, or requests of the (often) able-bodied researcher or practitioner. Acquiescence has implications for informed consent, since 'the assumption of competence may be as equally intrusive as the assumption of incompetence ... Therefore, any tendency to accept the acquiescence of an individual as consent when her or his competence is highly suspect has due process implications' (Lindsey, 1996: 174; see also Sigelman et al., 1981; Sigelman et al., 1982; Flynn, 1986). Third, acquiescence may be compounded by a wish to 'please the interviewer' (Biklen and Mosely, 1988: 159).

Incorporating Personal and Contextual Factors

In short, in designing informed consent researchers must anticipate and plan for the consequences of qualitative methods for participants with developmental disabilities, including participants' misconstruing a research relationship and sharing information too intimately. So, too, must they foresee potential compromised voluntariness, the role of institutionalization, lack of practice in making decisions, and passing. To build an informed-consent design that encompasses these factors, researchers have an array of tools: psychometric tests (see Tymchuk, 1997), the consent screening interview (see Lindsey 1994, 1996), a tape- or video-recording of the consent process, and consent auditors, monitors, and substitute decision-makers (Bach and Rock, 1996; Bonnie, 1997; Tymchuk, 1997).

Commonly in practice, the researcher administers these tools only once in any consent design – before the start of a project. Alternatively, sex education researchers, instructors, and policy-makers have recognized the need for both an initial and an *ongoing* consent measurement with respect to sexual acts between people with developmental disabilities (Kaeser 1992; Brown et al., 1994; Ames and Samowitz, 1995; Regional Residential Services Society and the Nova Scotia Department of Health, 1998; Young Adult Institute, no date). Conceivably, qualitative researchers investigating *any* aspect of the lives of persons with developmental disabilities need to consider tools that are ever-present and always available.

Ames and Samowitz (1995) suggest that the practitioner use these tools or indices as a guide, 'not an absolute checklist' (266), to determine the sexual consent of persons with developmental disabilities in intimate relationships. Admittedly, consent in sexual contexts is different from consent in research. As I have pointed out, however, persons with developmental disabilities may perceive a researcher–researched relationship as being something that it is not. So, rather than tailoring specific sexual-consent indices to research contexts, perhaps we, as qualitative researchers, might begin by asking the kinds of questions about relationships that sex educators and policy-makers have asked. Maybe we need to think about informed consent not as an inconvenience for researchers or, at best, a one-time deal, but as evolving guidelines to help maintain and clarify professional research partnerships and relationships with people with disabilities. To that end, I pose the following questions about capacity, voluntariness, and information:

How are participants to indicate their wish to abstain from all or part of the research project? Will they do so by verbal statements, behavioural or gestural indications (such as body language that indicates 'uncomfortableness' or a desire to escape), use of an alternative communication device, or American Sign Language? Is the researcher familiar with all these methods of abstaining (from research)? (see Shaddock et al., 1998: 280). How often does the researcher look for such abstaining signs – throughout the course of interviews or participant observations? Does there need to be a plan for participants to remove themselves? Who will help create and implement such a plan? Do participants require a trusted caregiver to be present throughout the project to help the researcher interpret the participant's particular communicative style? Do participants understand that quitting any part of the research endeavour will not affect any of the current or future community or social services that they receive and/or require? How does the researcher know this? Do participants understand that research interviews are not professional therapy sessions? In other words, do participants understand the boundaries of the researcher–researched relationship? How will the researcher make this plain? Do participants understand the conditions under which they agree to participate? This implies that if the aim and/or design and/or research strategy changes, participants must be informed of such changes and agree, in their own words, to continued participation. Do participants have the ability to know how to prevent unwanted outcomes in research situations? This prevention includes having the final say in where, when, what, and how research results are disseminated. Such considerations are necessary when the community from which participants are selected is small, and especially when such communities are oppressed. Knowledge 'control' is important, particularly in the area of confidentiality. Phtiaka (1994) notes that confidentiality is both *internal* and *external.* Confidentiality and participants' privacy within an institution or community, for example, may be defined as internal. How a community is publicly portrayed is an issue of external confidentiality. Furthermore, confidentiality in presenting findings may be the 'ultimate ethical test' (Woods, cited in Phtiaka, 1994: 159). Phtiaka (1994), for example, found that the usual 'assurances [for confidentiality] are almost totally useless, however, when findings are disseminated within the setting where the research has been carried out' (158). Khayatt (1992) conducted an extensive ethnographic study, in which internal and external confidentiality was paramount. In order to protect her participants, Khayatt 'agreed not to identify the quotations used' (101), and she avoided the use of mini-narratives, 'so that no [participant] would have a continuous presence in [her] work and thus be recognized by readers' (101). Above all, participants understand that they should regularly confer with a third party, such as an advocate, family member, or trusted confidant(e), about the progress, status, and nature of their participation in the research.

Conclusion

All research endeavours involve a level of risk for participants. The more vulnerable the participants because of the stigmatized character of their identities, and the more engaged the researcher is with participants, the greater the onus on the researcher to obtain and maintain informed consent. Qualitative researchers sometimes encounter unpredictable ethical problems. 'We prefer to solve our dilemmas situationally – perhaps justifying our choices in the belief that ethical and moral dilemmas are an inescapable (and therefore inevitable) part of the fabric of conducting social research' (Hertz, 1996: 4). The questions posed here may seem either like a veritable wish list for the perfect research situation or too bothersome and too overwhelming to implement. I believe that when we research persons and subcultures with less power in the world, we need more safeguards, not fewer. Safeguards may need to be thought of as ongoing codes of ethical conduct, with at least part of their focus constantly on participants' continued informed consent.

Note

Preparation of this essay was supported by Social Sciences and Humanities Research Council of Canada (SSHRC) Grant No. 752-98-1744 and by a grant from the Laurel Group, a community-based organization supporting people with autism, both awarded to S. Anthony Thompson. I am grateful to Mary Bryson, Suzanne de Castell, Pat Mirenda, and Allison Tom for their gracious and essential assistance in preparing this essay; however, I take full responsibility for the content.

9

Hazel the Dental Assistant and the Research Dilemma of (Re)presenting a Life Story: The Clash of Narratives

ERIN MILLS

Life history and narrative analysis have long been popular tools for qualitative researchers attempting to 'unpack,' appreciate, and move towards an understanding of the 'lived experience' of people. Narrative analysis puts them in direct contact with 'people engaged in the process of interpreting themselves' (Josselson and Lieblich, 1995: ix). It focuses on everyday social reality in a way that quantitative and even some qualitative methods do not. Yet, despite repeated calls to 'listen' to respondents' interpretation of their own lived experience, qualitative researchers continue to encounter numerous obstacles. Mishler (as quoted by Josselson and Lieblich, 1995: 1) notes that conventional methods of sociological interviewing and interpretation tend to suppress respondents' narrative accounts and ignore the stories' importance to the interviewees.

Narrative analysis does not, however, provide an unproblematic understanding of the complex life history of an individual or social group. Postmodern assaults on the concepts of the rational, ordered, coherent, and unified self and on narrative analysis itself need to be taken seriously. Their attacks on 'truth' and 'objectivity,' though melodramatic, have their own ironic 'truth-content' and warn us against imposing a narrative where none exists.

Still, if we are to take seriously the study of lived experience and respondents' interpretation of their own lives, life history and narrative analysis become essential tools. As Chase (1995: 2) notes: 'In-depth interviews should become occasions in which we ask for life stories. By life stories, I mean narratives about some life experience that is of deep and abiding interest to the interviewee. Furthermore, taking narrative seriously has consequences for how we use those life stories to pursue our sociological interests. A major contribution of narrative analysis is the study of general social phenomena through a focus on their embodiment in specific life stories.'

Narrative analysis provides an opportunity for the sociologist to both 'listen' to what the interviewee thinks is important to him or her in their everyday life and then to link that story with larger social processes – which is ultimately what is important to us as researchers. Used as a starting point, life history research forces us to look at actual practices and particular lived events of real people living out real lives within a specific historical and cultural period. Only after this data is collected and people have had the opportunity to tell their stories in their own words can we then begin the difficult task of providing the links between their lives and those of others. As Chase (1992) argues: 'By analysing the complex process of narration in specific instances, we learn about the kinds of narratives that are possible for certain groups of people and we learn about the cultural world that makes their particular narratives possible – and problematic – in certain ways. The significant point here is that the general (cultural and discursive resources and constraints) is not fully evident to us in advance; we know the general fully only through its embodiments' (180).

The need to concentrate the analysis at the level of lived experience requires that we listen carefully to the historical record and allow – for example – women dental assistants' own voices to speak wherever possible. Unfortunately, as Chodorow (1989) documents in her case study of early women psychoanalysts, this is not an easy task:

When a researcher wants to respect the voices of other women and is concerned about a history of dissolving differences into a hegemonic unity, she runs into problems when the voices she wants to respect seem not to recognize the central categories in her research. I was thus faced with two kinds of questions. First, how can and should we conceptualise the gender-consciousness of women for whom gender itself does not seem like a salient category? Second, does the discovery that the very topic of inquiry is not salient to research subjects raise problems for methodologies like qualitative and reflexive sociology or feminism that privilege the perspective and voice of the subject? Are we left imposing categories on people that are not otherwise important to them, implying false consciousness in a group of women and thereby undercutting one major reason why we were doing feminist sociology in the first place? (199–200)

Using a life-history case study, I explore below the complex relationship that develops between the biography of the research subject and the autobiography of the researcher and the ethical dilemma that this clash of narrative entails. The chapter has two sections. First, I present the life story of Hazel the dental assistant. I am attempting to develop an interviewing technique and a writing style that allows Hazel to tell her story in her own words. This is not a naïve empirical process, since I was aware that Hazel does not see her life as a 'story' and often allowed her thoughts to wander considerably during the two four-hour interview sessions. Furthermore, I knew that I had questions that I wanted answered and that my conception of 'narrative' and 'biography' would shape her telling of her own life. Given all these caveats, however, I still believed it possible to find and present the 'story' of another person. This section also discusses the problems that I encountered trying to take such a perspective into the field.

The second section reviews the interview experience and explores the problems involved in trying to allow an interviewee's 'voice' to speak and the tensions that emerge between researched and researcher in such a process. Critical to understanding the problematic nature of 'story' is the recognition that the research encounter involves two narratives – biography and autobiography. The extent to which this clash leads to harmony or discord depends on the researcher's ability to acknowledge the existence of competing stories and to engage in a critical process of self-reflection.

It is also at this point that we researchers confront an ethical dilemma. The issue is, however, not how do we tell a story, but how do we portray the voices of research subjects? In short, do we have an ethical obligation to the people who share their experiences with us to tell their stories as 'given'? As Crabtree and Millar (1999: 137) note, 'The challenge is to find a way to honestly represent the process, the participants, and the many interpretations generated, yet also recognize the political realities and the limitations in understanding.' I believe that the researcher has to be accountable to the voices of the participants and to the research process in reconstructing and re-presenting the events, but it is not a responsibility to be taken lightly or an issue that is easily resolved.

Hazel: A Dental Assistant's Life

This is an interview with Hazel (a pseudonym) about her life as a dental assistant. Hazel is sixty-three years old and left dental assisting in 1979.

She was part of the executive for the provincial dental nurses and assistants' association from 1964 to 1979, acting as president and board member. She was born in a small town in 1935 and has one brother. Her mother
still resides in the town, although her father passed away recently. Hazel
graduated from grade twelve in 1952 and immediately began working for
the town dentist. She remained in the same dental office until 1958, when
she left for another city to seek different employment. In 1962, she en-
rolled in the province's first certified dental assistant (CDA) course, and
she still has the newspaper clippings marking the event. She married in
1962 and returned to her hometown, where she worked in private practice until 1968. After a dispute with a dentist she quit and applied to work
as a dental nurse with the regional health unit, where she stayed until her
retirement.

I chose Hazel from a specific group of women who had been long-time
dental assistants. The information that she provided forms part of an
ongoing research project that I am currently conducting on the history
of Canadian dental assistants. Through interviews with older assistants, I
was hoping to gain insight into working conditions in the 1950s and 1960s
and to put together an oral history about the profession.

We began the interview by looking at pictures in one of Hazel's scrap-
books. She felt that I should see these photos to understand her experiences as a dental assistant. She was not sure why I was so interested in
discussing her experiences: 'Why would anyone want to know about these
things, they were so long ago, why me? I really did not do anything very
interesting or any different than anyone else would have.'

Like many dental assistants, Hazel does not remember 'choosing' to
become an assistant, but rather recalls having the 'choice' made more or
less for her:

> When I started here with Dr S. I was in high school, it was grade twelve and
> I had just finished and I thought which way should I go, you could either be
> a secretary or a nurse or go and marry a farmer, or whatever. Dr S. came
> over and said would you like to work for me? At least it's something. I did not
> know a thing about dentistry. The first day I was there, and this young gal, a
> big thing around here if you were French and were getting married, the
> wedding gift from the parents was to have all your teeth removed and get a
> set of plates, not dentures, plates. I believe he charged sixty dollars for the
> upper and lower. I can see this huge can, and he pulled it up behind the
> chair and he got the forceps and crack, back, crack, back, he more or less
> ripped those teeth out. I was just standing there shaking, I thought this is

not for me. I came home and I did not know whether or not I was going back.

Hazel did go back, since she saw few options available to women with a high school diploma in the early 1950s. Her mother was a nurse, her father worked in construction, and her brother was a general labourer. Her world was a working-class, rural community. Although she said that she had not thought much about a career while in high school, 'there was not much choice, and it was a good job for a girl to get right out of high school.'

Given my interest in how gender identity is constructed and lived, I attempted to pursue her view that 'you could either be a secretary or a nurse or go and marry a farmer,' but Hazel ignored my probes and started talking about her early days as an assistant. She was particularly keen to relate stories about the poor working conditions that assistants had in that period. She talked with amazement about the unsanitary conditions and poor hygiene practices:

Hygiene? They'd wash off the forceps and throw them into the boiling sterilizer. And if someone else would come in, you'd pull them out before they were done. You'd just rinse them. It's a wonder they didn't end up with more hepatitis and things. But what he would do is have anaesthetic in a can, you'd have to live it to believe it. And not the disposable syringe but the old stainless steel and no disposable needles, just the old needles and you could just hear them breaking through the tissue. Now there was no way they could be properly sterilized. The waiting room would be packed, and the next one would come in and get frozen. By the time you get them all frozen the first one would be ready to start over again, so how could you have the forceps and things ready? He [the dentist] never ended up with infection. It was unbelievable.

Hazel finds a picture of herself at work and shows it to me: 'That's me, no rubber gloves, no mask.' She could not wear gold rings while working 'because of the amalgam, it would take the gold right off,' and she had to work with mercury to mix the amalgam: 'It was very [dangerous], many dental offices would not want you to have carpet on the floor because the mercury would eat into the carpet.' The sanitary conditions often left her feeling 'sick to my stomach.'

She also talked about long hours, low pay, and demanding workloads. On pay and benefits, there seemed to be very little 'upside': 'When I was in private [practice], there were no benefits. If you were sick that was too bad, that's why I got out and got with the health unit. You worked your butt off for nothing. [We worked] on Sunday, if anyone called. I was just thinking that the medical doctor was here too and he'd come in and had dentistry done one Sunday. We worked all afternoon, and Dr S. [dentist] didn't pay me any extra. He figured fifteen dollars a week covered everything. This doctor handed me a dollar. I made more money babysitting with friends around than I did in dentistry. I really did.'

Benefits came in the form of presents or a Christmas bonus, but the assistants gave the dentist presents. 'Usually money, once I got a nice watch and some money. Just depends. With the health unit, all the girls gave the dentist something.' While she worked for a few dentists who provided paid sick leave (she missed work because of a tumour that necessitated a hysterectomy), there were 'a lot of girls that never, never got it.'

Hours were long and often unpredictable. During the 1950s and 1960s, Hazel worked six days a week and was also on call Sundays. She was on salary, so there was no extra pay for overtime worked, which she says was frequent: 'You worked until the waiting room was empty. The hours didn't matter.' As for lunch and other breaks, they seldom happened: 'If you ran late it was a given. No lunch. I think that's why I eat so fast today.'

Workloads were demanding. Hazel recounts life in a one-woman office, where she was responsible for every facet of the operation except pulling teeth: 'When you think back to keeping the office clean, emptying the garbage, doing the books, answering the phone, mixing materials, doing x-rays, putting them away, doing your charting, you had to be organized, look good, and be pleasant with the patients.'

Her duties were not limited to the office, however. At the start of her career, she would have lunch with the dentist, which 'was a big thing, but then I had to wash the dishes.' Even with my interest in the production of gender relations at work, I admit to being startled by this and asked her to elaborate: 'At noon, I had to wash up. Everything. The family dishes. The office was joined to the house. *Would his family eat lunch with you?* I'd eat with the family. On Wednesdays he would go to the sanatorium and I would have to dust and vacuum the house and clean all the dental office. *You would clean both places?* Yes. One day I finally said that was it. It's no wonder I hate house cleaning. Often I had to shovel the sidewalk in the winter with the snow.'

Oddly, she had nothing to say when I asked her how she felt about combining domestic chores with her assisting duties. She stated simply that 'girls' today would never do what she did, but she seemed to accept the fact that domestic work was part of the job. She appeared neither defensive nor uncomfortable when talking about this part of her job and was genuinely perplexed that I would be so interested. She offered no explanation, nor did she attempt to rationalize the domestic duties. A fascinating linking of occupational with domestic duties is to Hazel just part of her taken-for-granted work experience.

Having listened to what seemed to me a rather horrific story of working conditions in postwar dentistry, I began to ask Hazel about her role in the dental nurses and assistants' association. This body forms a key part of my research, and I am interested in learning what it did in its early history and how other assistants viewed it. Hazel spent fifteen years as an executive member and had always taken part in its activities. Given her poor working conditions, I believed that she would regale me with forgotten stories about the collective struggles of dental assistants.

Even though she had been a president of the provincial association, she had nothing to say about the politics of the group. At one point as I pursued this line of inquiry, she asked me to turn off the tape. I thought that she would begin to recount internal political battles and feuds, but she talked more about her working life. With the tape back on, I learned that she viewed the association as a social club, devoid of political strategy or intent. The executive meetings were more of a 'social bit and fun night, and we'd always go for dinner before or after.' She talked about the socials that the association planned and pulled out 'menus' that she and other members had made for their dinner parties: 'Look at how we made our menus for dances and for wine and cheese.'

She spoke about attending dentists' conventions, where the women from her town did quite well, winning first, second, and third prizes, but she could not remember what the prizes were for. They were required to dress in their assistants' uniforms, she and still had a copy of the letter outlining what they could wear – 'either a long sleeve or short sleeve uniform, white stockings and a cap, white shoes.' The provincial and national associations of assistants held their conventions at the same time and in the same place as the dentists' meetings but had to abide by the rules established by the dentists (a practice that continues to this day). The dentists allowed assistants to attend the conventions, but set the agenda and required assistants to serve as hostesses during the main daily sessions (meeting delegates, serving drinks, staffing information tables). Again, Hazel seemed more interested in telling me about the dinners, the music, and the dancing. She could not recall what issues were discussed at the meetings, nor did she have any minutes or convention agendas – except for the dinner menus.

When I asked her about other functions of the association, she continued discussing the social aspects, such as organizing bridal showers for association members and attending receptions. 'Any girl that was getting married from the association we'd have a bridal shower for them. In one of their homes they had a crystal shower for me, and the association presented me with a beautiful teapot that went with my good china.'

She talked about how executive members would be invited to many of the receptions held at dentists' conventions (never the meetings), including that put on by the board of governors for the Royal College of Dental Surgeons (RCDS) and the province's dental society. 'There would be invitations sent out ... by the Board of Governors ... For receptions. *Was it a meeting?* No, there would be hors d'oeuvres and entertainment. *Reception and a meeting attached?* No it was a social.'

But once again, she offered no comment, except to note how much fun the receptions had been.

When it became obvious that she was not going to talk about the political functions of the assistants' association, I asked her directly if she had ever had to deal with complaints from any of the assistants about dentists or working conditions. Her answer was surprising. 'If a girl wasn't being used properly, she'd go and complain to the association. We'd talked to them, usually told them just to get out. It's the job.' She offered no further explanations and resisted any other probes. To her if a woman was having problems, then she should find another job, because the job was not going to change and 'there is nothing the association could do.' Later in the interview, when I asked her about the association and what role it should play for assistants, she returned again to the theme of the 'socials': 'They should be there for support and encouragement. It's become so large, it's out of hand. We were there as a little group, and we had our own dinners and parties together and showers for the girls getting married and baby showers. There isn't any of that now, that was our life.'

The complete absence from Hazel's story of any notion of the 'political' is striking. Not only was she an executive member and past president of the association, but she had her own horror stories:

This Yugoslav took over Dr B.'s practice. In the contract Dr B. wanted me to stay. But he [the other dentist] was something else. In surgery in the mouth he'd be smoking. John P. [Canadian Dental Association president] phoned me up one night and said 'Hazel what the hell is going on there?' I said you don't want to know. He asked me, I said yes. He was on the board of the RCDS, there were complaints.

[The Yugoslav dentist was] just recently married to a Jewish girl and baby on the way. She'd come into the office in the morning and they'd have a fight, he'd push her up against the wall and off she'd go. I'd think, 'Just another day.' I was so fed up. My brother came in to get something done, and told Don [her husband] 'You're a darn fool to let Hazel work there.'

Anyway one day I said, 'I can't take it anymore, I'm leaving.' I didn't have a job or anything to go to. I just needed a break, so I gave him two weeks' notice. I wrote out my cheque, and I said, 'You can pay me.' He did sign the cheque. I went over to the Department of Labour, he tried to put a stop payment on my cheque, and he did have to pay me. I gave him two weeks, so he owed it to me. What a bugger.

Mixed in with this story she talks about working with some dentists who would physically abuse children who were difficult: 'He'd haul off and give them a cuff. This is true, and he'd shake them, oh my word.' Another time while working at the health unit, she was attacked by a patient who had just been released from prison: 'All at once he jumped out of the chair, and he grabbed me, and he rammed me in the corner and said, 'If I had a gun, I'd shoot you now you bitch.'

Given my interest in the early inability of the dental assistants' association to improve working conditions, I was perplexed by Hazel's story. Here is a women who had experienced harsh working conditions and been a member of the association for fifteen years. Yet she never talked about feeling the need to take action.

Part of the explanation for her behaviour may relate to how she viewed her early years in dentistry. Hazel does not appear to perceive the working conditions as onerous and often compared a romanticized notion of the 'old days' with a much harsher view of contemporary dentistry:

It's not only dentistry, it's everything, it's out of hand. It's a real mess out there. The old days are gone. Even with family and home life, families don't get together anymore. At Christmas we would have our little offices parties, but they don't care anymore. I remember Jim M. [dentist] saying to me, this is something else, 'Make sure you hire a good-looking bitch, because you have to look at her for eight hours; you don't have to see your wife that long.'

Dentistry to me has become a racket. The TLC [tender loving care] is not there the way it used to be. I can recall one family we had – four young children. The father dropped dead. He had just had two partials made, and the children had all their dentistry done, and it was quite a large bill. His wife was left with quite a problem. I remember Dr. B. said to phone her up and tell her instead of giving to the United Appeal we'll just write off her debt. You don't get that today.

In the same sentence Hazel can talk about doing the laundry for everyone at her office, while mentioning how kind the dentists used to be: 'When I was sick the number of flowers that were sent to the hospital. Bill and Linda [dentist and wife] at night would bring food and kindness. You just do not get that today. More personal years ago. I did the laundry too, towels, smocks, and uniforms, and I got paid well for it.'

The fact that domestic duties were combined with other tasks did not seem to bother her. Long hours, poor pay, and bad working conditions were offset by the 'kindness' and 'care' shown by dentists to both patients and assistants. Her own and other assistants' stories about the 'bad' dentists are ignored or treated as aberrations. The job was tolerable and even worthwhile because of the 'TLC' and the pride that dentists and assistants used to take in their work. For Hazel, all of that is gone now, and dentistry is little more than a 'racket': 'The dentists want to make money [now]. Before if we had a missed appointment, no problem. We would sit for a few minutes. But now it's, "How come that appointment wasn't filled? I'm wasting money." People lived years ago, today they are just existing. They are rushing, trying to produce. Money, money, money. I don't think it's for the better. Patients used to come in and sit in the chair, and the doctor would say, "and how are you today?" "How is your family?" Not today. [He has] to look at the chart to see what your name is.'

I could easily detect the bitterness and anger in her voice as she talks about how things have changed and what has been lost. She was proud of what she did, but she left dentistry when she saw how it was changing and how assistants were being treated by the younger generation of dentists. The commercialization of dentistry, with its almost exclusive focus on money, combined with a breakdown in the social networks between assistants and even with some dentists, transformed work relations for Hazel. 'If you came and said to me, "I'd like to go into dental assisting," I would say to you, "You better think of something else, it's not going to get better."'

Biography and Autobiography

Hazel constitutes an integral part of my overall research project on the history of dental assistants and their association. Yet the interview left me troubled and perplexed. The need to concentrate the analysis at the level of lived experience requires that one listen carefully to the historical record and allow women dental assistants' own voices to speak wherever possible. Unfortunately, as the quote above from Chodorow implies, this is not an easy task. Like Chodorow, I found myself seeking answers to questions that Hazel had different answers for or that she found irrelevant. I wanted to respect the voices of the women whom I was researching but found this principle difficult to realize when the woman whom I was interviewing had little or no interest in my research questions. She did not think like I do and gave me little insight into the concepts that I had theorized were important. Again like Chodorow, I was left struggling to understand how this could be and felt the need to fall back into theories of false consciousness, hegemony, rationalization, denial, defence, or anything else that would allow me to explain the absence of pattern, form, structure, and direct cause and effect in her story.

As a qualitative researcher and a feminist, I was apprehensive about the retreat to structure and away from 'real' women leading 'real' lives. It would not be difficult (or even all that inaccurate) to place Hazel's romanticization of the past into a framework of ideological domination in which gender-blindness is not simply a 'given,' but an active feature produced, reproduced, and fought over in the capitalist-patriarchal society of the 1950s and 1960s. Indeed, as I noted above in my introduction, part of the purpose of conducting life history analysis is to move from the particular to the general, in order to understand 'the relation between this instance of social action (this particular life story) and the social world the narrator shares with others and the ways in which culture marks, shapes, and/or constrains this narrative' (Chase, 1995: 20).

Nor do I have a problem with placing Hazel's narrative within such a context. What is problematic is the way in which such an approach will transform Hazel's specific life story. If we qualitative-interpretative-feminist researchers really are to 'listen' to what our interviewees say, then we must accept, at least in part, their notions of what constitutes an important event or significant historical change. In short, the relation between researcher and researched must become more equal if we are to avoid imposing our own narrative on that of our subjects. As Chodorow notes:

My suspicion of an analysis that invokes false consciousness as an explanatory category led me, finally, to relativize and expand my understanding of my own gender-consciousness and of the varieties of gender-consciousness and female self-understanding available to women of different eras and milieux. Drawing on a basic premise of the sociology of knowledge and on the feminist methodological injunction that we pay particular attention to the relationship of the researcher to researched, I came to see my ideas, as well as those of my interview subjects, were rooted in our different social conditions ... I came to conclude that my interviewees, rather than being gender-blind, had different forms of gender-consciousness and experienced a different salience of gender as a social category and aspect of professional identity. (Chodorow, 1989: 200)

Chodorow's point, when combined with postmodernist injunctions concerning the elusiveness of 'meaning,' forces us to remember that we cannot simply 'transcribe' 'lived experience' but must also interpret it. As Mauthner and Doucet (1998) note, neither data nor data analysis speak for themselves. Our acts of interpretation will always be problematic, but they become even more so when we forget the power that we have to shape our respondents' narratives in terms of our own.

And on reflection, I realize that I continued to do just that. When Hazel argued that the working environment was better in the 1950s than it is today, I challenged her to tell me how doing laundry and washing dishes as part of her assisting duties could be seen as 'better.' I was equally mystified as to why a woman who experienced long hours, bad working conditions, and low pay did not see the need to move the dental assistants' association into a more progressive position. Did she not see that their attending the dentists' conventions as 'hostesses' and being asked to wear their uniforms at formal receptions was demeaning? Could she really argue that assistants who were asked to serve as hostesses and wash dishes had more pride in their job than the women who work today?

Of course, Hazel did argue exactly that, and it took me quite some time to recognize the important story that she was relating. While I believe that all the questions that I pose above are legitimate, I should not use them to minimize Hazel's life and her contributions to the association. If we are interested in the 'lived experience' of women workers and their interpretations of their own lives, then we should not belittle what we get. My views on the political failures of the assistants' association were not the same as hers. She saw the association's role as that of offering 'support and encouragement' and organizing 'dinners and parties and showers.' Insisting on an analysis that suggests that having dinner parties did little to improve the wages of assistants may ignore the major role that these social networks played in their daily lives. Perhaps these 'socials' provided a forum for mutual support and understanding that was unavailable to them as assistants working in 'one-girl offices.' The association may have allowed women to take pride in their work as 'caregivers,' and the socials served to reinforce the importance of their work even in the face of awful working conditions.

I missed the essence of what Hazel was telling me by concentrating on my own research agenda (my own lived experience) to the neglect of hers. I had questions that are based clearly on a pre-conceived notion of what kinds of answers I would receive (or wanted to receive), and these hypothetical answers did not fit the story that Hazel wanted to tell. This situation led to frustration and confusion on both sides. I was frustrated at how difficult it was to get even the simplest of facts out of her and at how often I would have to revise 'my' story of 'her' life because of numerous inconsistencies and outright contradictions. I was frustrated at the gaps in her story, her refusal to dig for more information, and her stubborn denials that the association's political inactivity was important to her.

I now realize that part of my frustration was also the product of my own methodological assumptions about how a life story should be both told and lived. It is easy to read Langness and Frank (1995) and agree with them that 'biography' and life histories are literary genres that contain 'rules' of production governing the assumptions that we make about 'lives' and about how we are to construct and report on them: 'We expect a biography to present a unified life through anecdotes that reveal this unity while, at the same time, demonstrating change or growth. Westerners make a story out of a life, telling it chronologically from early childhood on, ferreting out the subject's own feelings and interpretations of events and centring it around a moral paradigm of cause and effect' (101).

It is quite another thing, however, to face these assumptions in the field. Like a biographer, I was searching for a coherent 'story' based on a set of easily recognizable 'facts.' Furthermore, I wanted to learn Hazel's interpretation of these events, their significance to her, and how they made her 'feel,' and I wanted her to relate them in a consistent manner.

I realized how much of a social construction a life story actually is and the active role that biographers play in this process. As a simple example, a comparison of the interview transcripts and the life history presented above quickly reveals how Hazel's life has been reconstructed. In recounting the working conditions that Hazel experienced, I wrote the following:

Beyond the poor and dangerous sanitary condition of the offices, which she says often left her feeling 'sick to my stomach,' she talks very candidly about the long hours, low pay, and demanding workloads she experienced during her work life. On the issue of pay and benefits, there seemed to be very little 'upside.'

'When I was in private, there were no benefits. If you were sick, that was too bad, that's why I got out and got with the health unit. You worked your butt off for nothing.'

'[We worked] on Sunday, if anyone called. I was just thinking that the medical doctor was here too, and he'd come in and had dentistry done one Sunday. We worked all afternoon, and Dr. S [dentist] didn't pay me any extra. He figured 15 dollars a week covered everything. This doctor handed me a dollar. I made more money babysitting with friends around than I did in dentistry. I really did.'

Presented this way, Hazel is telling a very coherent and interesting story about part of her work life. In actuality, these quotes came from different points in the interview. The quotation on the lack of benefits occurred early, sandwiched between her discussion of training and her decision to become an assistant.

Carolyn is from around here too, and she was having a tough time getting through, they would have been smart if they had of taken a marker to mark the models. I had all my models in a row, and I had done very well, so I said to Carolyn, here just slip these through, that was wrong, likes and dislikes, Dr. J. certainly had his favourites, that should not have been. I was his class leader.
How did this compare to being in the field?
When I was in private, there were no benefits. If you were sick that was too bad, that's why I got out and got with the health unit. You worked your butt off for nothing. When I started here with Dr. S. I was in high school, it was grade 12 and I had just finished, and I thought which way should I go, you could either be a secretary or a nurse or go and marry a farmer, or whatever. Dr. S came over and said 'Would you like to work for me?' At least it's some-thing, I didn't know a thing about dentistry. I went home. The first day I was there, and this young gal, a big thing around here if you were French and were getting married, the wedding gift from the parents was to have all your teeth removed and get a set of plates, not dentures, plates. I believe he charged sixty dollars for the upper and lower.

Babysitting arose half-way through the interview, during a discussion of working on Sundays and doing domestic chores for the dentist:

Did you get out on time on Saturdays?

Oh gosh, maybe 3 o'clock. And then on Sunday, if anyone called. I was just thinking that the medical doctor was here too and he'd come in and had dentistry done one Sunday, we worked all afternoon and Dr. S didn't pay me any extra. He figured 15 dollars a week covered everything. This doctor handed me a dollar. I made more money babysitting with friends around than I did in dentistry. I really did. I had my clique here and they would take off and leave me, and say they'd go Saturday afternoon and be back Sunday night or something. And I would say, 'I'm not going to be around, that's it.' But then I got raised up to 80 dollars a month, 20 dollars a week. I had my dinner with him, that was a big thing. But then I had to wash the dishes.

Every night?

At noon, I had to wash up, everything, the family dishes. The office was joined to the house.

Would his family eat lunch with you?

I'd eat with the family. On Wednesdays he would go to the sanatorium, and I would have to dust and vacuum, the house, and clean all the dental office.

You would clean both places?

Yes. One day I finally said that was it. It's no wonder I hate house cleaning.

Hazel had actually talked about her working conditions and doing domestic chores in the same time frame, but I imposed my own authorial vision and separated the quotes into different sections. The final quote about holidays happened near the end of the interview, after a discussion about her role in the association and whether assistants raised many complaints about their working conditions.

These examples do not necessarily indicate that Hazel does not view her life as coherent; they simply suggest that the academic author helps construct a research subject's life. The problem occurs when we lose sight of this fact and replace our research subject's story with our own narrative interpretation.

Following Fontana and Frey (1994), we need to develop a sensitivity to the problems presented in doing interviews by 'focusing increased attention to the voices and feelings of the respondents and the interviewer–respondent relation' (363). Kondo (1990), in her book on identity formation in a Japanese workplace, argues that the social construction of self and identity is extremely complex and involves a process of negotiation for both researcher and research subject: 'It is my contention that selves that are coherent, seamless, bounded and whole are indeed illusions ... The problematic of selfhood is thus the product of a complex negotiation, taking place within specific, but shifting, contexts where power and meaning, "personal" and "political" are inseparable. Identity is not a fixed 'thing,' it is negotiated, open, shifting, ambiguous, the result of culturally available meanings and the open-ended, power-laden enactment's of those meanings in everyday situations' (14, 24).

Kondo's insistence on understanding identity as a process of 'negotiation' appears to avoid the pitfalls of constructing a coherent life where either none exists or where it has a markedly different trajectory than what we, as researchers, want to give it. An interviewer should spend time exploring how a respondent 'negotiates' the various events of his or her life. If this negotiation takes place within multiple contexts, then these contexts should also be examined, and the researcher should attempt to determine if the respondent develops multiple 'stories' to handle the shifting personal and political demands that arise in these situations. In Hazel's case, for example, I would need to probe the process by which she 'negotiated' her understanding of why the assistants' association should not become active vis-à-vis the sort of working conditions that she herself encountered every day.

Placed in these terms, such a research approach would be able to draw on a rich tradition of previous ethnographic work that uses symbolic interactionism and ethnomethodology. Awareness of negotiation, after all, is not new to sociology or anthropology (impression management, dramaturgy, role theory, and so on). It is important for me to recognize that even with my tape-recorder and with a complete transcript of Hazel's interview, I engaged in a process of interpretation and reconstruction that Hazel might find appalling.

But what of the negotiation that occurs for the researcher and between the researcher and the researched? The issue of interpretation and negotiation becomes far more complex once we acknowledge the existence of multiple and possibly competing voices in the research process. As Langness and Frank note, a biography always contains (at least) two voices 'singing different versions of the same melody' (1995: 96). This elementary statement has surprisingly complex implications. We researchers need to realize that when we research and write a biography (life history, narrative), we also write our own autobiography, whether or not we explicitly admit or document this process. The research project becomes our 'story,' our narrative, and it is naïve to assume that it should be any more unified or coherent than that of our research subjects.

This is not a new point, and many feminist and non-feminist qualitative researchers have discussed the implications of competing narratives between researcher and researched (Stanley, 1992; Langness and Frank, 1995). But it is surprising how few reports document, in lurid, empirical detail, the labyrinthine connections that must inevitably exist when two lives clash during a research process aimed at producing a single life history. And perhaps that is the source of the puzzle. If we are to take self-reflexivity seriously, we must recognize that we are always producing two works – a research biography and an autobiography. Indeed, is it not possible that every biography is nothing more than an unacknowledged autobiography?

Note

Warm thanks to Andrea Doucet, Florence Kellner, Karen March, and Will van den Hoonaard for taking the time to read and comment on earlier drafts of this essay. Special thanks to Carryll Steffens for encouraging me to collect and appreciate life histories of dental assistants. I express my gratitude to Wallace Clement and Janet Siltanen for their support and guidance in the writing of this essay. Finally, I would like to thank 'Hazel' for sharing with me her stories and memories of a lifetime.

10

Breaking In: Compromises in Participatory Field Research within Closed Institutions

MARY STRATTON

This essay explores a case study of participatory action research (PAR) into the experiences and views of students as they enter and leave high school. Ethical issues are inevitably entwined in such an enterprise at both practical and epistemological levels. Formal institutions have ethical standards to be satisfied, which may or may not be compatible with the intrinsically ethical ideals of participatory research.

As the researcher, my ethical goal (and, sometimes, dilemma) was to find a way to allow the voices of the students to be heard. Despite considerable research policy and theoretical attention vis-à-vis educational transitions, very little has asked students directly about their experiences, reasoning, and decisions. Children and youths form subordinate groups in society because they are not considered fully competent to govern their affairs or act in their own best interests. Some of this attitude stems from grounded concerns related to physical and cognitive development; but much of it derives from stereotypical and unchallenged assumptions that crumble on close examination (Stratton, 2001). Thus our knowledge about children and adolescents tends to be formed by what 'expert' adults believe about them rather than by their actual social experiences and perceptions. Social researchers also mete out such treatment to groups of subordinate adults such as psychiatric survivors, prisoners, welfare recipients, the disabled, and ethnic minorities.

Participatory action research (PAR) is a method of critical knowledge designed to address this inequitable treatment of subordinate groups. It is generally agreed that PAR is a process with a socially transformative purpose, which consists of three parts: social investigation (research), education, and action (Maguire, 1987; Hall, 1993). Central to PAR, and setting it apart from ordinary action research, creating social knowledge must involve the researched community (especially subordinated groups) in order 'to develop critical consciousness, to improve the lives of those involved in the research process, and to transform fundamental societal structures and relationships' (Maguire, 1987: 3). This admirable, if lofty ideal has many ethical and practical implications that are challenging for any research project. When the actions of some members of the researched community are tightly controlled (which is not uncommon among oppressed or subordinated populations) the ideal may be unrealizable. Certainly, many levels of moral and ethical questions arise in the research process.

Research in a Total Institution

Accepting the value of applying PAR methods to research with children and youths is one thing – conducting PAR within a highly controlled and restrictive setting is another. Discussing this issue in the context of a mental asylum, Erving Goffman (1961) identifies a set of likely constraints in a total institution. Goffman considered the boarding school a total institution, but excluded day schools *because* the students left the site daily. None the less, the degree to which the organization and operation of a day school fit Goffman's elements is eerily striking.[1]

My argument is that these conditions and the barriers that they erect must be explicitly recognized and confronted by any field researcher attempting to 'break in' to such an institution. A researcher planning a PAR or moderated collaborative approach,[2] must consider how the constraints imposed by a total institution affect the validity of the data and the subsequent well-being of the research participants/collaborators. It is possible, however, to move towards a participatory model of research, even within total institutions, and, given inmates' lack of opportunity to speak of their experiences, there is an imperative to try. A muffled voice must surely be better than no voice at all – as long as the limitations, constraints, and ethical questions are made explicit.

I contend that each of the elements of the total institution described by Goffman (1961: 3–124) affects the conduct of any kind of research within such an institution and impedes implementation of the PAR ideal. The elements also contain tensions and contradictions (as Goffman shows) that can serve as 'cracks in the wall' to allow entry to the institution and its inmates.[3]

My observations suggest that the following characteristics describe conditions inside the average day school, which, like any total institution, purports to do one or more of the following things:

- enable an instrumental task
- protect the inmates
- protect the community

(Sociology of education literature contains arguments that mass schooling serves any or all of those three purposes.) To that end, total institutions have tightly scheduled daily activities that proceed at pre-arranged times, enforced from above by a system of explicit formal rulings and a body of officials.

All these daily activities take place in the

- 'immediate company of a large batch of others' (6), who are
- treated as a homogeneous group and
- required to do the same things
- under the same authority structure.

Breaking In

The conditions described above all apply (to some extent at least) to the high school. Breaking into and doing research in a total institution involve three factors. First, total institutions (especially schools) routinely move 'large batches' of inmates with a minimum of coercion and few disruptive incidents – imagine in contrast the chaos that would emerge at a commuter station if 1,000 or more passengers were suddenly instructed to go to different platforms inside five minutes. Tight scheduling, constant surveillance, and a status split between staff and inmates retain cohesion and control. This arrangement will influence any research conducted inside such an institution. Carving out and preserving opportunities for inmates' privacy and confidentiality will be a constant challenge. In schools, rules dictate that a teacher must be present in a classroom at all times. A room designated for conducting interviews will probably be close to a staff person. There will inevitably be sudden and unannounced interruptions and possibly changed locations at a moment's notice.

Second, for such research conditions to be possible, at least a few of the officials and members of staff must collaborate in the research process (as happened with Goffman). Goffman (1961) points out that even in total institutions there are some officials who are sympathetic and supportive of inmates. Many teachers are dedicated to the nobler aims of education and do not relish their more warden-like tasks.

Finally, the researcher (outsider or insider) presents a potential threat to both staff and inmates but must negotiate all the above conditions to gain, maintain, and balance the co-operation of officials and the trust of the inmates.

A Case Study

To present this case study I have divided that process into five stages: setting the research agenda (including identifying the research issue); designing the research instruments; collecting the data; analysing the data; and disseminating the resulting knowledge (reporting results). Action for change follows from the reporting of results.

Setting the Research Agenda

As I stated above, I do not think that the PAR ideal can be attained within a closed institution. Ideally, the researched community identifies its own research issues and the research team comes from within the community (or at the very least the community would select the researcher). Inmates of total institutions cannot do these two things. The best possibility for students in high school is that a concerned teacher with some research background will facilitate research on their concerns, despite the power dynamics and institutional constraints. An outside researcher is quite possibly both necessary and preferable, especially to ensure their anonymity and protection from reprisal.

An outside researcher could in theory adopt the research agenda of the insiders, but in total institutions this is unlikely, as regulations will demand that the researcher first gain pre-approved entry, by declaring – in detail – all aspects of the research project. In order to gain approval, the research proposal will need to include components that are of interest to the authorities.[4]

Designing the Research Instruments

As I noted above, some students were able to be part of the development of the research instruments. The project's methods included a questionnaire, in-depth recursive interviews, informal discussions, and observation. Full class and focus group discussions with the university-bound Ontario Academic Credit (OAC) students helped shape the content, wording, and design of the questionnaire, which reflected the focus of the in-depth interviews.

However, in order to gain formal access to a broad range of students I had first to fulfil the school board's regulations and have a proposal approved by a joint-board research review committee that met only three times a year. Application rules required the submission of a final version of the research instruments. The participation of the OAC students was extremely valuable in that regard, but they were not representative of the entire group to be researched. I initially explained the PAR approach, proposing that my submitted instruments were drafts to be adjusted in response to feedback from a set of student collaborators drawn from the participating schools in the 1997/98 school year (prior to the actual project year). The review committee rejected this proposal. It was interested in the focus of the project but did not seem particularly impressed with the participatory approach. It was prepared to allow the in-depth interviews but focused on the questionnaire's content. It wanted a finalized questionnaire (in which I was not allowed to ask about things such as ethnicity) and suggested that I use my personal network of contacts to identify some students who would volunteer as collaborators over the summer. I could resubmit the proposal in September 1998. From my point of view, time and resources were clearly under pressure.

That I was actually able to gain the collaboration of nine students (and a retired teacher) during their summer break attests to students' enthusiasm to speak about their experiences of entering and leaving high school. It would have been possible, if I had had sufficient time, to involve more students. The collaborators included students from several schools, who were either entering or exiting the target grades. They reported a range of academic achievement and ethnic and social backgrounds. As well as 'pilot testing' the questionnaire, they explored the best way to broach issues and why there might be different viewpoints among students. Their contribution was invaluable.[5] However, most of the collaborators were not in the schools that would ultimately form the research sites, and those who were had just completed high school.

The committee approved my revised proposal (including negotiated forms of background questions that allowed me to gather needed information), but I still did not have the 'insider' team of research collaborators for which I had hoped. Further, the review committee did not allow me classroom time.[6] It proposed that I gain the voluntary participation of students during lunchtime, 'spares,' or before or after school – a serious constraint on collecting data.

With board-level approval gained, I had one final entry barrier to negotiate. I had to persuade principals of four schools to allow me to conduct the research. Once I was actually permitted to contact the schools, this proved an easy task, which actively reduced some of the constraints on my access to students.

Collecting the Data

The board-imposed constraints on my access to a wide range of students and the time pressure of the school year were at this point somewhat daunting. Originally I had hoped to have a team of student collaborators who could help with the questionnaire sessions, especially some of the senior students to assist with the lower grades.[7] The PAR ideal meant that interviewers should also be trained from among the students themselves, but I had already decided that this would not be possible. Deirdre Kelly (1993) had tried to do this and had run into problems deriving from power dynamics and insufficient resources for training, and I had neither the time nor the resources even to attempt it. Besides, there is no convincing evidence that peer interviewers, especially with children and youths, are more successful in obtaining rich and valid data.[8] I am not convinced that such an approach is even desirable in a total institution, as it would make both interviewer and interviewee vulnerable to subsequent reprisals and threats to breach confidentiality. Training university students just out of high school would have been a possible compromise solution, but the clash between university and high school timetables, along with lack of training resources, made it impossible. I would suggest, however, that participatory researchers need to take a much closer look at this issue.

Another potential roadblock arose when I was informed that even though the research committee had approved my project, one of the participating boards still required its own internal review (which would not occur for some weeks). Quelling panic, I arranged meetings with the principals of two schools in the board where I had the go-ahead. Both were accommodating, and one was particularly enthusiastic about the project. This principal felt that taking part in the research would be excellent experience for students, that the issues were of concern to them, that the questionnaire provided a curriculum-related opportunity in language and numeracy literacy, and that taking part in the in-depth interviews would offer students a rare opportunity to use their communication skills (for which they could be released from class).

At the other school, I was given two twelve-minute assemblies (one for grade nines and one for grade twelve/OACs) and a follow-up five minutes in a number of home rooms. I did gain some participation from both grades, and most students who volunteered were prepared to do both the questionnaire and a follow-up interview. I invested as much time as I could afford at this site, but the constraint on in-class time was a barrier to participation, which was much lower than for the other three sites where I was eventually granted class time.[9]

An official at the other board advanced my proposal and formally supported use of class time if the principals were willing. I already had contact with one school in this jurisdiction (where I had previously interacted with the OAC class), and several teachers at that school supported me. In the end I was not held up waiting for access, although I had only a short window of opportunity at the final school. By the time I received official permission to approach this school, exams were approaching for the first semester. Class time was a valuable commodity, but I was granted the minimum number of students that I requested. Further problems ensued when a number of the grade niners neglected to return their consent forms on time and could not therefore take part.[10]

In the end, I gained about 214 completed, properly consented questionnaires and 52 in-depth interviews. I made every effort to include a representative cross-section of students, but it was harder for some to take part than others. I included students in difficult circumstances such as teenaged mothers and students with special needs. Although some researchers concerned with gaining data from inductive interviews and other ethnographic data dismiss survey-type questionnaires, in this instance the method facilitated access at several points. First, the board's review committee saw it as 'useful.' Second, principals also immediately recognized the value of some of the information that the questionnaire would collect and granted me class time. I was able to offer curriculum-related discussions following the questionnaire-completion sessions, and these allowed all students (even if they had not completed the questionnaire) to ask questions about it and to make comments on the issues that it raised. Teachers, students, and the researcher all enjoyed these sessions: they provided a participatory moment for far more students than would have otherwise been possible; students liked the questionnaire (which was all about themselves), which increased their willingness to participate in a lengthy personal interview and ninety-two students used a space for open comment at the end of the questionnaire and provided some excellent comments and reflections.

As well as providing background data, the pre-completion of the questionnaires allowed the random drawing of a subgroup of interviewees by site, gender, and grade. While interviewing all willing students would have been the ideal, neither time nor money was available. If I had relied on school staff members to identify willing students, the 'pet' factor, noted by Goffman, would have been a problem. After I had made the random selection and gained the consent of the required number of students, I checked the remaining questionnaires for any written requests to be interviewed. This added two extra interviews. One non-selected student approached me while I was interviewing at his school. I offered him an interview, but he chose to be an informal collaborator and spoke with me on several occasions outside school time.

Recursive interviews help to maximize the interviewee's participation. As the interviewer starts with very broad questions and uses neutral prompts based on the interviewee's responses, the interview develops collaboratively. I got the students to explore their experiences of entering and exiting high school, and the resulting data are extremely rich. Many of the students clearly welcomed the full attention of an adult. The data make it clear that adolescents value the attention and opinions of adults whom they respect. Seldom does the school (or the rest of society) allow them sixty to seventy minutes to talk about their experiences and views. The interviews were supposed to take one period, and in most cases this was a comfortable time frame. At the school where interviews occurred at lunchtime there was only about forty minutes available, and this was sometimes not enough, but it was difficult to arrange a second session.

In summary, I did everything that I could to maximize students' input during data collection, but what I achieved was far from the PAR ideal. Not being allowed to establish in advance a specific group of in-site collaborators was a major constraint. With more time and financial resources I could have involved students further, but the PAR ideal of insider interviewers was unattainable – and possibly something that the students did not want.

Analysing the Data

The data collection produced a daunting task of data analysis. Entry and analysis of questionnaire data demand a large amount of time, as does transcription of fifty-two hour-long interviews. The university could not provide even transcribing equipment. Available funding to support field research covered just a fraction of the costs, and the schools, while keen to receive the research results, had no budget to support their development.[11]

Student involvement could have been maximized in data analysis. There is, however, a fine line between allowing students to participate and exploiting their labour. It would be unethical to have them enter data and transcribe interviews without compensating them, and there were no resources to pay them. I would have liked to arrange some co-op placements for students to analyse data, but the university offered few support resources, and the funded portion of my doctoral program had expired, forcing me to take paid work elsewhere.

I did, however, find students who were willing to be recontacted and to consult with me on possible interpretations of the data, and I will be requesting their input as raw data are analysed. Lack of time and resources has slowed this phase and inhibited the continued participation of students. These delays have been obstacles to dissemination of the resulting knowledge, and so, inevitably, to any action for change.

Disseminating the Results

Despite the problems in completing data analysis, I have been able to disseminate fragments of resulting knowledge as they occur. One particular area involves the students' views and experiences concerning course and career choices. Students and staff members in Ontario high schools are very aware of this issue because the new curriculum forces grade nine students to make important early choices of courses that amount to academic streaming. I was able to present some of the comments and concerns expressed in the research data at an in-school career fair for students in grades nine and ten. I involved student volunteers from the audience – but not the original research participants – in presenting relevant quotes. A presentation at a national conference on career development, complete with student collaborators from the researched group, has been scheduled. This essay itself allows me to speak out about both involving students in creating knowledge about themselves and the lack of resources to do so.

Students who participated in the research were promised feedback and received it in the following school year, but because the analysis has taken longer than planned they did not receive a final summary. Instead I gave them a contact address and invited them to keep me updated on their whereabouts so that I can send them the final summary. I had hoped to return to their classrooms (especially the grade nines) and to involve them in further discussions of the results. I will still seek to do so, and to involve other students in evaluating the knowledge that has been created, but meeting those goals under resource-scarce conditions is difficult.

Action for Change

The PAR ideal equates action for change with the dissemination of the new knowledge and anticipates the involvement of the researched community in both. The nature of school is such that the 'inmate' population constantly changes. Thus the knowledge created by a group of inmates is more likely to benefit others in the future than to assist the participants. In my study, many senior students have already left the institution. I am convinced, however, that their insights will be of benefit to younger students. I am also certain that many teachers will learn from the knowledge generated by this study. Unfortunately, getting everything of value back to the students and out to the adults who have the power to respond constructively is neither easy nor quick, and an additional obstacle arose. Local school boards rotate principals every few years, and a wave of scheduled and early retirements among teachers and administrators has created turmoil. As of January 2001, none of the original principals remained at the research sites, and only one of the vice-principals. Two of my four student liaison teachers have retired, and a third has transferred to another school.

The dissemination phase of the project is only just beginning, and despite the problems I remain hopeful for positive change at least at the level of the school. Further, many students indicated that they had learned from their own participation in the study. Examining their own experiences and thoughts helped them to think through upcoming choices, but they also hoped that other people would listen to them.

Conclusion

Even with generous support, it is probably impossible to attain the PAR ideal in a closed institution, but that goal may not be attainable in *any* research community. Too little attention is generally paid to what Hansen et al. (2001) call the 'trap of pseudo democracy' – that is, assuming that everyone in a community is equally able to participate once invited to do so. The structure of a total institution exacerbates such problems and perhaps makes them easy to identify.

Questions emerge that make me wonder whether the PAR ideal is really ideal in all respects, in all situations. The most notable issue concerns the matter of insider versus outsider researchers. While lack of resources influenced my decision in this area, training insiders might not have been the best approach. Once again, the matter cries out for more analysis and attention.

Despite the problems, I do not think that the attempt to 'democratize' research should be abandoned. I acknowledge the imperfections of my attempt and the always-inherent danger of raising the hopes of subordinated groups, only to see governing authorities take away gains.[12] I do not believe, however, that this is a reason to abandon the effort to give such communities a research voice. In total institutions, if outsiders make no attempt to break in and find ways to release the voices of the captive populations, how will they ever be heard? The outside researcher need not be an academic, but, given scarce university resources, members of this group are still the most likely to be able to muster sufficient freedom and support for such an enterprise.

I suggest that bringing to light the problems involved is one way to help address them. Terminology can affect our conceptualization of possibilities and limitations. If the PAR ideal is unattainable, how should we categorize projects that recognize this fact but still set out to maximize the involvement of a researched community? 'To participate' means literally 'to take part,' a requirement satisfied by merely filling out a survey. To *collaborate*, however, involves working with another on a joint project. While the PAR ideal provides a useful ideal type, against which to measure the degree of collaboration achieved, I find the latter term more useful for evolving research models for the social constructionist's world. I can then claim a project that allowed me to work with a number of students on a project to create knowledge about their experiences – albeit in a process fraught with problems.

I still believe that the possibilities make the effort worthwhile – a conclusion conveyed also by many of the students whom I interviewed: 'Will our answers affect the way our schools are? Will we know the results of this ... who will know the results? Can we do the interview if we want? (25F9). 'I think it is good to have [this research] for students so the school board can maybe make some changes for the students' (03M9). 'I think this whole thing was an excellent idea. Please get back to me as soon as possible. I am very anxious to see the results' (44F12). 'Thank you for taking the time and for caring enough to do this – hopefully it will help' (79F12).

I too hope that it will help, and I continue to strive for that outcome, but the constraints are real and ongoing. As the researcher 'breaking in,' I had to be sufficiently positive and encouraging to motivate the students to participate. While I tried also to be honest and realistic, there is an ethical, and possibly irresolvable, dilemma involved in raising consciousness and expectations for transformative outcomes. I can only hope that in the long term the students' voices will be heard and acted on and that in the interim being part of the process was reward enough for most of the students.

Notes

Stephen Richer provided comments on an earlier draft of this essay and expert advice and support throughout the research process, for all of which I am most grateful. Thanks also to Will C. van den Hoonaard for editorial comments and advice. I first presented elements of this chapter at the 17th Qualitative Analysis Conference in Fredericton in May 2000.

1 There is definitely room for detailed descriptive comparison and theoretical debate about the elements of total (or closed) institutions, but the focus of this essay is on breaking through the barriers to conduct meaningful research. Suffice it to say, therefore, that Goffman notes that Etzioni (Goffman, 1961) also describes educational institutions as 'total' and 'closed,' and both Apple 1990: 136 and McLaren 1993: 191 specifically remark on (but do not pursue) the relevance of Goffman's description to a consideration of the structure and practice of education.

2 A critical examination of PAR literature reveals that in practice there is no clear conceptual application of the term 'participatory action research.' It is used interchangeably with 'participatory,' 'collaborative,' and 'transformative,' among others (for one examples see Reason, 1994). Detailed analysis and discussion of this are outside the scope of this essay, but I return briefly to terminology in the conclusion below.

3 I refer in this essay to some of the main elements. There are other comparisons to be made, and I discuss these elsewhere.

4 All these issues are further complicated when the researcher is required to meet the regulations and constraints of the university organization, particularly as they apply to graduate students.

5 There is of course always a question about who does and does not partici-

pate. Students who volunteered were undoubtedly among a relatively articulate group frequently willing to speak up. But this is an inevitable condition of research – even if subjects are legally compelled to respond, some still will not do so, and others will not do so truthfully. There is no solution other than to be aware of who may be 'missing' from resulting data.

6 The reason given for refusing me classroom time and previously for disallowing my access to collaborators was that too much school time had already been lost to the 1997 teachers' strike. How class time was used was a 'hot' issue at this point.

7 As noted above, the researcher needs to consider issues of development, and, in a school, age adds a further constraint, both because of a need to consider the developmental skills of students and because laws govern what a child may personally consent too.

8 A personal communication with Deirdre Kelly (7 January 1996) was helpful in this regard. Research that actually systematically examines the role of different interviewers is lacking. In the available examples of recursive interviewing (Tesson, Lewko, and Bigelow, 1987, 1990; Boutilier, 1994; Stratton, 1994) adult interviewers had been very successful in initiating and expanding dialogue with children and youths.

9 There may have been a site factor beyond the requirement to volunteer, because at all three of the other sites many of the senior students *chose* to do the interview on their own time rather than miss important classes. For grade nines getting out of class was a definite 'reward,' however!

10 Students over eighteen could sign their own forms, but younger students required parental consent. Failure to return these forms by the younger students was a perpetual problem. At two sites I was able to add a couple of extra grade nine classes to compensate, and teachers allowed students who wanted to take part but had forgotten their forms to do so. However, if they did not return the forms subsequently I had to destroy those surveys, and they could not be included when I drew up the interview group.

11 At the time of the research, because of provincial funding cuts the schools could not always afford to pay for a substitute teacher in the event of staff illness, and students would have to spend the period in the cafeteria. Photocopy budgets for in-school materials ran out, and students frequently had to share text books.

12 See both Apple 1990 and Kelly 1993 for examples of this with prisoners and school students, respectively. In both cases it was an agonizing experience for the researcher, but Apple's account suggests that the researched population may still benefit from the experience.

11

The Harmony of Resistance: Qualitative Research and Ethical Practice in Social Work

MICHAEL UNGAR AND GILLIAN NICHOL

Words belong to nobody, and in themselves they evaluate nothing.

– M.M. Bakhtin (1986)

There is a widespread, but poorly organized, call for ethical research methods that can generate new knowledge while respecting the diversity of knowledge claims from marginalized individuals and groups (for example, Maddocks, 1992; Gorman, 1993; Weis and Fine, eds., 1993; Gilchrist, 1997). If, as Janice Ristock and Joan Pennell (1996) explain, research is 'the search for answers to questions in a way that is made open to the appraisal of others' (116), then researchers must ensure these 'others' authentic representations of their local realities. The difficulty in responding has been the lack of support for researchers' use of qualitative methods in human service disciplines such as social work.

We argue in this essay that for those of us working in human services, the goal of our interventions is similar to that of the qualitative researcher – to enhance the discursive power of silenced voices. However, the dominant research discourse most in evidence in academe promotes traditional 'scientism,' which denigrates qualitative research in human service–related disciplines. Recent international conferences on qualitative research made evident to us the need for supportive environments in which to nurture an alternative research discourse that celebrates the fit between qualitative methods and progressive human services. Through our collective experience as presenters and participants at these conferences, we helped develop methods that are particularly relevant to the exploration of diverse knowledge claims concerned with personal and social 'problems.' As we show below, these methods are also congruent with ethical practice in social work.

Specifically, conferences and other forums that deal with qualitative methods support our continued role in academe while strengthening the voices of those with whom we work. This discursive empowerment reflects the orientation of professional social workers who 'believe in the intrinsic worth and dignity of every human being and are committed to the values of acceptance, self-determination and respect of individuality' (Canadian Association of Social Workers [CASW], 1994: 7). Participation in these forums improves in three ways our understanding of the applicability of qualitative research methods to the human services in general and to social work in particular.

First, the multiplicity of methods and diversity of research contexts discussed by conference presenters demonstrate the central place of qualitative research in any movement to resist social hegemony. Qualitative researchers who share their work at such events can extend the localized discursive power of silenced individuals.

Second, through their participation they collectively resist the positivist scientific discourse, which devalues the knowledge claims of marginalized individuals and groups typically served by the social work profession. And third, the range of social issues and the multiple points of view so evident at the conferences suggest that qualitative research can provide research methods that generate trustworthy and authentic knowledge. In our concluding remarks below, we look at how to enhance these collective experiences in academic meetings and better meet professional obligations for an ethical and empowering social work practice.

Our discussion refers to two exemplars of a supportive environment – the sixteenth and seventeenth annual Qualitative Analysis Conferences held in Fredericton, New Brunswick, in May 1999 and May 2000, respectively. Each conference brought together 200 international participants. Each year, individuals and groups of researchers made over 100 presentations on the theory, practice, and outcomes of qualitative research. The range of topics covered each year was immense, including, at the 1999 conference, 'Building Bridges: The Collaborative Development of Culturally Appropriate Definitions of Child Abuse and Neglect for the South-Asian Community' (Maiter, 1999), 'Witch Wars: The Tensions between Ideology and Practice in Neopagan Communities' (Reid, 1999), 'Between a Rock and a Hard Place: Gay and Christian Identity Integration' (Walton, 1999), and 'Home-less-ness: Linking Contributing Factors, Interventions and Mediating Factors' (Jeffery, 1999). Researchers came from a range of disciplines, including anthropology, economics, education, medicine, nursing, psychology, social work, and sociology. Though diverse in their methods and topics, participants shared their commitment to exploring an alternative research paradigm and enhancing the discursive power of marginalized groups.

This chapter looks at the gestalt shift that led to the Fredericton gatherings; the emerging method of resistance, which emphasizes qualitative research; quantitative research and the helping professions; and the road ahead.

A Time and a Place for Marginalized Voices:
The Road to Fredericton

Their code of ethics obliges social workers to engage people in processes that enhance their personal and social empowerment (CASW, 1994; Lee, 1994; Ife, 1997). The professional, in the course of his or her duties, is instructed to attend to 'the wishes, desires, motivations, and plans of the client ... as the primary consideration in any intervention' and cautioned 'that all actions and interventions of the social worker are taken subject to the reasonable belief that the client will benefit from the action' (CASW, 1994: 4). While these ethical injunctions do not explicitly address the research endeavour, they demonstrate the need by practising social workers for knowledge of the lived experiences of marginalized people if interventions are to be in tune with local realities. The empowerment of individuals whose opportunities for power are delimited by their broader social circumstances requires both a time and a place for the expression of their voices in the detailed description of their lives. Research, by providing a forum in which these voices are heard, is explicitly a social intervention. As such, it requires a method that is congruent with the ethical obligations of the profession that the research seeks to inform. The notion of reflexivity (Lather, 1991; Fine et al., 2000; Olesen, 2000) typical of critical qualitative research ensures a 'give and take, a mutual negotiation of meaning and power' (Lather, 1991: 57) such that the voice of the research participant is privileged like that of the researcher. Just as, ethically, the practitioner must not purposefully impose his or her values on clients, so too must the researcher account for his or her pre-determined biases or perceptions.

bell hooks (1989) writes eloquently and passionately of the time in her life when she was ready to present her voice but found no place for what she had to say in the social conditions of experience constituted by those around her. Nor did she receive the support of others who might have added their voices to hers: 'It is precisely these voices that are silenced, suppressed, when we are dominated. It is this collective voice we struggle to recover' (31). When qualitative researchers speak together and make a time and a place for silenced voices, those voices become a little louder, a little less fragmented (see, for example, Weis and Fine, 1993). When these voices from the margins are juxtaposed in such quantity, as occurred at the two qualitative research conferences, we are forced to reconsider what is 'marginal' (see Kirby and McKenna, 1989). In this way, the collective efforts of researchers can enhance the discursive power of both themselves and the participants in their studies.

In creating a time and a place for the expression of normally silenced voices, the researchers challenged themselves to protect these marginalized discourses from intrusion. Michelle Fine (1994) has explored this connection between the self of the researcher and the 'other' whom we call the 'participant,' arguing that researchers must remain conscious of the 'hyphen' between self-other and of how what they do affects those whom they study:

> Self and Other are knottily entangled. This relationship, as lived between researchers and informants, is typically obscured in social science texts, protecting privilege, securing distance, and laminating the contradictions. Despite denials, qualitative researchers are always implicated at the hyphen. When we opt, as has been the tradition, to simply write *about* those who have been Othered, we deny the hyphen. Slipping into a contradictory discourse of individualism, personalogic theorizing, and decontextualization, we inscribe the Other, strain to white out Self, and refuse to engage the contradictions that litter our texts.
>
>   When we opt, instead, to engage in social struggles *with* those who have been exploited and subjugated, we work the hyphen, revealing far more about ourselves, and far more about the structures of Othering. Eroding the fixedness of categories, we and they enter and play with the blurred boundaries that proliferate. (72)

This chapter extends Fine's analysis from the actions of the individual researcher to the collective actions of qualitative researchers.

The conference format in Fredericton promoted a collegial environment, mirroring the collegiality and equality encouraged in the study of human lived experience. In a large number of diverse sessions, 'experts' made presentations alongside new scholars and an eclectic mix of bachelor's, masters', and doctoral students who shared their work. While the conferences began in 1984 as a forum devoted to symbolic interactionism, they now include many disciplines and approaches to qualitative research. This celebration of methodological and topical diversity allowed for the creative and stimulating juxtapositioning of studies reflecting an international mix of marginalized discourses without the domination of one over the other. A number of presenters made transparent their efforts to avoid 'colonizing' the voices of those whom they studied by authenticating what study participants had to say during the research process (Cutajar, 1999). Through the abundant use of narrative and the succinct but 'thick' description of data, presenters and audience interacted in forums typically numbering between ten and forty participants, during which the broader meanings of findings were constructed.

The act of creating layer upon layer of alternative discourse through such collective efforts makes the speech acts of the individual participants in each of their studies more credible as political and emancipatory forces. It does not matter that participants in different studies are unaware of each others' voices. At one of the conferences, a woman in one study on sex-trade workers insisted that she and other strippers did control and manipulate to their advantage the men who came to see them (Egan, 1999), while in another study women in Mexico's Chiapas region explored their experiences of oppression living with abusive husbands (Vega-López and Gonzalez-Perez, 1999). In both cases, it was through the praxis inherent in qualitative research that each study's participants became part of both a localized discourse which, they told us, their communities deny them and of a broader social discourse of emancipation. In the global community of the research forum, voices – in this instance, of women – could be heard in opposition to the cultural norms of their communities. This experience of empowerment reflects the expressed goals of social work and allied professions that are ethically obligated to address oppression. For the research participants whose voices were presented, their marginality became a place of resistance.

As participant observers within an alternative academic discourse, we are not simply a passive audience to these expressed localized truth claims. Our responsivity, whether articulated or not, allows consumers of qualitative findings to join a movement of resistance. Our listening acknowledges the authenticity of each study's findings. As conference attendees, we engaged dialectically with speakers in a process that created new meanings that expand our capacity to perceive our world. Although research reporting tends to fix meaning, the presentation may also improve praxis and social action through its catalytic effect on others (Lather, 1991). As the audience, we learn new names for our own experiences. Critical discourse says that speech acts change power relations. 'Performativity' helps explain what took place at the conferences. Enunciation has a way of affecting what has been enunciated. In practice, if we say 'it,' 'it' becomes a little more real.

A Method of Resistance

As a group, qualitative researchers' voices are marginal within the dominant scientific discourse, especially that of health-related sciences such as social work. And yet, in a world where the forces of a global economy homogenize and privatize local social issues, documenting diversity and preserving indigenous knowledge have never been more essential. How then are we to explore the challenges facing professional human service workers as they seek to empower individuals and groups without methods sensitive to the 'politics of location' of participants (Dominelli and McLeod, 1989)? Academic forums that celebrate an alternative research paradigm become vehicles to express sufficient discursive power to challenge the principles of conventional science.

For example, many of the presenters at Fredericton noted the influence of feminist research principles on their work. They acknowledge the contributions of people such as Lena Dominelli and Eileen McLeod (1990), who noted: 'Feminist work has demonstrated that substantial, though otherwise inaccessible, evidence as to the nature of social problems and the suffering this entailed is opened up by legitimizing the analytical standing of the accounts of those immediately affected' (32). Arguably, qualitative methods are grudgingly accepted when the dominant discourse that defines a social problem (for example, spousal abuse, sexual assault of children, racism) faces a significant challenge from a large and well-organized group of advocates who define the problem within a broader social context that makes quantitative investigation difficult. In such instances, professionals are ethically mandated to respond to these alternative definitions as they become better articulated. Research methods that foster this articulation and forums that support their expression can therefore further the social agendas of disempowered groups.

For example, the social work literature on the ethics of practice with marginalized peoples, such as northern and remote or Aboriginal populations, has noted the need for researchers and practitioners to check their conceptual 'baggage' at the door before they proceed to intervene and instead to attune themselves to local definitions of problems (Delaney and Brownlee, 1996; Gilchrist, 1997). Roger Delaney and Keith Brownlee (1996), in their writing on northern practice models, caution against 'social workers who are southern in their orientation, metaphors and conceptual systems and who operate in northern areas in a manner congruent with their metaphors' (47–8). When the worker must transpose himself or herself contextually, the challenge is the same as that confronting the qualitative researcher who must attend to the variations in context in which data are generated: 'Social workers must clearly understand the descriptive, evaluative and prescriptive meaning of a belief system if they are to assess if their actions are imposing upon a client system or not. In other words, when a social worker refers to concepts like self-determination, empowerment, respect and non-judgement, then that social worker needs to clearly understand what these concepts mean or run the risk of ethically violating a client system not by intent but by ignorance. Acting in ignorance is a violation of social work's *Standard of Practice* (3–3.6)' (50). An ethical practice is one that intervenes in ways that demonstrate respect for local definitions and solutions, which are documented best through the lengthy engagement and contextually sensitive research typical of qualitative work.

Qualitative Research as First Choice

Once understood this way, the study of problems necessitates accounting for myriad confounding variables. In such cases, researchers will sometimes propose exploratory studies (often qualitative) to cope with a problem too complex for immediate investigation through quantitative methods. This approach, we feel, relegates qualitative methods to the status of 'second best,' as we seldom see quantitative researchers refer to the epistemological drawbacks of positivist research. Neal Newfield and his colleagues (Newfield et al., 1996) make a similar point in regard to ethnographies in family therapy research. While arguing that qualitative and quantitative methods are complementary, they highlight the usual bias against qualitative work:

> Although the results of ethnographic studies can be tested later in quantitative designs, this does not mean that they must be tested. To treat such ethnographic studies as incomplete is discriminatory. This is still most obvious in many graduate programs in which students interested in doing qualitative research are permitted to do so, by ambivalent thesis and dissertation committees, as long as they do 'real' quantitative research as well. Such an approach results in the student doing two research projects. Investigators using quantitative research strategies could follow up their statistical descrip-

tions and prediction with a purposive sampling of rich descriptions of the phenomenon under measurement. The fact that they do not does not make the research inferior. (33)

A survey of the literature on postmodern and qualitative techniques reveals the extensive time and energy devoted to justifying these techniques rather than to celebrating the large and diverse bodies of knowledge that qualitative methods have generated. Qualitative research forums that bring together the collective efforts of investigators provide a safe place to celebrate an alternative research paradigm. The ubiquitous notion that we as qualitative researchers must justify what we do is, in our experience, always present at traditional research conferences, as well as in other academic forums such as promotion and tenure committees and editorial boards of many of the leading journals in the social sciences. Such was not the case in Fredericton, where presenters were unabashed about their preference for qualitative methods and their benefits for both researchers and study participants. A scientific community that valued the products of qualitative research more highly would have to understand the relativism of what it holds to be true and its grounding within a particular paradigm. 'Methodological awareness' (Seale, 1999: 49) would require positivist researchers to acknowledge the same issues of interpretation in their choice of criteria for rigour.

Clive Seale (1999), in looking for a middle ground between relativism and objectivity, urges the community of scientists who act as gatekeepers to professional knowledge to adopt much greater tolerance for each other's definition of rigour. He sees the need for mutuality in this endeavour. Perhaps we can learn from one another. The community generated through a qualitative conference in which each person is critically constructive of the work of others is aware of standards of practice. The old positivist approach assumed the uncontroversial existence 'of shared meanings, but ended up imposing meanings that were resisted by many individuals. The alternative qualitative paradigm, investigating how shared meanings are constructed and celebrating their diversity, can lead to a condition of profound uncertainty and distrust. It seems time for qualitative researchers to establish a new consensus around exploring shared meanings for positive purposes, drawing on the strengths of a constructed, imagined research community' (Seale, 1999: 29).

In the conference setting, what Seale imagines became real. The conference forums promoted establishment of conventions for ethical qualitative inquiry reminiscent of those for more realistic and positivistic approaches, but encouraging exploration of multiple voices and realities competing for discursive presence. In the broader community, however, the ethics of good research are judged within competing discourses, ones which often reward only some knowledge products and most certainly treat with disdain the relativism so obvious in qualitative generation of ethical knowledge.

As researchers, we are caught between the paradigm of modernism, which tells us how science is done, and postmodernism, which de-professionalizes the researcher by adding power to individuals' and groups' descriptions of their lived experience. Our experience at two qualitative research conferences that offered a critical but supportive environment for our work was that of engagement in a struggle. At its best it is a challenge to the dominant research paradigm and an earnest attempt to do science differently; at its worst, the conferences were a paternalistic presentation of the voices of participants framed within the presenters' honest efforts to promote the struggles of others.

Qualitative Research and the Helping Professions

Our experience as both presenters and participants in forums that celebrated the discovery of indigenous knowledge made evident the fit between qualitative research and the helping professions. Social workers and their colleagues in other disciplines have an explicit goal to make the world a better place. This is more than rhetoric, as social work professionals must find appropriate, contextually sensitive ways to help those whom they serve. Understanding and responding to local definitions of problems and solutions are issues of accountability that underlie ethical practice.

Jim Ife (1997), in his consideration of a critical practice, explores top-down, managerial-style accountability. Social work practice that vests outside experts with the power to make decisions for individuals and their communities is antithetical to the work of respectful front-line practitioners. As Ife notes: 'The current environment of practice does not readily allow for the kind of dissent, creativity and seeking of alternatives that are a natural consequence of social work's primary commitment to a value position' (11). This same battle for accountability is shared by the researcher seeking to document alternative service paradigms indigenous to local realities. The solution, in both instances, is remarkably similar.

Just as the qualitative researcher's methods promote reflexivity, the social worker who practises in ways that respect marginalized voices seeks reflexivity through accountability.

As Joe Kincheloe and Peter McLaren (1994) explain, qualitative methods value silenced voices and avoid the pitfalls of mainstream research practices, which, 'although most often unwittingly, are implicated in the reproduction of systems of class, race and gender oppression' (140). While we share much with allied health professionals, we social workers work with people in context. We need knowledge that recognizes the contextual bias present during its generation. As Mary Rodwell (1998) explains in her discussion of constructivist research methods, benefits accrue to the social worker who engages in ethical research that is attentive to context and voice: 'Because of this constant attention, not only to research ethics, but also to contextual ethics, a fascinating consequence of constructivist inquiry develops. The social work researcher/practitioner will become even more attentive to use of self in a professional sense. The focused attention to managing paradoxes and the potential for ethical dilemmas in the research process adds another level to the researcher's practice sophistication' (221). Social work needs this sophistication if it is to produce authentically relevant research that is supports empowering change.

Katherine Wood (1990) notes how we have tended not to consider which research is most relevant to our field: 'Social work is the practice profession that deals with contexts, more so than any other helping profession; if the research findings are based on context stripping, to that degree will their utility to practice be compromised' (377). We believe that social workers have tended to avoid theory because much of what is available is divorced from the context of those with whom they work. Jim Ife (1997) explains: 'Theory for social work emerges from practice; the "client" has as much of a role in formulating that theory as the social worker, and any idea of "theory" being accessible to the social worker but inaccessible to the client is unacceptable ... this is a very different understanding of theory, and indeed of knowledge from the traditional social work perspective, and it requires a very different relationship between worker and client' (139–40). From this perspective, Ife notes that all our work is inherently political and cannot avoid examining who exercises power over the knowledge that guides that work. Participation in collective forums with other qualitative researchers takes some of this power away from the conventional research paradigm and reinvests it in alternative discourses.

While social work in particular professes to celebrate diversity, the profession has struggled with developing a research base that honours the experiences of clients, most of whom come from marginalized social positions. The ethics of an objective stance idealized in the positivist paradigm becomes suspect when one is accounting for the marginalized position of the knowledge of those whom we seek to help. As Joe Kincheloe and Peter McLaren explain, research's credibility is questionable except when participants judge it to be reflective of their lives: 'Critical researchers award credibility only when the constructions are plausible to those who constructed them, and even then there may be disagreement, for the researcher may see the effects of oppression in the constructs of those researched – effects that those researched may not see' (151). Accounting for a client's context-based experience and understanding of his or her world challenges the social scientist who must tolerate a diversity of knowledge claims. Working together with like-minded researchers, one finds that this tolerance becomes normative rather than problematic. At the conferences, a plethora of competing discourses were embraced and critically discussed. Arguably, documenting this alternative knowledge and giving it volume through its presentation make the research process part of a plan of intervention with marginalized groups of people.

The postmodern qualitative researcher in health-related disciplines embraces the paradox inherent in contextually sensitive research. The explicit ways in which context affects results confirm the ethical necessity to account for the messiness of people's lives and the divergent understandings of those lives. Put simply, that which is discovered has everything to do with where and how it is discovered. This should be good news to social workers and allied professionals who work in material ways that must reflect the indigenous knowledge of those being helped. By way of illustration, Pamela Cotterill (1992) has written about interviewing women and her vulnerability as the researcher. The contexts in which interviews occur are not the sanitized research relationships often seen in texts:

> Three of the single parents had pre-school children, and a problem I never fully resolved was how to interview whilst entertaining a 3-year-old. Small children have a short concentration span and are extremely difficult to keep occupied long enough to conduct an in-depth interview with their mothers. In desperation I have stocked up with chocolate, colouring books and other goodies to use, unashamedly, as bribes and I have interviewed women whilst nursing a child on my knee, sitting on the floor building 'Lego' houses and painting pictures at the kitchen table. I have, in the space of an hour, been amused, frustrated, and exhausted, emotions which came flooding back later

during the transcription of tapes when the respondent's voice was inaudible, completely drowned by a vociferous child. (602)

For us as social workers, Cotterill's experience sounds unremarkable: an average day in an often-chaotic work environment. But there is something synergistic about the untidiness of research, the way it intrudes into the researcher's personal spaces, its lack of control or regimentation. It leaves us, the consumers of the research, sensitized to the realities of the participants in the study and to the theory that they collectively generate. It makes the knowledge discovered appear more congruent with the work that we do. The diversity of experiences embodied in the collective work of qualitative researchers demonstrates a similar postmodern tolerance for chaos: gone is the paternalism of experts determining normative functioning. Instead, a finely textured fabric of ideas is woven using a few key themes as threads: empowerment, oppression, diversity, and resistance. These four concepts are foundational to social work ethics and practice (CASW, 1995).

Hearing the alternative discourses of those with whom we work requires a commitment to humility on the part of the researcher and practitioner in order to see his or her knowledge as simply one of many ways of knowing. 'Not knowing' frees the researcher to reach a deeper understanding of the localized experience of the 'other.' It is this type of knowledge generation that social work needs.

Unfortunately, for most social workers, enculturation into the professional discourse brings with it reliance on teleological theories that posit singular ends (see Reamer, 1994). This, of course, strikes at the heart of a debate within the helping professions as they struggle with postmodernism in its many forms: how do we help if there are no predetermined goals, no metatheories to guide our work, and all truth is relative (see Scott, 1989; Sands and Nuccio, 1992; Howe, 1994; Ristock and Pennell, 1996; Brotman and Pollack, 1997; Leonard, 1997)?

We take an optimistic orientation towards the challenges posed by postmodernist thought. Similar to Jane Gorman (1993), we see ourselves as 'affirmative postmodernists [who] acknowledge the value of the consensual reading of a text or the shared understanding of a human experience and thus avoid the extreme nihilistic relativism characteristic of skeptical postmodernists' (250). We believe that the social worker's material day-to-day occupation confronts the disembodied theory of postmodernism. Further, qualitative research is the best vehicle to help social services staff understand the diverse contexts in which policy and practice decisions are enacted.

Take, for example, research shared at one of the Qualitative Analysis Conferences regarding the needs of women street workers. We were shown how complicated it is to address in policy what the women themselves identify as needs – safer working conditions, health care, political power (Hancock, 1999). Other groups have an interest in solving the problem of street workers in other ways. Although street workers are seldom heard, their position is not irreconcilable with that of other constituents. Intervention is more difficult, however, when the 'clients' or 'patients' oppose the well-intentioned efforts of the service provider to solve the perceived problem (i.e., getting women off the streets). Qualitative methods can account for these different social agendas and act as part of the process of empowerment for voices that our political discourse tends to silence.

Discourse about the 'real world' is embedded in sets of material practices, including those of researchers who speak about the experiences of others: 'Research that breaks social silences fractures the very ideologies that justify power inequities' (Fine, 1994: 221). The postmodern social worker cannot rely only on individual accounts of private concerns to inform action. Discourse is not a private act, nor is discursive resistance. To study problems ignoring their social construction is at best shortsighted and may harm those whose realities are being objectified. Furthermore, the 'truth' is implicated in a set of political arguments that includes 'What is to be done?' – a question answered only through detailed inquiry that is attentive to the sociopolitical and historical contexts in which action is to be taken.

Discourses, in other words, are constructed through linguistic rules and social practices that direct attention to the politics of knowledge-producing activities. It is this connection between what we know and how we came to know it that often goes unquestioned in the human services. By its nature, qualitative research deconstructs this position of power. Many of the voices discovered through its methods challenge conventional wisdom espoused by social workers. At one of the Fredericton conferences, attendees helped Ayalah Aylyn (1999) to understand how pyramid-like bureaucracies or 'triangles' are incongruous with Inuit culture, where circular organizational structures are more reflective of indigenous social organization.

Future Implications

We were humbled and inspired by the collective voices of the hundreds of people represented in the research shared at the two conferences.

However, qualitative forums for sharing these voices can be as shrouded by the fog of academe as more mainstream venues. Our reflections on this experience made us think that this tension between the need to hear the participants in the studies speak and the way we as researchers talk to each other in our professional language reveals the transitional nature of qualitative work. As Patti Lather (1986, 1991) observes, qualitative methods facilitate research as praxis that encourages dialectical practices which prevent 'imposition and reification on the part of the researcher' (265). As qualitative interveners/researchers, we add power to subjugated knowledge. While in most instances we do so benignly, it is not the final step in the process. Do we need to do more than bring to these academic forums the artefacts of informants? Can we truly represent what participants say when the language of the social sciences is itself delimited by discourse (DeVault, 1990)? How do we avoid the 'ventriloquy' (Fine, 1994) caused by academic presentation of research findings?

Perhaps, we speculate, the next stage is for us to bring the people themselves to the forums in which their words are to be shared. This has taken place in other contexts. A recent effort to document women fishers' experiences in the economically turbulent atmosphere of Atlantic Canada brought together women's voices, both in print and through conference presentations (Woodrow and Innes, 1994). While the model was based on participatory action research, informants were involved in dissemination. Collaboration between researchers and participants, which also includes such activities, can give participants first-hand experience with discursive resistance. Such an initiative would fulfil the ethical obligation of making research useful, even emancipatory, for participants.

Lather's concept of catalytic validity is particularly relevant in this regard. Research is valid, Lather points out, to the 'degree to which the research process re-orients, focuses and energizes participants toward knowing reality in order to transform it' (68). In the case of marginalized communities such as those of Aboriginal peoples, research is ethically justifiable only to the extent that it is 'relevant.' In order to be relevant, information generated from research must be made accessible and shared freely if participants from marginalized positions are to be 'equal participants and co-owners of the research endeavour' (Gilchrist, 1997: 71). These issues of relevance and control are as applicable to the qualitative as to the quantitative researcher. Ian Maddocks (1992), in his discussion of the ethics of research with Aboriginal people in Australia, notes that mainstream medical researchers find it much more difficult to carry out studies when they have to negotiate with Aboriginal groups for owner-ship of data and control over publication of the findings.

Therefore we envision future conferences that encourage reflection on the ethics of qualitative (and quantitative) research and its relation to emancipatory praxis. We might also see autobiographical accounts of the research participants' experiences and forums in which to challenge the dichotomous thinking inherent in the researcher–participant dyad, per-haps opening up to debate our role as researchers in the oppression of others.

Conclusion

A strong case can be made for the synergy between qualitative research and the human services. Within an emerging understanding of post-modernism's applicability to such fields of practice as social work, there is need for a research paradigm that can account for the aspirations of practitioners while authenticating the knowledge claims of those with whom they work: 'Research thus becomes a transformative endeavour unembarrassed by the label "political" and unafraid to consummate a relationship with an emancipatory consciousness' (Kincheloe and McLaren, 1994: 140). As such, the research process is representative of the profes-sional's ethical obligation to act in ways that are of use to those whose lives they affect. Validity in the research process, as Ristock and Pennell (1996) define it, consists of 'the integrity, accountability, and value of a research project, achieved through accountability both to the participants and to those who will be affected by the outcome' (116). Research, whether quali-tative or quantitative, that disregards its consumers must be judged ethi-cally suspect. While many social workers have been self-conscious about aligning themselves with that which challenges the objective and typically positivist approaches to their discipline, this timidity has not served the profession well. Instead we feel that we need make no apology for our enthusiastic embrace of methods that celebrate diverse knowledge claims. Qualitative research is an integral part of an anti-oppressive practice.

Note

Special thanks to Professor Carolyn Campbell, Dr Ross Klein, and Dr Eli Teram for their helpful comments on earlier drafts of this essay. We presented parts of this essay at the 17th Annual Qualitative Analysis Conference in Fredericton in May 2000.

12

Pace of Technological Change: Battling Ethical Issues in Qualitative Research

BARBARA THERESA WARUSZYNSKI

Advances in technology, particularly in information-based systems, are increasingly influencing the conduct of qualitative research. With the advent of the internet, social scientists continue to explore what constitutes ethical concerns or dilemmas in the application of innovative research methods (for example, analysing correspondence via e-mails and chat rooms). As a result, academic researchers are increasingly scrutinizing attempts to reconcile the critical issues and methods employed in the conduct of internet research. Has the 'information age' changed qualitative research? Are we moving away from more traditional research methods in qualitative research, or is the internet an adjunct to current-day research? Does the internet provide a valid and reliable venue for conducting social science research? How do we reconcile the discourse between private and public information? In general, are researchers responsible and accountable for using electronic information? These questions exemplify some of the current concerns and critical thinking among social scientists.

In this chapter, I examine some of the implications of conducting qualitative research via the internet and the ethical considerations that arise from the application of innovative research methods. Its aim is to provoke thought and discussion about ethics in cyberspace qualitative research. I suggest questions to help determine if certain research methods and activities in cyberspace would violate our professional ethics in conducting social science research (for instance, ethics in on-line ethnography). I also examine the ethical implications of conducting ethnographic fieldwork in studying virtual communities by focusing on a more comprehensive review of ethical standards in electronic qualitative research.

Technological Change and Ethics in Qualitative Research

In an information-based era, the rapid pace of changing technologies is affecting the conduct of social science research. With the advent of new technologies, researchers are examining how to employ specific examples in qualitative research. Technological innovations such as the internet (for example, listservs, newsgroups and bulletin boards, chat rooms, e-mail, data-mining/searching capabilities), interactive computer-based systems, and video-conferencing are easily accessible for researchers. However, how effective are they in research? What, if any, are the ethical issues facing researchers who are using them in qualitative research?

The internet is a technological on-line communication medium designed to ease the transmittal of data and information. On-line research can serve as a primary source for information on specific topics. Through the use of various search engines and effective search techniques, researchers are able to conduct extensive research on various topics; communicate directly with others through e-mail, chat lines, and newsgroups; and use or analyse publicly posted messages (for example, newsgroups). As a result, researchers are engaging in extensive research in on-line communication systems. The data are readily available for studying 'natural discourse' on the internet. Ethical issues in the conduct of on-line research have typically focused on how study participants are being examined by researchers.

This chapter focuses on three issues raised by Sharf (1999) – private versus public information, informed consent, and misinterpretation of information. These issues have received much debate and continue to pose questions about the 'researched' and the 'researcher.' First, I introduce each issue, and then I put forward several questions about ethics to generate thought and discussion among cyberspace researchers in ethnography.

Three Issues

Private versus Public Information

The internet, as a medium of communication, has raised a number of methodological issues, notably in the area of public versus private information. When do we consider information to be private, and at what point does the information become public? There is a growing belief that once information is posted on the internet, it becomes public. How do researchers resolve the matter? For instance, Waskul and Douglass (1996) argue that private interactions persist despite public access. We need to redefine what we consider to be public. When ethics in cyberspace research faces social scientists, it is unclear what is the 'right thing to do.' How do researchers define private and public domains in cyberspace? Should they be employing conventional social science methods of research in examining the ethics of internet research within public and private domains? Should they be engaging in attitudinal studies (such as focus groups), focusing on subject-to-subject and subject-to-researcher? Should they deal with listserv discussion groups on the ethics of using cyberspace discussions in social science research?

Informed Consent

Another issue concerns exploitation of research results. Sharf (1999) has reported the dilemma of investigating subjects via the internet (for example, chat rooms, listservs) without the informed consent of the participants. Possible dangers include identifying study participants through e-mail, chat lines, and newsgroups and disclosing one's participation after the fact. In Sharf's research on breast cancer, she considered it important to get informed consent from the people (listserv) participating in her research. Although listserv correspondence occurs within a public forum, Sharf sought informed consent from the people whom she quoted.

Conducting on-line research may pave the way for future methodological problems, which in turn, may create additional dilemmas in social science research. The whole issue of public versus private domains comes into play. Do researchers draw the line in specific circumstances in obtaining informed consent from diverse electronic forums (for example, obtaining informed consent from all group participants within a listserv)? If this is the case, how do they obtain 'group informed consent' or 'group consensus'? What are the methodological implications of obtaining or not obtaining informed consent?

Misinterpretation of Information

Researchers' validation of information is also crucial – checking the integrity of information. How, for example, do they authenticate information? Nigohosian (1996) speculates whether it is the responsibility of both teachers and students to validate all sources used in scholarly research in order to build a new way of thinking for using the internet. Sharf (1999) states that once a researcher imposes his or her own framework of analysis in interpreting others' words, the ownership and validity may become questionable. The interpretation can distort the meaning behind the words. Who owns the story? From an ethical standpoint, there is a need constantly to validate the information used as research – the researcher must check its integrity and authenticity. There is a potential to damage reputations, livelihoods, and personal relationships.

In examining these three issues – private versus public information, informed consent, and misinterpretation of information – we need to ask the following questions. Should researchers be responsible for safeguarding participant's anonymity, privacy, and/or confidentiality? What are the responsibilities and obligations of independent researchers to themselves as well as to study participants? What are the fundamental principles for internet research? We need to examine these questions from an ethnographic perspective, focusing on ethical and social considerations in conducting internet research.

Ethics in On-line Ethnography

Perspectives of ethnography and the related fields of ethnomethodology, symbolic interactionism, cultural-historical theory, and phenomenology require us to re-examine the ontologies and epistemologies dealing with how people function (Bannon, 1997), especially in observing individuals and groups conducting research on the internet. Ethnography, also referred to as observational research or naturalistic inquiry, examines human interaction in its natural setting. Ethnographic research provides very explicit descriptions or accounts of social phenomena and human interaction by making observations and inferences, interviewing participants, asking questions, and constructing hypotheses about people in their natural environment. Interest in ethnography and in its application to internet use has prompted researchers to focus on how people are using and responding to the internet (for example, discourse analysis, literary criticism, conversation analysis). For example, Neuage (1999) has been researching 'Discourse Analysis on the internet,' focusing on the ethics of studying conversation within chat rooms and on the establishment and construction of social relations within these virtual environments. The aim of his research is to examine how conversations are carried out through specific media. Similarly, Sharf (1999) also focuses on 'The Ethics of Doing Naturalistic Discourse Research on the internet,' using a breast cancer listserv.

Study of ethnography and internet use necessitates focus on tools and techniques, decision-making, group dynamics (social actions and interactions), group make-up (classification/position, group size), individual characteristics, methods, work practices, and activities. In studying communication and qualitative research in internet use, there is a need to examine how people use the internet to communicate and make decisions and how researchers promote qualitative research of the ethical foundations of using technological innovations. How does the internet affect interpersonal communication and social interaction in cyberspace, and how do we discern public and private domains? For instance, how do we explore ethical considerations concerning privacy in communication (for example, public versus private domains for data storage and discussion)? Questions of this nature have led researchers studying natural discourse to lay out ethical guidelines to ensure ethical participation of participants under study.

Guidelines in Internet Research

Ethical implications that arise from the application of innovative methods such as the internet have raised questions for researchers. Is research on the internet based on the highest possible standards? Do researchers have a responsibility to identify themselves and their research objectives within a public forum? What are the responsibilities of researchers who are conducting research on ethics in cyberspace research?

Current ethics guidelines insist that individual researchers must ensure that subjects under study are made aware of their participation from the onset. Guidelines in conducting ethical qualitative research have been proposed by many researchers, although this chapter focuses on only two of these authors – Schrum (1995) and Sharf (1999). Schrum (1995, 323–4) has put forward a synthesis of what researchers consider to be ethics standards/guidelines in conducting electronic research (Erickson, 1986; Guba and Lincoln, 1989; Lather, 1991; Reinharz, 1992; Erlandson et al., 1993; Kincheloe and McLaren, 1994).

According to Schrum's guidelines (1995: 323–4):

1 Researchers must begin with an understanding of the basic tenets for conducting ethical qualitative research.
2 Researchers should consider the respondents and participants as owners of the materials that are created; the respondents should have the ability to modify or correct statements for spelling, substance, or language.

3 Researchers need to describe in detail the goals of the research, the purposes to which the results will be put, plans of the researcher to protect the participants, and recourse open to those who feel mistreated.

4 Researchers should strive to create a climate of trust, collaboration and equality with the electronic community members, within an environment that is non-evaluative and safe.

5 Researchers should negotiate their entry into an electronic community, beginning with the owner of the discussion, if one exists. After gaining that entry, they should make their presence known in any electronic community (for example, a listserv, specialized discussion group or class format), as frequently as necessary to inform to all participants of their presence and engagement in electronic research.

6 Researchers should treat electronic mail as private correspondence that is not to be forwarded, shared or used as research data unless express permission is given.

7 Researchers have an obligation to begin by informing participants as much as possible about the purposes, activities, benefits and burdens that may result from their being studied.

8 Researchers must inform participants as to any risks that might result from their agreeing to be a part of the study – especially psychological or social risks.

9 Researchers must respect the identity of the members of the community, with special efforts to mask the origins of the communication, unless express permission to use identifying information is given.

10 Researchers must be aware of the steep learning curve for electronic communications. Information about the research should be placed within a variety of accessible formats.

11 Researchers have an obligation to the electronic community in which they work and participate to communicate back the results of their work.

In discussing the dilemma of private versus public information, Sharf (1999: 253–4) offers a set of ethical guidelines:

1 Before starting an investigation and throughout the duration of the study, the researcher should contemplate whether or not the purpose of the research is in conflict with or harmful to the purpose of the group. Conversely, the researcher should consider whether the

research will benefit the group in some way – for example, helping to legitimize the group's function.

2 The researcher should clearly introduce himself or herself as to identify the role, purpose, and intention to the on-line group or individuals who are the desired focus of study.

3 The researcher should make a concerted effort to contact directly the individual who has posted a message that he or she wishes to quote in order to seek consent.

4 The researcher should seek openness to feedback from e-mail participants being studied.

The implications for conducting research on the internet are continuously plaguing researchers. Once information is on the internet, is it public or private information? Any interpretive inquiry is based on observations made of the virtual communities under study. Fernback (1999: 216) states: 'The same concerns about validity in the interpretive approach that have plagued ethnographers all along are applicable to research in the virtual realm as well. Ethnographers working in cyberspace must be careful to attempt a measure of reflexivity, to separate oneself from the subjects being studied; they must develop a sense about the truthfulness and candor of their informants, just as ethnographers of the nonvirtual must; and they must use a theoretically informed framework for their research, just as ethnographers have traditionally done.'

All professionals engaging in humanistic or scientific research need to demonstrate their commitment to understanding and demonstrating their ethical responsibilities in conducting qualitative and quantitative research. We need to consider standardized guidelines in the conduct of cyberspace research. Are these guidelines being exercised among researchers engaged in cyberspace research? If so, how effective are they? Would standardized guidelines exacerbate current ethical dilemmas? Would standardized guidelines inhibit the study of natural discourse, or would they resolve the many critical issues plaguing social scientists?

Conclusion

The pace of technological change has influenced the conduct of social science research. The impact of technologies on ethnographic fieldwork has demonstrated new methods and approaches in the conduct of qualitative research. As a result, ethical standards in qualitative research are being addressed to ensure that study participants will not suffer as a result of their participation in electronic research. The conduct of qualitative research (for example, participant observations, face-to-face interviewing) may be taking on a new direction, where researchers are focusing on new ethical concerns and dilemmas in conducting social science–style on-line research. This chapter has introduced some of the dilemmas encountered in conducting internet-based qualitative research, including private versus public information, informed consent, and misinterpretation of information. Through ethnographic studies on electronic forums, social scientists will be able to explore in more depth the critical issues revolving around ethics in cyberspace research.

Ethics in qualitative research is not a new phenomenon; however, the integrity of qualitative research is contingent upon ethical issues in social science research. The advance of internet technology is generating more discussion on putting current research practices into context. For instance, how are social scientists, among other researchers, working with participants? What are they doing to ensure ethical practices and standards? What assurances do participants have that their involvement in cyberspace research will not divulge their identity? These are some of the challenging areas that this essay has introduced for further discussion.

13

The Tri-Council on Cyberspace: Insights, Oversights, and Extrapolations

HEATHER A. KITCHIN

This essay examines the *Tri-Council Policy Statement: Ethical Conduct for Research Involving Humans* (MRC, NSERC, and SSHRC, 1998d) in an attempt to fathom the document's implicit position on the use of cyberspace material as a source of data for academic research. Funding by the councils is 'conditional on research organizations' adherence to guidelines' (Grubisic, 1998: 1). Thus, learned research in Canada is expected to abide by the statement's specifications. Data captured through cyberspace can now be used for such research methods as ethnography, including observation and participant observation, case studies, content analysis, linguistic studies, biography, and discourse and textual analyses. Thus cyberspace may pose new and exciting possibilities to researchers.

Researchers are now beginning to use the internet for data collection (see, for example, Denzin, 1995; Schneider, 1996; McKie 1997; Kayany, 1998). Some sociologists, moreover, are now arguing for the expansion of targeting Usenet[1] newsgroups (NGs) as sources of data (Denzin, 1995: 249). NGs allow researchers access to thousands of potential research 'subjects'[2] at a mere click of a mouse. Researchers may now also look at populations traditionally difficult to locate through the internet – for example, atheists (alt.atheist), wiccans (alt.religion.wicca), drug users (alt.drugs.hard; alt.drugs.pot; alt.drugs.psychedelic), 'swingers' (alt.swingers), persons considering and championing suicide (alt.suicide), impotent men (alt.support.impotent), balding men (alt.baldspot), and transgendered persons (soc.support.transgendered).

Clearly, the use of cyberspace material and garnering data from chatrooms, listservs, and Usenet and websites are treading new research ground. As yet, however, there is little discussion or debate about the ethics of using internet data for research. In this essay I try to decipher the Tri-Council's position on exploitation of such data. I apply one of my doctoral research methods – obtaining data from a particular Usenet NG. Does the use of NG data for research qualify for exemption from ethics review and approval of research ethics boards (REBs)?

This essay first discusses the extensive role of the internet in presenting new forms of data as the background for research. Second, it offers research on Alt.Recovery.AA as a case study of ethical dimensions involved in doing research on the internet. Third, it considers the issue of converting internet data into public data. Fourth, it examines the extent to which the Tri-Council policies apply to internet data. Fifth, it reveals the emerging issues that any researcher must consider when using internet data.

Internet Data as Background for Research

Schwimmer (1996: 562) observes that 'e-mail has created a unique form of academic activity through distributed discussion lists.' Subscription to e-mail discussion groups gives people access to all messages posted to an NG. Individuals may also 'submit queries, answers, comments, notices, and longer pieces and follow trains of postings from other contributors' (562). E-mail presents new forms of data through the multiplicity of discussions distributed through listservs.

A mailing list, as defined by Gormley (1998: 33), is a discussion group on the internet that links together people with a common interest, while a 'newsgroup ... is a virtual area reserved for the discussion of a certain topic.' As Schwimmer (1996: 562) notes, 'there is usually little screening because of ... the conviction that internet communication should not be restricted according to any standards, including those of propriety, taste, or relevance.' Such latitude, and perhaps tastelessness, are clearly evidenced through the enormous breadth and diversity of topics found in public NG discussion groups.

Not unlike e-mail discussion groups, individuals may also subscribe to Usenet (short for Unix User Network) NGs (Kayany 1998: 1135). As Schwimmer (1996: 563) observes, NGs are discussion groups that are stored in an open central depository or bulletin board rather than distributed to subscribers. There exist thousands of NGs, each focused on a specific topic, ranging from rape, through feminism, to support for obesity. Each NG poses the potential for hundreds of daily postings. Indeed, as Schneider's (1996: 380) research attests, over a twelve-month period one Usenet NG alone yielded 46,592 articles posted by 3,276 authors.

Kayany (1998: 1136) further points out that 'according to some estimations, there are over 10 million users of Usenet who exchange over 25 million bits daily in ... newsgroups.' Thus a great deal of conversation now occurs in cyberspace (Kayany, 1998: 1136). These NG conversations serve, moreover, as potential data.

According to Schwimmer (1996: 561), the internet 'promises, or perhaps threatens, to transform the character of academic work.' As the use of computer technology increases, so too does reliance on it. Researchers will increasingly rely on the internet for data. As one of the methods that I used for doctoral research demonstrates, NGs can provide new and exciting approaches to research and analysis. The NG examined here – Alt.Recovery.AA (2000) – like all NGs, is organized and driven by its own guidelines and policies for use.[3]

Research on Alt.Recovery.AA

An internet NG that provides a place/space for discussion related to Alcoholics Anonymous (AA) served as one source of data for my doctoral research. Denzin (1995: 250) calls analysis of such a site 'interpretive interactionism' – the examination 'is a cultural studies approach to the media and everyday life which focuses on those narratives and stories people tell one another as they attempt to make sense of the epiphanies, or existential turning-point moments, in their lives.'

The original goal of my research on AA was to organize focus groups from which to gather data in response to specific questions concerning program philosophies and social practices within AA. This goal was a compromise over breaching trust by entering meeting sites unannounced as a researcher. Historically, AA has been a target of deceptive research, and I was not interested in reproducing unethical research on the organization. My concern was to satisfy my research goals without exploiting members and AA as a whole by covertly or deceptively gathering data. The best way to accomplish this goal, I reasoned, was by publicly recruiting members and having them participate first in focus groups and then in individual interviews. I could not conduct conversational analysis from naturally occurring group discussions within regular meeting sites.

One day, however, much to my delight, I happened across a Usenet NG named Alt.Recovery.AA, where AA members post their 'experience, strength, and hope'[4] with one another. This NG provided rich material, ordinarily inaccessible through overt collection of data. Indeed, I could use its multiplicity of ongoing conversations regarding AA's philosophy and members' social practices to conduct discourse analysis. Moreover, using the NG data did not violate privacy, as participants had given up their privacy, and even their anonymity, by posting to a public NG.

Furthermore, a pre-test of the NG data revealed that the discussions sometimes dealt with the very questions that I was preparing to ask of focus groups. Gathering data from the NG proved also much more expedient and less troublesome than advertising for research participants, locating meeting sites, and mutually agreeing on times to produce and gather the data. It completely obviated the tedious chore of transcribing audio tapes.

Because the data occur naturally, I did not have to factor in the possibility of a Hawthorne effect. Clearly, using the NG data is extremely efficient, as the data have been previously manufactured and require minimal time and energy to transpose from their original source. Thus, not only are the data extremely rich and easily accessible, but capturing them is both economical and quick. The preliminary test of data retrieval revealed that two days of NG discussions, including follow-up postings, delivered approximately three hundred pages of text. Computer technology, in contrast to traditional methods of audio-taping and transcribing, lends itself to extremely proficient data collection. In the end, I merely downloaded hundreds of threads, cleaned the raw data by removing sections of the headers, and printed more than a thousand pages of text – all without typing a single word.

While the data are gleaned efficiently, practically, and naturally, persons who post – those whom Denzin (1995: 254) calls 'speakers-as-writers' – may not be representative of the larger AA population, as only members who own, or who have access to, computers with internet capabilities can be active members of the NG. Having appropriate hardware, software, and computer knowledge may reflect higher levels of income and formal education. As Schwimmer (1996: 567) notes, 'Although seemingly limitless, the computers, networks, and storage devices on which information structure is based are expensive, and their accessibility is already restricted according to class, race, ethnicity, geography, and gender.' None the less, NG data can prove valuable.

Through threads, or specific topics/dialogue, I followed NG participants as though I was gathering their communications through traditional interviews or linguistically, from meeting discussions. I began by asking of the text a series of questions, which eventually served as a preliminary coding strategy. For example, one part of the analysis was an ethnomethodological examination of rules of conduct, which on analysis led to my discerning sites of resistance.

Exploitation of NG data is also useful for discourse analysis, which can involve both micro-examinations of the linguistic dynamics of conversation and broader studies of texts and documents (Potter and Wetherall, 1987). Gubrium and Holstein (1997: 55) point out as well that conversational analysis (CA) seeks to 'recover the structures that [undergird] interaction.' Its 'aim is to document the systemic practices used to achieve social order' (55). Thus the dynamics of interaction within the NG site may be analysed for systemic practices underlying its social order. To this end, CA can look at NG discourse as local narrative, which occurs as a public text or document. Textual deconstruction or other postmodern-informed analyses can potentially analyse the discourse for dynamics of power.

Following Gubrium and Holstein (1997), CA also makes it possible to draw out the 'hows' of 'method talk' in the dynamics of the construction of discourse and reality within the NG discussions – that is, the ways by which the conversation is structured linguistically – and to examine the technical rules of that structuring. CA may further discern the 'whats' in NG conversation. What is being constructed? What is occurring? Answering 'what' questions requires examination of social interaction as it is mediated through culture (Gubrium and Holstein, 1997: 14). Thus, indexicality, or cultural context, must be an integral component of the analysis. NG data may also assist such cultural examinations.

The NG data from Alt.Recovery.AA revealed further a related question concerning the changing face of AA. For example, a traditional principle of AA is not to state one's 'dry date,' especially if one has been sober for a long time. One states rather that one has been around 'the rooms' for 'a few twenty-four hours.' Or members will say that whoever got out of bed earlier on a given day has been sober the longest, given the principle/slogan of 'one day at a time.' Yet a common trend found within the AA discussion group is the inclusion of one's dry date in the signature profile.

Members are now frequently rejecting traditional AA etiquette, as the following quote demonstrates: 'In AA there is sobriety and there are catch phrases and there are stories, but in these meetings there is a very strong sense of futility and very little joy and very little spirit. Surely, sobriety is the prerequisite for a new beginning, but AA promises this new beginning but robs with the other hand. The catch is that you must spend the rest of your life listening to tales of woe and misery and reliving your own over and over again. What is worse is the intellectually stifling atmosphere in AA. I cannot accept that in order to stay sober I must reduce my vision of myself and most of my experience of life to something consistent with the twelve steps and a bunch of phrases that make my skin crawl.' Thus clear forms of resistance to AA appear within Alt.Recovery.AA.

Finding such sites of rich and unconventional data is significant for researchers who wish to explore previously unchartered territory. Without Usenet texts, resistance within AA might not have been identified as overtly as it may be through autobiographical text. There is no academic literature that examines AA as a site of resistance.[5] Clearly, NGs are useful in opening discursive space previously unavailable to social actors.

Today, websites provide copies of AA literature, allowing people access to AA texts and discourses without their even attending meetings. AA discussion groups and websites evidence change within the organization. Indeed, the internet now offers global cyberspace meeting places for AA's NG posters.[6] No longer are members' discussions localized at the level of group, private membership, fellowship, and/or sponsorship. A member can participate in the AA program solely through cyberspace. Availability of literature and of other members on the web and in chat rooms now means that a person who 'has a desire to stop drinking' (that is, on the basis of AA's third tradition) never has to enter an AA meeting room or experience face-to-face contact with other members. These developments are indicative of both the quality and the nature of life as it changes within and through cyberspace.

The Issue: Converting Internet Data into Public Data

Schneider (1996: 376) observes that people with no previous public voice can, when posting to Usenet NGs, 'suddenly find themselves in a public forum, offering their opinions, and having other people respond to them.' Posting to NGs places one's post within a public domain. Thus one's participation becomes constituted as a public voice. In turn, as with NG postings, such public voice becomes public text, public documents, and hence, I would argue, public data.

As Schwimmer (1996: 562) writes, 'The efficiency, versatility, and power of internet facilities have created new possibilities for communication, publication, and instruction and engendered a growing body of electronic literature, primarily because of low production and distribution costs.' The efficiency and versatility of capturing data from the internet serve specific goals of researchers. As the simplicity of gathering, and the richness of, such data become more widely recognized, so will the exploitation of cyberspace information bases, especially NGs.

Individuals who gain access to the internet may also do so for NGs, either to participate in discussions or merely to lurk and observe. Thus a researcher may easily become a systemic observer of an NG community. In their discussion of the ethics of gathering data from the internet, Mann and Sutton (1998: 211) suggest at least three reasons why traditional research ethics of natural observation do not apply there: 'First, participants in newsgroups are fully aware that their conversations are being watched by many people who do not reveal themselves ... Secondly, some members believe they are actually being monitored by the police or other officials ... Thirdly, it is not always possible to infer from a participant's email address the jurisdiction in which they are located.' Not knowing the location of a poster prevents true identification of a participant. Thus anonymity, one of the criteria by which the Tri-Council regulates ethics clearance, may be more assured.

Miller (1995: 9) points out that in Canada committee review as a standard requirement for regulating research on human subjects began in 1966. The most recent Canadian effort to revise and standardize academic research guidelines rests on the *Tri-Council Policy Statement* (MRC et al., 1998d), which informs and systematizes research ethics through otherwise-independent research ethics boards (REBs). Thus it has become important to ensure a particular quality of ethics when conducting research on 'human subjects.' As I show below, however, cyberspace voices may escape the statement's formal designation of 'human subjects.'

Mann and Sutton (1998: 210) note specific advantages of collecting data from NGs: 'On the Net there is no need to be present at the time when important postings, discussions or events actually happen. ... Also, with newsgroups, there are no real problems gaining access to the setting ... Useful research can be undertaken without the need to interact with the group ..., or influencing the behaviour of the group ... There is no need to strike up a rapport, or establish empathy with the group. Consequently, there is less risk of "going native."'

Thus research conducted through NG data can circumvent several of the more traditional problems related to observational studies, such as access to a population and loyalty to one's research group. I would add three more benefits: a researcher need not travel to the study site, may avoid exposure to potentially threatening or dangerous populations, and, most important, can obtain information generally unavailable from traditional data-gathering techniques.

NG data present a merging of oral and written expression. Whereas traditional interviewing of life experiences is generally recorded on audio-tape and then transcribed, NG posters offer already-transcribed 'subject' histories, attitudes, and behaviour. The final product is located in an oral story subsequently transcribed into textual form by the 'research subject.' The internet offers tremendous possibilities of readily available data with immense analytical potential. Use of such data, according to the *Tri-Council Policy Statement* (MRC et al., 1998d), appears to escape the ethics review normally required for work with human subjects.

Miller (1995: 9) comments: 'Research Ethics Boards exercise wide discretion to approve or reject research protocols ... before giving their approval for research to proceed.' Nevertheless, the *Tri-Council Policy Statement* provides guidelines for researchers' conduct. Thus Miller (1995: 13) observes that 'research in Canada is ... governed on the basis of moral-suasion, rather than on the basis of legislative authority.' Indeed, morality is central to the Tri-Council's statement, although it remains largely undefined there.

The statement completely fails to consider the ethical implications of data drawn from the use of information technologies (ITs). Thus academic researchers must extrapolate ethical principles from the document.

The Tri-Council on Cyberspace

As we saw above, this essay seeks to determine whether the *Tri-Council Policy Statement* (MRC et al., 1998d) exempts from ethics review use of NG data for research purposes, since NG data become public text/documents. The statement (i.3) seeks 'to encourage continued reflection and thoughtful consensus around more contentious ethical issues.' Moreover, it aims '(a) to outline guiding principles and basic standards and (b) to identify major issues, and points of debate and consensus.' Non-traditional modes of data collection thus present new challenges to research ethicists.

According to the statement, three primary grounds exempt collection and use of data from NGs from ethics review: 'minimal risk,' NG data as public texts, and cyber inhabitants as other than 'human subjects.'

Minimal Risk

The *Tri-Council's Policy Statement* (MRC et al., 1998d: i.6) asserts that 'a principle directly related to harms–benefits analysis is ... the duty to avoid, prevent or minimize harms to others. Research subjects must not be subjected to unnecessary risks or harm, and their participation in research must be essential to achieving scientifically and socially important aims that cannot be realized without the participation of human subjects.' The researcher must guarantee minimal harm to human research subjects. As for NG data, however, cyber participants place their experiences and attitudes in the public arena, so a researcher's use of the data does not violate a poster's privacy or pose risk of harm beyond that posed by the cyber participant. In much the way that authors of letters to editors 'de-anonymize' themselves, posters frequently position themselves as public material. Their texts thus are public, and so to use or reproduce them fails to violate a normal state of privacy.

Just as a formally published author opens himself or herself to potential criticism, review, and reproduction by virtue of his or her printed text, so too does an NG poster, a chatroom participant, or an internet contributor, vis-à-vis public consumers. Furthermore, just as authors of magazine articles need not be consulted for consent to use their printed text, the element of consent is moot for texts made publicly available by NG posters.

The Tri-Council's document states further: 'The standard of minimal risk is commonly defined as follows: if potential subjects can reasonably be expected to regard the probability and magnitude of possible harms implied by participation in the research to be no greater than those encountered by the subject in those aspects of his or her everyday life that relate to the research then the research can be regarded as within the range of minimal risk' (1.5). Persons within cyber communities post to NGs as an everyday activity; use of their texts can thus be estimated to pose as little harm as that encountered normally in their everyday lives. Others' using NG data therefore poses minimal risk to posters, especially when the researcher conceals the identity of participants.

The *Policy Statement* explains too (2.5): 'In considering research involving naturalistic observation, researchers and REBs should pay close attention to the ethical implications of such factors as: the nature of the activities to be observed; the environment in which the activities are to be observed ...; and the means of recording the observation ... Naturalistic observation that does not allow for the identification of the subjects, and that is not staged, should normally be regarded as minimal risk.' Again, use of NG data falls well within the Tri-Council's parameters of exemption. Thus naturalistic observation of NG communities both appears to be acceptable research and requires no ethical review. Thus, in the event that an NG participant posts anonymously, as long as the researcher does not reveal his or her identity, the research does not violate the Tri-Council's standards.

NG Data as Public Documents

The *Tri-Council Policy Statement* proposes: '*Research about a living individual involved in the public arena,* or about an artist, *based exclusively on publicly available information, documents,* works, performances, *archival materials* or third-party interviews, *is not required to undergo ethics review*' (MRC et al., 1998d: 1.1; emphasis added). Clearly, as cyber participants place their experiences, attitudes, and behaviour in the public eye with the goal of public consumption, their self-produced data become public documents/texts. Thus, by virtue of their public nature, their use requires no special ethics approval.

The Tri-Council states:

> Identifiable personal information means information relating to a reasonably identifiable person who has a reasonable expectation of privacy. It includes information about personal characteristics such as culture, age, religion, and social status, as well as their life experience and educational, medical or employment histories. *However, Article 1.1(c) excludes from REB review research that is based exclusively on publicly available information. This includes documents, records, specimens or materials from public archives, published works and the like, to which the public is granted access.* REB approval is not required for access to publicly available information or materials, including archival documents and records of public interviews or performances. (MRC et al., 1998d: 3.2, emphasis added)

Thus, because NG postings are publicly available, largely archived, and easily reached by the public, the data released by the postings are available for public consumption. Use of such data therefore requires no ethics approval.

Exploitation of publicly available information 'only requires ethics review if the subject is approached directly for interviews or for access to private papers, and then only to ensure that such approaches are conducted according to professional protocols and to Article 2.3 of this policy' (MRC et al., 1998d: A2). As autobiographers have already provided public information about themselves, the Tri-Council's requirement of direct approach is moot. 'REBs should recognize that certain types of research – *particularly biographies,* artistic criticism or public policy research – may legitimately have a negative effect on organizations or on public figures in, for example, politics, the arts or business. *Such research does not require the consent of the subject,* and the research should not be blocked merely on the grounds of harms/benefits analysis because of the potentially negative nature of the findings' (i.9; emphasis added). Clearly NG posters, as public figures, may be researched without ethics review.

Furthermore, article 2.3 reads: 'REB review is normally required for research involving naturalistic observation. However, research involving observation of participants in, for example, political rallies, demonstrations or public meetings, should not require REB review since it *can be expected that the participants are seeking public visibility*' (A5; emphasis added). Thus there is no need to approach 'speakers as writers' (Denzin, 1995: 254), as the data already exist, being previously produced by cyber inhabitants. Indeed, the public nature of NG postings serves to exempt the use of NG data from ethics review, according to the Tri-Council.

Definition of Human Subject

The *Tri-Council Policy Statement* leaves 'research subject' largely undefined. 'Subjects' are implied to be both physically and emotionally involved at some level of a research enterprise. Research subjects are 'those persons, on, or about whom, research is carried out' (MRC et al., 1998d: i.3). They 'are unique amongst the many participants [of a research enterprise] because it is they who bear the risks of research' (1.3). Cyber inhabitants, however, do not bear risks of research as long as they remain anonymous, if they so desire.

As a means of naturalistic observation, NGs present dynamic and novel sites in which to conduct naturalistic research. In the light of traditional risks involved with such observation, the Tri-Council (2.5) advises, 'Naturalistic observation is used to study behaviour in a natural environment. Because knowledge of the research can be expected to influence behaviour, naturalistic observation generally implies that the subjects do not know that they are being observed, and hence can not have given their free and informed consent. Due to the need for respect for privacy, even in public places, naturalistic observation raises concerns of privacy and dignity of those being observed. These concerns are accentuated if, for example, the research records permit identification of the subjects, or if the research environment is staged.'

Although some naturalistic means of observation may threaten the privacy of individuals who prefer to remain unobserved, public self-promotion shows that cyber participants cleary do not value privacy. Rather, NG posters whose anonymity would normally be protected by a researcher forgo their privacy and anonymity by public participation in their cyber community(ies).

Do cyber inhabitants constitute 'research subjects,' as envisioned and protected by the *Tri-Council Policy Statement*? That is, do NG posters constitute 'living, human subjects'? The Tri-Council assumes that there are potential risks involved for the subjects of research; however, cyber inhabitants are not physically and emotionally connected to the research conducted through their texts, especially in cases where the cyber person is unaware of the use of his or her texts. If a cyber person's identity and geographical location are not revealed, then the NG poster suffers no risk. And, as research on public figures does not warrant ethics review, research on or about a self-positioned public figure, such as an NG poster, is similarly exempt.

Emerging Issues

According to the *Tri-Council Policy Statement* (MRC et al., 1998d: i4), all research must advance both knowledge and human welfare. Although these criteria appear noble and feasible, their accomplishment is largely speculative. How, for example, do we ascertain that research has increased knowledge and human welfare? Must the political agenda be immediately accomplished, or identifiable? Who, or what, determines whether a research plan or enterprise represents the advance of knowledge and human welfare – the Tri-Council? the researcher? the research participants? Clearly, the answers are highly subjective. Thus the *Tri-Council Policy Statement* remains largely interpretive, requiring levels of extrapolation to discern and determine more clearly ethics guidelines regarding the use of IT data, including NG data.

Computer technology is expanding human communication and communicative possibilities. Indeed, it now proffers changing techniques of research. As Schwimmer (1996: 566) observes, 'The creation and expansion of internet communication services ... [allow] for ethnographic presentations expanded and embellished by inclusion of visual images, case studies, complementary texts, and field notes. It also opens the possibility for new forms of expression that can better capture the multilevel referencing and interrelatedness of complex symbolic and behavioral systems. Accordingly, postmodernists might more easily realize their objectives of articulating numerous voices and perspectives without the restraints of linear exposition.' The research potential of cyberspace presents researchers with a vast range of possibilities and problems.

The future of exploitation of data from the internet may bring with it new legal issues. Once cyber inhabitants come to realize that their written texts are being used as data, we may see questions about copyright of intellectual property. For example, NG posters may begin to copyright their texts in order to prevent reproduction without their consent. We may see NG postings preceded by notification that they may not be quoted or reproduced without the author's express permission. Infringement of copyright may then lead to civil, or eventually perhaps even criminal, cases concerning ownership of property. Until such copyright claims to NG text are practised, however, researchers may apparently exploit NG texts and analyse data without formal ethical review. It will be interesting to see when NG posters start to deny access to their public texts. How will the Tri-Council address the increasingly popular use of internet material for research?

Conclusion

The *Tri-Council Policy Statement* (MRC et al., 1998d: i1) 'welcome[d] comment and discussion' and promised 'regular updates.' That ITs are redefining research protocol and opening new modes of data collection is unquestionable. That we do not assess the implications and ethics of such redefinitions begs the question of whether there are ethics involved in such research at all.

The *Policy Statement* reads that 'REBs should not reject research proposals because they are controversial, challenge mainstream thought, or offend powerful or vocal interest groups' (1.6). Thus research on or near to controversial or otherwise-sensitive areas is not to receive more scrutiny or more stringent review that other research. My critical research on Alcoholics Anonymous, then, or any research that challenges mainstream thought carries the same legitimacy and authority as less-threatening forms of research.

Given the 'evolving' nature of the *Tri-Council Policy Statement* (MRC et al., 1999d: 1), we can expect shifts and amendments to its 'guiding principles and basic standards' (Grubisic, 1998: 1). As the importance and breadth of ITs expand, garnering of data from sites such as Usenet NGs will, I predict, expand substantially. The free access, efficiency, and simplicity of such data capturing increase the attractiveness of exploiting naturally occurring NG discussion data.

As we saw above, NG data can be exploited with a variety of methods, including ethnography, discourse analysis, textual analysis, content analysis, and natural observation. Researchers are now exploring the potential of cyberspace. Over time, the use of such data may well increase, and so the implicit criteria of the *Policy Statement* demand more study.

My own research has shown how NG communities connect researchers with previously inaccessible populations. Unconventional NG data also reveal forms of resistance. NG data conform to the Tri-Council's definition of public documents, and their use falls within the Tri-Council's definition of 'minimal risk'; as well, cyber inhabitants probably do not constitute 'human subjects.' Thus again the use of NG data circumvents the requirement for REB approval. In many cases, eliminating ethical review facilitates research. Usenet NG data becomes increasingly attractive to researchers who view the *Tri-Council Policy Statement* as overly restrictive and possibly ineffective in much of qualitative research.

Notes

I presented an earlier version of this essay to the 17th Qualitative Analysis Conference in Fredericton in May 2000. I would like to thank Dr Lee Chalmers and Dr Florence Kellner for their helpful comments regarding some of the issues examined here.

1 NGs were originally Usenet-based but are now available through web programs such as Netscape and Outlook Explorer.
2 'Subject' is used here as adopted by the *Tri-Council Policy Statement*. However, the authors (MRC et al., 1998d: i3) explain that 'subject' was the term chosen only after a great deal of discussion and debate. None the less, the language serves to impose positivist terminology over the more participatory methods of working with 'participants' preferred by many qualitative researchers. Thus the language of the Tri-Council's document appears to favour positivism over other methods.
3 The Alt.Recovery.AA FAQ (frequently asked questions) outlines the newsgroup's purpose and realm of discussion and provides a disclaimer that the file is not intended to be a complete description of AA. Questions that the newsgroup engages include: What is Alt.Recovery.AA? Is Alt.Recovery.AA a group or meeting? How can I get sober through AA? Can Alt.Recovery.AA

help? What about anonymity? Is Alt.Recovery.AA public? The newsgroup's formal definition is as follows: AAlt.Recovery.AA is a USENET newsgroup. Its purpose is to discuss [AA] and the program of recovery from alcoholism.' In response to whether Alt.Recovery.AA is a group or meeting, the FAQ reads: 'Alt.Recovery.AA lacks a few things common to many "live" groups and meetings.' This implies to the subscriber that solidarity with the AA program can be found within the site. The dynamics of the newsgroup reveal, however, a great deal of dispute, "flaming," and resistance to both specific elements of AA and to AA as a whole.

4 'Experience, strength, and hope' is a phrase used in AA to guide and inform participants' group discussion. It is meant to discourage members from lecturing each other. Rather, members are to reflect on their own experiences in order to contribute to the common strength of AA and the hope required for personal recovery from 'alcoholism.'

5 One chapter of my doctoral research examines sites of resistance within AA. Without an analysis of a particular NG it is highly doubtful that such clear resistance could be traced.

6 Although the internet continues to be largely a mechanism and tool of privileged Western persons, in time computer technology will probably permeate the globe. The newsgroup data examined here stem from primarily North American and European posters.

Some Concluding Thoughts

WILL C. VAN DEN HOONAARD

The qualitative, or inductive researcher's wish for alternatives to the current practice of formal ethics review may well be needless, for many forces countenance other approaches. Litigiousness and the continuing force of quantitative, or deductive research will no doubt hamper qualitative research for the foreseeable future, aided and abetted by the work of research ethics boards (REBs) in Canada and institutional review boards (IRBs) in the United States. The boards can withhold funds if the researcher has not sought ethics review, and the university loses money. The resulting and widespread 'culture of fear' gives added impetus to these enactments, born from the horrors of medical experimentation in the Holocaust, and promulgates, legally and socially, a culture of ethics review. We cannot point to many other instances in history when legal norms and culture overlapped so completely. Asking researchers to conform to the norms of a legally and socially constituted ethics board just seems to make eminent sense. But does it?

Those on the margins respond creatively to situations that appear inexplicably concrete. In the run of things, even solid social structures can melt and make way for alternative explanations or make room for peaceful coexistence. This concluding essay does not present the current approach to ethics review of research as definitive, even if that method seems lodged so inflexibly in legal texts, institutional discourse, and the popular mind. Aside from the fact that all structures change – and some of them as suddenly and radically as the flock of birds changing its course in mid-air – (Elizabeth Rochester, personal communication [p.c.]), we must give credit to countless qualitative researchers who have delivered work of the highest moral order. Countless people without privilege may also insist that their voices and their life chances be heard through qualitative research, because it is that sort of research that can resonate those voices and those life chances. Ironically, we may wonder whether a research participant may lose his or her right to be interviewed if he or she, even though eager to be interviewed, refuses to sign the consent form.

In might seem a daunting task to reset the course of formal ethics review of research – the template of medical research and the stirring of a moral panic seem to work against the benefits of qualitative research. Qualitative researchers, however, have too much to offer to go quietly into the night and not raise their voices. As qualitative research is growing in many fields, it is not likely to disappear. Rather, more friction can be anticipated.

Friction is already in evidence. As Melanie Pearce (chapter 4) claims, research morale is low. According to Florence Kellner (chapter 2), qualitative researchers do not trust the adjudication by REBs, and REBs think that qualitative researchers are too cavalier and not as responsible as they should be. I first cast this discussion in the larger context of what it means to be doing qualitative research as distinct from 'conventional' forms of research. Then I pull together the suggestions offered in this volume to improve the situation of qualitative researchers vis-à-vis the REBs.

The Salient Aspects of Qualitative Research

The reader will have already noted from almost every essay that ethics review of research tends to reflect the standards of quantitative, medical research as the norm. A number of authors ask if it is unethical for those unfamiliar with qualitative research to pass judgment on proposals for qualitative research. Let us consider how qualitative researchers see the differences that make ethics review of their work entirely different.[1]

Part of the difficulty for qualitative researchers is that their quantitative counterparts have colonized qualitative work. Qualitative researchers must explain their epistemology in quantitative language (Becker, 1996). The discourse of inclusion and exclusion exemplifies this process. Quantitative researchers speak of the importance of including qualitative researchers to create a complete picture of a social phenomenon; one seldom hears the obverse (D. van den Hoonaard, p.c.). This situation echoes the position of other minority groups, whether Natives in North America vis-à-vis the central government or 'desk-top' cartographers vis-à-vis people trained in geographic information systems (GISs). It appears to make quantitative researchers more generous and inclusive than qualitative researchers. Colonization extends into ethics review of research and grant applications, where quantitative research is seen as the norm.

But there is more to the difference than just language: it centres around the nature of data and the way we collect and analyse them. Palys's (1997) definition is key – namely, that the nature of induction is to 'engage a phenomenon of interest on its own terms and to let theory emerge from the data' (46). Engagement with the data makes a large difference in the conduct of research.

This section outlines six distinctive epistemological features of qualitative research:

- recognizing the complexity of social settings
- not knowing in advance the extent of data to explore
- avoiding as much as possible advance knowledge of the literature
- reversing the order of writing up the data and analysis
- emphasizing accuracy
- seeking out deviant or negative cases (Becker, 1998: 208)

There are, no doubt, other notable features, but these seem to be threshold ones for REBs. This section ends with a look at characteristics common to qualitative and quantitative research methods.

First, a qualitative researcher, by moving away from 'variable research,' recognizes the complexity of social settings. Here is an excerpt from Howard S. Becker (1996: 46) referring to the sort of questions that fieldworkers ask about delinquent activity:[2] 'Fieldworkers usually want something quite different: a description of the organization of delinquent activity, a description which makes sense of as much as possible of what they have seen as they observed delinquent youth. Who are the people involved in the act in question? What were their relations before, during, and after the event? What are their relations to the people they victimize? To the police? To the juvenile court? Fieldworkers are likewise interested in the histories of events: how did this start? Then what happened? And then? And how did all that eventually end up in a delinquent act or a delinquent career? And how did this sequence of events depend on the organization of all this other activity?'

Second, a qualitative researcher does not know in advance the full range of data that he or she will collect (Becker, 1996). A qualitative research project is never finished, especially where data gathering is done expertly. Take, for example, interview data. Some researchers transcribe and analyse each interview before moving on to the next. If the interviews are done well – i.e., yield rich data – the researcher may have to conduct

more interviews. One can simply imagine the difference between analysing ten interviews only after all ten have been transcribed *after* they have
been conducted, as opposed to a research effort in which each interview
builds on the previous one. The latter approach flies in the face of standard question-and-response questionnaires used by quantitative researchers, who find it important to maintain the format from beginning to end,
to enhance the reliability of the research.[3]

Third, a qualitative researcher, by habit, tends to conduct a review of
the literature late in the data-gathering stage; this treatment of the literature ensures a broader scope of discovery. As Nils Christie (1997), one of
the world's leading criminologists, points out, it is vital to engage first in
empirical research and to review the literature later: 'Libraries are for
what is already known ... Later comes the time for ... libraries, [and] critique' (18). This highly distinctive element poses the greatest challenge
to those who use quantitative techniques. Abandoning the advance review of the literature counter to common sense. Yet everyone enters
research settings with assumptions – some sadly strengthened by a too-
early review. Such a review may close the researcher's eyes to what should
be investigated. Even reviewing the literature to ascertain what specific
substantive areas have not yet been explored carries the assumption
that social institutions do not alter and do remain unchanged over the
years.

Fourth, the foundational differences are also revealed in the fact that
qualitative researchers in their practice often reverse the order of 'writing up the data' and analysis. Many researchers find it helpful to start the
analysis by writing up the data. Those using a quantitative approach conceive of research as following the sequence of data collection, analysis,
and writing. The elements of this sequence, however, are neither discrete
nor undirectional. For qualitative researchers, they occur at the same time,
with varying intensity, but analysis will go much further and deeper if it
starts with the data.

Fifth, a qualitative researcher strives for accuracy. A good many of them
seek to find out 'from people what meanings they are actually giving to
things' (Becker, 1996) as things that they either say or do. The goal goes
beyond accurately rendering a social setting. The qualitative researcher
takes the time to understand a phenomenon that is beyond his or her
own realm of experience and circumstances. In Becker's words, 'we should
not invent the viewpoint of the actor' (1996). Much of current research
funded by governmental, social, and corporate agencies favours ready-
made questions and answers (I call this 'supermarket sociology' – i.e.,
when the questions are 'packaged' and when we know what to expect) to

mounting social problems, rather than accuracy. Given any urgency to solve these problems, 'errors of attribution' (Becker, 1996) will of course increase significantly.

This process speaks to the 'eager state' of research employees who 'know what they want from research' and where the answers are implicit (Christie, 1997: 18, 19). REBs may well see a problem in the qualitative researcher's not specifying in advance either the motives or the hypotheses needed to explore the motives of research participants. Qualitative researchers, according to Linda Snyder, who has contributed to this volume, are not always aware of how the research design will unfold. As chapter 3 above, by the Adlers, makes clear, qualitative researchers rely heavily on everyday knowledge to start and to further their work. Many will agree that 'it is often not exactly clear when, where, and how research begins.'

Sixth, a qualitative researcher deviates from a deductive researcher in another way: he or she seeks deviations in the studied group. A quantitative researcher is in the business of confirming (or rejecting) hypotheses; a qualitative researcher discovers and explores (Stebbins, 2000) and is keen to find deviations from the norm. Such deviations tell us as much, or maybe even more, about a given setting. The search for deviation also acknowledges that every setting contains a hierarchy of credibility that a qualitative researcher must take into account. Such a hierarchy suggests 'that the superiors of any hierarchical setup will be conceived of by everybody who accepts that legitimacy of that setup as knowing more about it than anyone else. Their questions, their proposed answers, their notion of what constitutes the area being looked at, all of that will be taken as obviously correct and sensible' (Becker, 1986: 39). This hierarchy can dictate the kinds of questions asked, circumscribe the setting studied, and make research political. Researchers question institutional information (such as official statistics) and, by taking interest in groups that are probably not represented in formal social accounting, inadvertently poke some people in the eye.[4]

There are, however, a number of essential elements that qualitative researchers share with other social science researchers and which should determine how REBs adjudicate applications. Researchers in the social sciences adopt a more passive role vis-à-vis intervention, if any, than medical researchers and practitioners (Homan, 1991: 13). As Kellner (chapter 2 above) suggests, the criterion of minimal risk should exempt some proposals from ethics review.[5] Moreover, unlike the medical field, confidentiality in social research is not legally defensible. Thus REBs' insistence on confidentiality is legally wasted in the social sciences (a number of essays in this volume recount the willingness of qualitative researchers to go to jail rather than reveal the identity of research participants). Further, social science researchers are interested not so much in individuals as in the social processes that characterize the life of groups. Some qualitative researchers maintain that 'the data collected from private situations, therefore, need not be recorded or regarded as private data' (Homan, 1991: 46). Unlike the medical field, non-co-operation of subjects – as a sanction – is quite possible (Homan, 1991: 25, 46). Eliot Freidson emphasized that social researchers do not render services to a 'helpless and ignorant clientele' who are not in a position to refuse personal services (1964: 410).

A New Discourse

We now turn to some specific suggestions that can be part of a new discourse between qualitative researchers and REBs.[6] I look at three issues. How can qualitative researchers heighten the ethical tone of their work? What might REBs consider useful when working with qualitative researchers? How can qualitative researchers and REBs help each other? Many of these suggestions issue from the essays in this volume.

Heightening Ethical Tone

Qualitative researchers do not want to be above the law or not fulfil their ethical obligations. They are in fact eager to foster an ethic of care that should permeate the research enterprise, following Weinberg (chapter 7 above). Some researchers, like Mary Stratton (chapter 10), want to extend this ethic of care and make their work more credible as a political and emancipatory force for the good. Such self-reflections can go a long way to formulating a solid ethical stance in research, whether qualitative. Merlinda Weinberg proposes that we become aware of competing hierarchies within the research setting. In her experience, there are contradictions, and one needs to assign the highest priority to the most vulnerable group(s) in making decisions about anonymity and confidentiality. Her suggestion follows Thompson's observation (chapter 8) that the more stigmatized the participants, the greater the onus on the researcher to obtain and maintain informed consent. As qualitative researchers develop loyalty to their research subjects, they must practise self-censorship, according to Patti and Peter Adler (chapter 3). These researchers 'do not advance [their] careers at the expense of [their] subjects.' Five suggestions follow.

First, qualitative researchers ought to deal with ethics more explicitly in their proposals. Ideally, such discussion should be part of a 'method' section, rather than an appendix. Every qualitative researcher who has examined research ethics in a published work has experienced the wider value of such a discussion, as it permeates method and theory.

Second, qualitative research needs to be conspicuous by its awareness of whose voice is, after all, represented in the research process. The issue of 'voice' will always serve as a backdrop to such work. Erin Mills (chapter 9) speaks of two lives' clashing: the researcher and the researched. Whose voice carries the research? It is easy for research to become distant from the lives of participants. Linda Snyder (chapter 6) reminds us that we should clarify with each participant the personal distance inherent in research and its resulting limitations. Somehow, as Michael Ungar and Gillian Nichol assert (chapter 11), we need to hear the participants speak and the way they hear researchers talk to each other in their professional language. These two authors want safeguards against 'imposition and reification on the part of the researcher.'

Third, researchers might also consider submitting relevant portions of their drafts to the members of the community that they have studied. Factual errors are then minimized, and the opinions or observations of the researched community can be incorporated into either the main text or endnotes. Such a dialectic provides a rich store of findings. I would like to cite some examples from my own research projects. The first involved a study of a religious community that led to the publication of *The Origins of the Bahá'í Community of Canada, 1898–1948*; the second pertains to a recent study of women cartographers.

With respect to the Bahá'í, I included the community in several stages. I returned to a number of Bahá'í groups, including members whom I had previously interviewed, to present my preliminary findings. I reworked my preliminary findings to include the insights that emerged from those meetings. I submitted the first draft of the book to two circles of Bahá'í readers (one consisted of older members; the other, of younger). My aim was to elicit their reactions and encourage them to suggest what should or should not be included in the book. They all submitted written comments, which I then extracted and shared with all other members of the groups. We met over a working dinner, where for many hours we discussed many facets of the book.

I cannot describe the impetus and the encouragement that this consultative process engendered. The attentiveness of these Bahá'ís made me believe that I had a manuscript worth researching and writing. The writing style had to appeal to both the formally educated and the 'not-so-educated' element of the community. These categories are, I realize, artificial, but they forced me to put the manuscript into a narrative style, with details packed into the footnotes for those who wanted to explore the issues and sources more deeply. As I believed it important to be as sensitive as possible to gender in research, I made sure that the circles of readers included both women and men. I have found it most helpful to receive the views of readers who spot a particular blind spot or bias on my part. Margrit Eichler's work on non-sexist research (1987) has, in particular, moved me to consider carefully such bias in research: circulating the manuscript was simply one way of fulfilling this particular goal.

In my other project – a study of women in cartography – I followed my habit of sending all interviewees a copy of my written preliminary analysis, which amounted to a chapter for *The Dark Side of the Moon: Gender in Historical and Contemporary Cartography* (van den Hoonaard, n.d.). I invited each of the thirty-eight interviewees to send me their comments and suggestions. The process brought many benefits, not the least of which was catching errors, factual and imaginary.

There are countless other ways to realize this process of checking. Linda Snyder (chapter 6) found 'member checking' of critical value in all her research, so that participants can review preliminary findings. Sending the final report of one's research might be ethically doubtful, because participants have been left out of the full loop. On a wider scale, we should be prepared to come up with alternative definitions of social problems, especially of disempowered groups (Ungar and Nichol, chapter 11), which may hold an alternative view of the given 'social problem.'

Fourth, teachers in courses on method might consider teaching their students using an inductive perspective. They send their students out to collect field data in relatively safe places (such as in public or semi-public places, such as malls), return to class, and discuss what students have noted about ethical dilemmas and possibilities. Rather than adopting a top–down approach, teachers would commence the instruction of research ethics at the experiential level, moving on later to higher-order constructs of ethics. In more unfamiliar settings, students would regularly report back to their supervisors about the ethical implications of their collecting and analysing data and discuss them as a means of improving ethical sensibilities. Ethics then is not routine, but an ongoing social concern.

Fifth, according to Linda Snyder (chapter 6), a researcher must try to understand 'the degree of anonymity, confidentiality, and/or identification desired by each participant' or group. There are multiple realities at work. Anonymity is not always a prerequisite. Some research proceeds without the need to hide the identity of the interviewee, as in studies of famous people (Patrick O'Neill, p.c., 25 Jan. 2001). Even studies of ordinary people are criticized by readers when fictitious names are used (Anonymous F, 2001: 11). A qualitative researcher may well feel that he or she has to be careful in choosing a suitable pseudonym. One can assign names that speak to the time, era, or temperament of the participant or adopt a name chosen by the participant.

Finally, qualitative researchers should collectively avail themselves of the opportunity to explore with REBs on their campus the nature and purpose of their research. These symposia can be held regularly.

How REBs Can Facilitate Ethics Appraisal

As Arthur Kleinman (cited by Charbonneau, 1984: 21) proposes, we should not rely on 'supposedly universal moral codes' promulgated by clinical researchers. Instead, he advocates bringing in anthropologists to denote the ethnographic moral context. Such an approach, he avers, is 'more likely to resolve ethical problems than are philosophical debates on moral and legal codes for universal participation' (21). Four suggestions seem relevant.

First, rather than looking at a research setting from the perspective of 'universal' moral codes, REBs should consider looking at research proposals from the perspective of the populations being studied. While some populations deserve a hearing, others will resist, even though research on them might be the moral thing to do (one thinks of far-flung organizations, such as white supremacists, terrorists, or multi-level marketing organizations, whose activities are sheltered by corporate lawyers). Ethics codes seem to be situationally determined.

Second, REBs should be looking at educating, not policing. They might consider, on an annual or semi-annual basis, a colloquium on ethical questions in research. Such a forum would bring together the best ideas on research ethics, rather than 'educating' the researchers in the prevailing paradigm. In the same light, REBs should concentrate on ethical issues, not scientific, legal, or confidential ones, according to Melanie Pearce (chapter 4).

Third, the university should provide legal representation if a study is taken to court. A number of essays in this volume noted that universities do tend to leave social researchers high and dry when these researchers face legal challenges or conundra. It is a matter of pride to qualitative researchers that, so far, very few research cases have necessitated this sort of legal help, but it has happened, as Patrick O'Neill (chapter 1) so clearly demonstrates.

Fourth, O'Neill proposes that jurisdictions give advance immunity to researchers from having to break confidentiality. To assist researchers in maintaining confidentiality, the Jackson–MacCrimmon formulation ensures that the university will provide legal representation until all court processes have been exhausted – a solution advocated by O'Neill.

How REBs and Qualitative Researchers Can Help Each Other

REBs and qualitative researchers can make each other's work more useful and constructive. I offer seven propositions to that end.

First, proposals from qualitative researchers must be evaluated for their ethical soundness by peers. Because membership in some REBs is biased heavily towards quantitative and medical research, there needs to be a deliberate attempt to open membership to bona fide, recognized qualitative researchers. The fact that more and more boards are now also considering the 'scholarly merit' of proposals is, as one contributor said, quite 'bizarre.' Melanie Pearce suggests (chapter 4) that ethics review be delegated to other qualitative researchers.

Second, the ethnographic researcher will not need to offer a consent form to be signed by the participant. Instead, he or she will provide an information sheet, if appropriate, explaining the research and the needed verbal consent to continue with the interview. To assure anonymity, the researcher will not use real names on transcripts of interviews (such pseudonyms can be of either the researcher's or the participant's own choosing). It is the researcher who signs the information sheet, not the interviewee or the research participant. The granting of verbal permission will be indicated as such on the transcription. As I mentioned above, when a participant refuses to sign a consent form (which we would discourage in any case), he or she will still be allowed to be interviewed when he or she expresses a desire to take part in the research.

Third, the matter of informed consent needs to be re-examined. The requirement should be flexible. For example, researchers can individualize the consent form to reflect the wishes of specific participants. As many qualitative researchers see their goal as alleviating the oppression of marginal groups, researchers and participants should be brought closer together. The requirement of signed consent will invariably pose a formidable obstacle to that goal. It is not uncommon for a researcher to be a member of the same group as he or she is studying. Barbara Waruszynski (chapter 12) points to some of the innovative directions in this regard. At the same time, Scott Thompson reminds us of the special place of people with developmental disabilities who require special consideration. These sentiments underscore Florence Kellner's advice (chapter 2) that REBs need to be flexible regarding informed consent; in some cases, as Linda Snyder (chapter 6) mentions, consent forms should be individualized to reflect the specific wishes of research participants. Captive inmates, whether of nursing homes or of prisons, might be quite reluctant to sign such a form.[7]

Fourth, REBs might consider using terms that are more meaningful to qualitative researchers. For example, such terms as 'protocols' and research 'subjects' do not correspond to any that most qualitative researchers use. In a similar vein, REBs could scale down such evocative, aggressive terms as 'destroying' audio-tapes (after an interview has been transcribed) and keeping the tapes in a 'locked' cabinet. These terms instil fear in research participants about projects that usually carry minimal 'risk.' There is no reason why REBs cannot use more friendly, open expressions when inviting researchers (including quantitative researchers) to participate in the ethics review of their proposals. Moreover, adjudicating research proposals quickly not only expresses courtesy but is also practical, as Melanie Pearce (chapter 4) points out. Qualitative researchers typically undertake fieldwork during the summer, and if ethics review is not complete before then, a whole cycle will be missed and research will have to wait for another year, carrying with it funding and other implications.

Fifth, REBs can exempt certain types of naturalistic observation from review. As with observation in public spaces, including listservs, on the internet, there should be no ethics review for observations of public life. As well, the criterion of minimal risk should absolve some proposals from ethics review. Even several types of historical research that rely on research participants to provide information can be exempt. At my university, a historian received such exemption before conducting research on policies related to the provincial potato industry: he interviewed scientists and policy makers. As Florence Kellner (chapter 2) hopes, minimal risk should absolve some research proposals from ethics review.

Sixth, REBs need to accept a wider range of research methods. There are a few possibilities once ethics bodies decide to use a more comprehensive model of research. In short, I suggest a more variegated policy of review of ethics in research, which entails the need for more research methods and goals than is currently the case. Johnson and Altheide (chapter 5) demonstrated our collective ability to rethink and revise ethical approaches and to develop models that seem to fit better with the needs of qualitative researchers, among others. The effort is in the hands of both REBs and qualitative researchers. Both groups can take initiatives in promoting ethics review appropriate for qualitative research.

Seventh, to overcome qualitative researchers' distrust of REBs, REBs should consider learning more about the collective, but still diverse perspectives of qualitative researchers. The University of New Brunswick's REB accepted an invitation from the organizers of the seventeenth Qualitative Analysis Conference (Fredericton, 2000) to attend sessions on ethics in research. Across campuses in North America, groups of qualitative researchers can organize even modest gatherings to make the case for qualitative research in general. These symposia should extend a special invitation to members of REBs, and they can draw on the interests of a wider circle of researchers, including those undertaking cyber research, in order to clarify the kinds of issues raised by Barbara Waruszynski (chapter 12) and Heather Kitchin (chapter 13). Through this process of educating others, we too become better apprised of their interests and thresholds of 'ethical pain.' Who knows? Perhaps in the foreseeable future universities and research agencies will realize that distinctive REBs might well be a good alternative to the frightening process that is currently under way.

Towards a Separate Structure of Ethics Review?

These arguments lead to the inevitable conclusion that the current practice of ethics review of qualitative research (and more generally of social science research) by boards in thrall to the medical and quantitative model of research is inappropriate. Oddly enough, no REB has ever admitted the unethical nature of judging work by people not versed in the methods and principles of the research of the applicants. REBs can silence qualitative researchers when members of REBs claim to 'know' about qualitative research. Not uncommonly, their assertions are based on these researchers' having included open-ended questionnaire items – a far cry from doing *bona fide* qualitative research! These assertions virtually deny that there exists more than open-ended questions on surveys.

There is enough evidence in this volume to argue for creation of a distinct, separate structure to adjudicate proposals for social research, and for qualitative research in particular. Unfortunately, the issue of a separate, distinct REB for social scientists is not cut-and-dried. For one thing, social science researchers differ in approaches and intentions. A qualitative researcher may not want his or her project to be evaluated by members of a board who are steeped in survey research, even though they are social scientists. And even if some of the disciplines are formally designated as 'social sciences' (such as psychology and economics), would that situation not continue to vex qualitative researchers? One would almost want a local panel – one that is in many ways closer to the interests and locale of the qualitative researcher-applicant – as a way out of the dilemma. Under these circumstances, *ethics* review can also become *ethical.*

It is clear that the ethics review dust has been agitated. The contributors to this volume have explained painstakingly why the dust has been agitated. They have also offered solutions that would transmute the current low morale among qualitative researchers attributed to the process of ethics review into a situation that benefits everyone.

Notes

1 I presented elements of this section at the Tema Institute of Technology, Linköping, Sweden, in October 2000 (van den Hoonaard, 2000).

2 Field researchers are interested not so much in *delinquents* as in *delinquent activity*. The shift to what people *do* rather than *who* they are helps researchers to focus on social processes rather than on individual traits of social actors (Becker, 1998: 44–6).

3 In this vein, members of REBs often refer to the inclusion and analysis of answers to open-ended questions as 'qualitative research.' A qualitative researcher would cringe at such a reference.

4 My own work, *Working with Sensitizing Concepts* (van den Hoonaard, 1997), addresses the benefit of keying in to expressions used by social actors, especially those in disadvantaged positions.

5 Unlike in medical research, the main risk of some qualitative research may come after publication of findings (Homan, 1991: 13).

6 Part of this subsection and the next appears in van den Hoonaard 2001. Copyright permission, *Canadian Journal of Sociology and Anthropology.*

7 There is an extended discussion on signed consent forms in my 'Introduction' in this volume.

References

Adler, Patricia A. 1985. *Wheeling and Dealing.* New York: Columbia University Press.

Adler, Patricia A., and Peter Adler. 1993. 'Ethical Issues in Self-Censorship: Ethnographic Research on Sensitive Topics.' In Claire M. Renzetti and Raymond M. Lee, eds., *Researching Sensitive Topics,* 249–66. Newbury Park, Calif.: Sage.

– 1998. *Peer Power: Preadolescent Culture and Identity.* New Brunswick, NJ: Rutgers University Press.

– 1999. 'Do University Lawyers and the Police Define Our Research Value System?' Paper presented at the Annual Meetings of the Pacific Sociological Association, San Diego, Calif.

Agosin, Marjorie. 1987. *Scraps of Life: Chilean Arpilleras – Chilean Women and the Pinochet Dictatorship.* Trenton, NJ: Red Sea Press.

Alberti, K. George 1995. 'Local Research Ethics Committees.' *British Medical Journal* 311: 639–40.

Alberti, K. George. 2000. 'Multicentre Research Ethics Committees: Has the Cure Been Worse than the Disease?' *British Medical Journal* 320: 1157–8.

Alt.Recovery.AA. 2000. <http://well.com/~dhawk/AA.FAQ.html>.

Ames, Thomas, and Perry Samowitz. 1995. 'Inclusionary Standards for Determining Sexual Consent for Individuals with Developmental Disabilities.' *Mental Retardation* 33: 264–8.

Anderson, K., and D. Jack. 1991. 'Learning to Listen: Interview Techniques and Analyses.' In S. Gluck and D. Patai, eds., *Women's Words: The Feminist Practice of Oral History* – 26. London: Routledge.

Anonymous A. 2000. Conversation with a colleague in gerontology. January.

Anonymous B. 2000. E-mail from <[name omitted]@unbsj.ca> to <will@unb.ca>, subject:/notes re informed consent, 16 April.

Anonymous C. 1999. E-mail from <[name omitted]@brunnet.net> to <will@unb.ca>, subject: consent forms, 29 Dec.

Anonymous D. 2000. Detailed description of an application to the Social Sciences and Humanities Research Council of Canada.

Anonymous E. 2000. 'Official Statement. Report of the Review into the Research Framework in North Staffordshire.' *Bulletin of Medical Ethics*: 20–5.

Anonymous F. 2001. 'Alone Again, Naturally: Women on Coping with Widowhood.' *Atlantic Books Today*, 34 (fall): 11.

Apple, Michael W. 1990. *Ideology and Curriculum.* New York; Routledge.

Aylyn, Ayalah. 1999. 'Inuit Narrative as Text of Tool of Empowerment.' Paper presented at the 16th Annual Qualitative Analysis Conference, Fredericton, NB, May.

Bach, Michael, and Melanie Rock. 1996. 'Seeking Consent to Participate in Research from People Whose Ability to Make an Informed Decision Could Be Questioned: The Supported Decision Model.' Paper presented at 'Deciding for Others: Power, Politics and Ethics.' Canadian Bioethics Society, 8th Annual Conference, Roeher Institute, North York, Oct.

Bakhtin, Mikhail M. 1986. *Speech Genres and Other Late Essays.* Trans. V.W. McGee. Austin: University of Texas Press.

Bannon, Liam. 1997. 'CSCW: A Challenge to Certain (G)DSS Perspectives on the Role of Decisions, Information and Technology in Organizations?' In P. Humphreys, S. Ayestaran, A. McCosh, and B. Mayon-White, eds., *Decision Support in Organizational Transformation*, 92–121. London: Chapman and Hall.

Barber, Bernard. 1976. 'The Ethics of Experimentation with Human Subjects.' *Scientific American* 234 (Feb.): 25–31.

Bauman, Zygmunt. 1993. *Postmodern Ethics.* Oxford: Blackwell.

Baumrind, Diana. 1964. 'Some Thoughts on Ethics of Research: After Reading Milgram's Behavioral Study of Obedience.' *American Psychologist* 26: 887–96.

Becker, Howard S. 1967. Whose Side Are We On? *Social Problems* 14: 239–48.

– 1986 [1970]. 'Dialogue with Howard S. Becker.' In Howard S. Becker, *Doing Things Together: Selected Papers*, 25–47. Evanston, Ill.: Northwestern University Press.

– 1996. 'The Epistemology of Qualitative Research.' In Richard Jessor, Anne Colby, and Richard Schweder, eds., *Ethnography and Human Development: Context and Meaning in Social Enquiry*, 53–71. Chicago: University of Chicago Press.

– 1998. *Tricks of the Trade: How to Think about Your Research While You're Doing It.* Chicago: University of Chicago Press.

Benhabib, Seyla. 1987. 'The Generalized and the Concrete Other: The

Kohlberg–Gilligan Controversy and Feminist Theory.' In Seyla Benhabib and Drucilla Cornell, eds., *Feminism as Critique: On the Politics of Gender,* 77–95. Minneapolis: University of Minnesota Press.

Biklen, Sari, and Charles Moseley. 1988. '"Are You Retarded?" "No, I'm Catholic": Qualitative Methods in the Study of People with Severe Handicaps.' *Journal of the Association for Persons with Severe Handicaps* 13: 155–62.

Bogdan, Robert, Steven Taylor, B. de Grandpré, and S. Haynes. 1974. '"Let Them Eat Programs": Attendants' Perspectives and Programming on Wards in State Schools.' *Journal of Health and Social Behavior* 15 (June): 142–51.

Bonnie, Richard. 1997. Research with Cognitively Impaired Subjects: Unfinished Business in the Regulation of Human Research.' *Archives of General Psychiatry* 54: 105–11.

Booth, Tim, and Wendy Booth. 1994. *Parenting under Pressure: Mothers and Fathers with Learning Difficulties.* Buckingham, UK: Open University Press.

– 1996. 'Sounds of Silence: Narrative Research with Inarticulate Subjects.' *Disability and Society* 11: 55–69.

Bouchard, Camille. 1998. 'Recherche épidémiologique sur la violence envers les enfants: enjeux ethiques.' *Canadian Journal of Community Mental Health* 17: 79–90.

Boutilier, Susan. 1994. 'The Developmental Experience of Cancer.' Master's thesis, Laurentian University, Sudbury, Ont.

Brajuha, Mario, and Lyle Hallowell. 1986. 'Legal Intrusion and the Politics of Fieldwork: The Impact of the Brajuha Case.' *Urban Life* 14 (4): 454–78.

Brotman, Shari, and Shoshana Pollack. 1997. 'Loss of Context: The Problem of Merging Postmodernism with Feminist Social Work.' *Canadian Social Work Review* 14 (1): 9–21.

Brown, Gail, Pat Carney, Joan Cortis, Lori Metz, and Anne Petrie. (Human Sexuality Advisory Committee). 1994. *Human Sexuality Handbook: Guiding People toward Positive Expressions of Sexuality.* Springfield, Mass.: Association for Community Living.

Brown, Hilary, and David Thompson. 1997. 'The Ethics of Research with Men Who Have Learning Disabilities and Abusive Sexual Behavior: A Minefield in a Vacuum.' *Disability and Society* 12: 695–707.

Bulmer, Martin, ed. 1982. *Social Research Ethics.* London: Macmillan.

Burgess, Ian. 1984. *In the Field.* London: Routledge.

Canadian Association of Social Workers (CASW). 1994. *Social Work Code of Ethics.* Ottawa: CASW. <www.web.net/~oasw/ENG/ETHICS.HTM>

– 1995. *Standards of Practice in Social Work.* Ottawa: CASW.

Centre on Governance. 2000. *Governance of the Ethical Process for Research Involving Human Subjects.* Ottawa: University of Ottawa.

Chahal, Kusmindar. 2000. 'What Will You Do with this Information?' Ethical Issues and Sensitive Research. Unpublished.

Charbonneau, Robert. 1984. 'Ethics in Human Research.' *The IDRC Reports* 13 (1): 20–1.

Chase, Susan. 1992. 'The Family as an Overwrought Object of Desire.' In G.C. Rosenwald and Richard Ochberg, eds., *Storied Lives: The Cultural Politics of Self-Understanding*, 000–000. New Haven, Conn.: Yale University Press.

– 1995. 'Taking Narrative Seriously: Consequences for Method and Theory in Interview Studies.' In Ruthellen Josselson and Amia Lieblich, eds., *Interpreting Experience: The Narrative Study of Lives*, 1–26. Thousand Oaks, Calif.: Sage.

Child and Family Services Act. 1996. *Revised Statutes of Ontario of 1990. Office Consolidations.* Toronto: Queen's Printer for Ontario, June.

Chodorow, Nancy. 1989. *Feminism and Psychoanalytic Theory.* New Haven, Conn.: Yale University Press.

Christie, Nils. 1997. 'Four Blocks Against Insight: Notes on the Oversocialisation of Criminologists.' *Theoretical Criminology* 1 (1): 13–23.

Coffey, Amanda, and Paul. Atkinson. 1996. *Making Sense of Qualitative Data.* Thousand Oaks, Calif.: Sage.

Cohen, Stanley. 1972. *Folk Devils and Moral Panics: The Creation of the Mods and Rockers.* New York: St Martin's Press.

Comarow, Murray. 1993. 'Are Sociologists above the Law?' *The Chronicle of Higher Education* 15 (Dec.): A44.

Cotterill, Pamela. 1992. 'Interviewing Women: Issues of Friendship, Vulnerability, and Power.' *Women's Studies International Forum* 15 (5/6): 593–606.

Crabtree, Benjamin, and William Millar. 1999 *Doing Qualitative Research.* Thousand Oaks, Calif.: Sage.

CRIAW (Canadian Research Institute for the Advancement of Women). 1995. *Feminist Research Ethics: A Process.* Ottawa: CRIAW (Nov.).

CSAA (Canadian Sociology and Anthropology Association). 1994. *CSAA Statement of Professional Ethics.* <http//www.unb.ca/web/anthropology/csaa/englcode.htm#top>

Cutajar, Josephine A. 1999. 'When an Insider Is Transformed into an Outsider.' Paper presented at the 16th Annual Qualitative Analysis Conference, Fredericton, NB, May.

Dalton, Melville. 1959. *Men Who Manage.* New York: John Wiley & Sons.

– 1964. 'Preconceptions and Methods in Men Who Manage.' In Phillip E. Hammond, ed., *Sociologists at Work*, 50–95. New York: Basic Books.

Delaney, Roger, and Keith Brownlee. 1996. 'Ethical Dilemmas in Northern Social Work Practice.' In Roger Delaney, Keith Brownlee, and M. Kim Zapf, eds., *Issues in Northern Social Work Practice*, 47–69. Thunder Bay, Ont.: Lakehead University, Centre for Northern Studies.

Denzin, Norman K. 1978. *Sociological Methods*. New York: McGraw-Hill.
– 1995. 'Information Technologies, Communicative Acts, and the Audience: Couch's Legacy to Communication Research.' *Symbolic Interaction* 18 (3): 247–68.
Department of Health (United Kingdom). 1991. *Local Research Ethics Committees*. London: Department of Health.
DeVault, Marjorie L. 1990. 'Talking and Listening from Women's Standpoint: Feminist Strategies for Interviewing and Analysis.' *Social Problems* 37 (1): 96–116.
Diesing, Paul. 1972. *Patterns of Discovery in the Social Sciences*. London: Routledge and Kegan Paul.
Dominelli, Lena, and Eileen McLeod. 1989. *Feminist Social Work*. Houndmills, England: Macmillan.
Douglas, Jack D. 1976. *Investigative Social Research*. Beverly Hills, Calif.: Sage.
– 1979. 'Living Morality versus Bureaucratic Fiat.' In Carl B. Klockars and Finnbar W. O'Connor, eds., *Deviance and Decency: The Ethics of Research with Human Subjects*, 13–33. Beverly Hills, Calif.: Sage.
Edgerton, Robert. 1967. *The Cloak of Competence*. Los Angeles: University of California Press.
– 1993. *The Cloak of Competence*. Rev. ed. Berkeley: University of California Press.
Egan, R. Danielle. 1999. 'Fractured Narratives and Alternative Discourses: The Complex Storytelling of Sex Work.' Paper presented at the 16th Annual Qualitative Analysis Conference, Fredericton, NB, May.
Eichler, Margrit. 1987. 'The Relationship between Sexist, Non-sexist, Women-centred and Feminist Research in the Social Sciences.' In Greta Hofmann Nemiroff, ed., *Women and Men: Interdisciplinary Readings on Gender*, 21–53. Montreal: Fitzhenry and Whiteside.
Ellis, James. 1992. 'Decisions by and for People with Mental Retardation: Balancing Considerations of Autonomy and Protection.' *Villanova Law Review* 37: 1779–1809.
Epstein Jayatne, Toby, and Abigail Stewart. 1990. 'Quantitative and Qualitative Methods in the Social Sciences: Current Feminist Issues and Practical Struggles.' In Mary Margaret Fonow and Judith Cook, eds., *Beyond Methodology: Feminist Scholarship as Lived Research*, 85–106. Bloomington: Indiana University Press.
Erickson, Frederick. 1986. 'Qualitative Methods in Research on Teaching.' In Merlin C. Wittrock, ed., *Handbook of Research on Teaching*, 119–61. New York: Macmillan.
Erikson, Richard V. and Kevin D. Haggerty. 1997. *Policing the Risk Society*. Toronto: University of Toronto Press.
Erlandson, David A., Edward L. Harris, Barbara L. Skipper, and Steve D. Allen. 1993. *Doing Naturalistic Inquiry*. Newbury Park, Calif.: Sage.

Evans, Donald, and Martyn. Evans. 1996. *A Decent Proposal: Ethical Review of Clinical Research.* Chichester, England: Wiley.

Ferguson, Dianne. 1993. 'Something a Little out of the Ordinary: Reflections on Becoming an Interpretivist Researcher in Special Education.' *Remedial and Special Education* 14 (4): 35–43, 51.

– 1995. 'Celebrating Diversity.' *Remedial and Special Education* 16: 199–202.

Fernback, Jan. 1999. 'There Is a There There: Notes toward a Definition of Cybercommunity.' In Steve Jones, ed., *Doing Internet Research: Critical Issues and Methods for Examining the Net*, 203–20. Thousand Oaks, Calif.: Sage.

Festinger, Leon, Henry W. Riecken, and Stanley Schachter.1956. *When Prophecy Fails.* New York: Harper and Row.

Fine, Michelle. 1994. 'Working the Hyphens: Reinventing Self and Other in Qualitative Research.' In Norman K. Denzin and Yvonna S. Lincoln, eds., *Handbook of Qualitative Research*, 70–82. Thousand Oaks, Calif.: Sage.

Fine, Michelle, Lois Weis, Susan Weseen, and Loonmun Wong. 2000. 'For Whom? Qualitative Research, Representations, and Social Responsibilities.' In Norman K. Denzin and Yvonna S. Lincoln, eds., *Handbook of Qualitative Research*, 2nd ed., 107–32. Thousand Oaks, Calif.: Sage.

Flynn, Margaret. 1986. 'Adults Who Are Mentally Handicapped as Consumers: Issues and Guidelines for Interviewing.' *Journal of Mental Deficiency Research* 30: 369–77.

Fontana, Andrea, and James Frey. 1994. 'Interviewing: The Art of Science,' in Norman K. Denzin and Yvonna S. Lincoln, eds., *The Handbook of Qualitative Research*, 000–000. Thousand Oaks, Calif.: Sage.

Freidson, Eliot. 1964. 'Against the Code of Ethics.' *American Sociological Review* 29: 410.

Furey, Eileen. 1994. Sexual Abuse of Adults with Mental Retardation: Who and Where? *Mental Retardation* 32: 173–80.

Gans, Herbert. J. 1962. *The Urban Villagers: Group and Class in the Life of Italian-Americans.* New York: Free Press.

Getty, Grace. 1999. E-mail from <getty@unb.ca> to <will@unb.ca>, subject, personal ltr to qualitative researchers at UNB and STU, date sent: 24 Nov.

Gilchrist, Lauri. 1997. 'Aboriginal Communities and Social Science Research: Voyeurism in Transition.' *Native Social Work Journal* 1 (1): 69–85.

Gilligan, Carol. 1982. *In a Different Voice. Psychological Theory and Women's Development.* Cambridge, Mass.: Harvard University Press.

Goffman, Erving. 1961. *Asylums.* New York: Anchor.

Gorman, Jane. 1993. 'Postmodernism and the Conduct of Inquiry in Social Work.' *Affilia* 8 (3): 247–64.

Gormley, Myra Vanderpool. 1998. 'Exploring Mailing Lists and Newsgroups.' *Heritage Quest* 75 (May/June): 33–5.

Gouldner, Alvin. W. 1968. 'The Sociologist as Partisan: Sociology and the Welfare State.' *American Sociologist* 3: 103–16.

– 1970. *The Coming Crisis of Western Sociology.* New York: Basic Books.

Grubisic, Katia. 1998. 'Ethics in Research.' *Imprint Online* 21 (10) (Friday, 25 Sept.) <http:// imprint.uwaterloss.ca/issues/092598/News/news07.shtml>

Guba, Egon G., and Yvonna S. Lincoln. 1989. *Fourth-Generation Evaluation.* Newbury Park, Calif.: Sage.

Gubrium, Jaber, and James Holstein. 1997. *The New Language of Qualitative Method.* New York: Oxford University Press.

Hall, Budd. 1993. 'Introduction.' In Peter Park, Mary Brydon-Miller, Budd Hall, and Ted Jackson, eds., *Voices of Change: Participatory Research in the United States and Canada*, xiii–xxii. Toronto: OISE Press.

Hancock, Karen. 1999. 'London's Sex Trade Industry: The Politics of the "Problem."' Paper presented at the 16th Qualitative Analysis Conference, Fredericton, NB, May.

Hansen, Helen P., Jennaya Ramstead, Stephen Richer, Susan Smith, and Mary Stratton. 2001. 'Unpacking Participatory Research in Education.' *Interchange* (forthcoming).

Harding, Sandra. 1991. *Whose Science? Whose Knowledge? Thinking from Women's Lives.* Ithaca, N.Y: Cornell University Press.

– 1992. 'Rethinking Standpoint Epistemology: What Is Strong Objectivity?' *Centennial Review* 36 (3) (fall): 437–70.

– 1997. Paper presented at a public lecture, University of Toronto, 12 Nov.

Hertz, Rosanna. 1996. 'Introduction: Ethics, Reflexivity, and Voice.' *Qualitative Sociology* 19: 3–9.

Hickson, Linda, Harriet Golden, Ishita Khemka, Tiina Urv, and Salifu Yamusah. 1998. 'A Closer Look at Interpersonal Decision-making in Adults with and without Mental Retardation.' *American Journal on Mental Retardation* 103: 209–24.

Homan, Roger. 1991. *The Ethics of Social Research.* London: Longman.

hooks, bell. 1989. *Talking Back: Thinking Feminist, Thinking Black.* Boston: South End Press.

Horowitz, Irving L. 1970. 'Sociological Snoopers and Journalistic Moralizers.' *Transaction* 7: 4–8.

– 1974. *The Rise and Fall of Project Camelot: Studies in the Relationship between Social Sciences and Practical Politics.* Cambridge, Mass.: MIT Press.

Howe, David. 1994. 'Modernity, Postmodernity and Social Work.' *British Journal of Social Work* 24: 513–32.

Hsiung, Ping-Chu. 1996. 'Between Bosses and Workers: The Dilemma of a Keen Observer and a Vocal Feminist.' In Diane L. Wolf, ed., *Feminist Dilemmas in Fieldwork*, 122–37. Boulder, Col.: Westview.

Humphreys, Laud. 1970. *Tearoom Trade: Impersonal Sex in Public Places*. Chicago: Aldine.

Hunt, Morton. 1982. 'Research through Deception.' *New York Times* (Sunday, 12 Sept.), section 6: 66–7.

Ife, Jim. 1997. *Rethinking Social Work: Towards Critical Practice*. South Melbourne, Australia: Longman.

Jackson, Michael, and Marilyn MacCrimmon. 1999. 'Research Confidentiality and Academic Privilege: Implications for the New Ethics Policy at SFU.' <www.sfu.ca/pres/research confidentiality.htm>

Jeffery, Heather. 1999. 'Home-less-ness: Linking Contributing Factors, Interventions and Mediating Factors.' Paper presented at the 16th Annual Qualitative Analysis Conference, Fredericton, NB, May.

Jenkins, Graham C. 1995. 'Problems of Students Must Not Be Ignored.' *British Medical Journal* 311: 1571.

Jenkinson, Josephine. 1993. 'Who Shall Decide? The Relevance of Theory and Research to Decision-making by People with an Intellectual Disability.' *Disability, Handicap and Society* 8: 361–75.

Johnson, John M. 1975. *Doing Field Research*. New York: Free Press.

Jones, James H. 1993. *Bad Blood: The Tuskegee Syphilis Experiment*. 2nd ed. New York: Free Press.

Jones, Paul. 1998. 'Consultation Underway at Simon Fraser Following Coroner's Inquest.' *CAUT Bulletin* (24 Oct.): 24.

Josselson, Ruthellen, and Amia Lieblich. 1995. *Interpreting Experience: The Narrative Study of Lives*. Thousand Oaks, Calif.: Sage.

Kaeser, Fred. 1992. 'Can People with Severe Mental Retardation Consent to Mutual Sex?' *Sexuality and Disability* 10: 33–42.

Kayany, Joseph. 1998. 'Contexts of Uninhibited Online Behavior: Flaming in Social Newsgroups on Usenet.' *Journal of the American Society for Information Science* 49 (12): 1135–41.

Kelly, Deirdre. 1993. 'Secondary Power Source: High School Students as Participatory Researchers.' *American Sociologist*. (spring): 8–25.

Kessler, Seymour. 1997. 'Genetic Counselling Is Directive? Look Again.' *American Journal of Human Genetics* 61: 466–7.

Khayatt, Didi. 1992. *Lesbian Teachers: An Invisible Presence*. Albany: State University of New York Press.

Kimmel, Allan J. 1988. *Ethics and Values in Applied Social Research*. Applied Social Research Methods Series, Volume 12. Newbury Park, Calif.: Sage.

Kincheloe, Joe L., and Peter L. McLaren. 1994. 'Rethinking Critical Theory and Qualitative Research.' In Norman K. Denzin and Yvonna S. Lincoln, eds., *Handbook of Qualitative Research*, 138–57. Newbury Park, Calif.: Sage.

Kirby, Sandra L., and McKenna, Kate. 1989. *Experience, Research, Social Change: Methods from the Margins.* Toronto: Garamond.

Klein, Renate Duelli. 1983. 'How to Do What We Want to Do: Thoughts about Feminist Methodology.' In Gloria Bowles and Renate Duelli Klein, eds., *Theories of Women's Studies,* 88–104. London: Routledge.

Klockars, Carl B. 1979. 'Dirty Hands and Deviant Subjects.' In Carl B. Klockars and FinnbarW. O'Connor, eds., *Deviance and Decency: The Ethics of Research with Human Subjects,* 261–82. Beverly Hills, Calif.: Sage.

Kondo, Dorrine K. 1990. *Crafting Selves: Power, Gender and Discourse of Identity in a Japanese Workplace.* Chicago: University of Chicago Press.

Langness, Lewis L., and Gelya Frank. 1995. *Lives: An Anthropological Approach to Biography.* Novato, Calif.: Chandler and Sharpe.

Lather, Patti. 1986. Research as Praxis. *Harvard Educational Review* 56 (3): 257–77.

– 1991. *Getting Smart: Feminist Research and Pedagogy with/in the Postmodern.* New York: Routledge.

Lee, Judith A.B. 1994. *The Empowerment Approach to Social Work Practice.* New York: Columbia University Press.

Leo, Richard. 1995. 'Trial and Tribulations: Courts, Ethnography, and the Need for an Evidentiary Privilege for Academic Researchers.' *American Sociologist* 113: 126–7.

Leonard, Peter. 1997. *Postmodern Welfare: Reconstructing an Emancipatory Project.* Thousand Oaks, Calif.: Sage.

Levine, Felice J. 2001. 'Weighing In on Protecting Human Research Participants: Let Our Voices Be Heard.' *ASA Footnotes* 29 (1) (Jan.): 2.

Lincoln, Yvonna S. 1995. 'Emerging Criteria for Quality in Qualitative and Interpretive Research.' *Qualitative Inquiry* 1 (3): 275–89.

Lincoln, Yvonna S., and Egon G. Guba. 1985. *Naturalistic Inquiry.* Newbury Park, Calif.: Sage.

Lindhout, D., Pedra G. Frets, and Martinus F. Niermeijer. 1991. 'Approaches to Genetic Counselling.' *Annals of the New York Academy of Sciences* 630: 223–9.

Lindsey, Pam. 1994. 'Assessing the Ability of Adults with Mental Retardation to Give Direct Consent for Residential Placements: A Follow-up Study for the Consent Screening Interview.' *Education and Training in Mental Retardation and Developmental Disabilities* 29: 155–64.

– 1996. 'The Right to Choose: Informed Consent in the Lives of Adults with Mental Retardation and Developmental Disabilities.' *Education and Training in Mental Retardation and Developmental Disabilities* 31: 171–6.

Lofland, John F. 1971. *Analyzing Social Settings.* Belmont, Calif.: Wadsworth.

Lowman, John, and Ted Palys. 1998. 'When Research Ethic and the Law Conflict.' *CAUT Bulletin* (June): 6–7.

MacDonald, Heather. 1999. E-mail from <keith@worrall17.freeserve.co.uk> to <will@unb.ca>, subject: re: personal ltr to qualitative researchers at UNB and STU, date sent: 24 Nov.

McKie, Craig. 1997. *Using the Web for Social Research.* Toronto: McGraw-Hill Ryerson.

McLaren, Peter. 1993. *Schooling as a Ritual Performance: Towards a Political Economy of Educational Symbols and Gestures.* 2nd ed. London: Routledge.

Maddocks, Ian. 1992. 'Ethics in Aboriginal Research: A Model for Minorities or for All?' *Medical Journal of Australia* 157 (Oct.): 553–5.

Maguire, Patricia. 1987. *Doing Participatory Research: A Feminist Approach.* Amherst: Massachusetts University Press

Maiter, Sarah. 1999. 'Building Bridges: The Collaborative Development of Culturally Appropriate Definitions of Child Abuse and Neglect for the South-Asian Community.' Paper presented at the 16th Annual Qualitative Analysis Conference, Fredericton, NB, May.

Malinowski, Bronislaw. 1967. *A Diary in the Strict Sense of the Term.* New York: Harcourt Brace.

Mann, David, and Mike Sutton. 1998. 'Netcrime: More Change in the Organization of Thieving.' *British Journal of Criminology* 38 (2): 201–29.

Marshall, Catherine, and Gretchen Rossman. 1995. *Designing Qualitative Research.* 2nd ed. London: Sage.

Martindale, Kathleen. (Chair of panel). 1987. 'Panel Two: Developing an Ethical Methodology for Feminist Research.' *Feminist Ethics* 2 (2): 30–51.

Marx, Gary. 1980. 'Notes on the Discovery, Collection and Assessment of Hidden and Dirty Data.' Paper presented at the Annual Meetings of the Society for the Study of Social Problems, New York.

Mauthner, Natasha, and Andrea Doucet. 1998. 'Reflections on a Voice-centred Relational Method.' In Jane Ribbens and Rosalind Edwards, eds., *Feminist Dilemmas in Qualitative Research,* 119–46. London: Sage.

Maykut, Pamela, and Richard Morehouse. 1994. *Beginning Qualitative Research: A Philosophic and Practical Guide.* London: Falmer.

Michie, Susan, and Therese Marteau. 1996. 'Genetic Counselling: Some Issues of Theory and Practice.' In Therese Marteau and M. Richards, eds., *The Troubled Helix,* 104–22. Cambridge: Cambridge University Press.

Michie, Susan, Therese Marteau, and Martinet Bobrow. 1997. 'Genetic Counselling: The Psychological Impact of Meeting Patients' Expectations.' *Journal of Medical Genetics* 34: 237–41.

Mies, Maria. 1983. 'Towards a Methodology for Feminist Research.' In Gloria Bowles and Renate Duelli Klein, eds., *Theories of Women's Studies,* 117–39. London: Routledge.

Milgram, Stanley. 1963. 'Behavioral Study of Obedience.' *Journal of Abnormal and Social Psychology* 67: 371–8.

– 1965. 'Some Conditions of Obedience and Disobedience to Authority.' *Human Relations* 18: 57–76.

Miller, Catherine. 1995. 'Protection of Human Subjects of Research in Canada.' *Health Law Review* 4 (1): 8–16.

Mitchell, Richard G., Jr. 1993. *Secrecy and Fieldwork.* Newbury Park, Calif.: Sage.

Morgan, David, and Margaret Spanish. 1984. 'Focus Groups: A New Tool for Qualitative Research.' *Qualitative Sociology* 7 (3): 253–70.

MRC, NSERC, and SSHRC (Medical Research Council, Natural Sciences and Engineering Research Council, and Social Sciences and Humanities Research Council) 1998a. *Context of an Ethical Framework.* <http:// www.sshrc.ca /english/programinfo/policies/Intro03.htm#C>

– 1998b. *Privacy and Confidentiality.* <http:// www.sshrc.ca/english / programinfo/policies/Sec03.htm>

– 1998c. *Requirement for Free and Informed Consent.* <http:// www.sshrc.ca/ english/programinfo/policies/Sec02.htm>

– 1998d. *Tri-Council Policy Statement: Ethical Conduct for Research Involving Humans.* <http:// www.sshrc.ca/english/programinfo/policies/Intro01.htm>

National Association of Social Workers. 1999. *Code of Ethics.* (Database on line) cited 26/09/2000. <http://www.naswdc.org/Code/ethics.htm>

Neuage, Terrell. 1999. 'Discourse Analysis on the Internet.' <http:// se.unisa.edu.au/e.htm>

Newfield, Neal, Scott P. Sells, Thomas E. Smith, Susan Newfield, and Faye Newfield. 1996. 'Ethnographic Research Methods: Creating a Clinical Science of the Humanities.' In Douglas H. Sprenkle and Sidney M. Moon, eds., *Research Methods in Family Therapy*, 25–63. New York: Guilford.

Nicholl, Jon. 2000. 'The Ethics of Research Ethics Committees.' *British Medical Journal* 320: 1217.

Nigohosian, Robert. 1996. 'Scholarly Internet Research: Is It Real?' Paper presented at the Conference of Ethics and Technology, Loyola University of Chicago, Chicago, March.

Oddens, B., and D. De Wied 1995. 'Committees Should Devise Special Forms for the Social Sciences.' *British Medical Journal* 311: 1572.

Ogden v. Simon Fraser University. 1998. Provincial Court of British Columbia (Small Claims Court). No. 26780 Burnaby Registry.

Olesen, Virginia. 2000. 'Feminisms and Qualitative Research at and into the Millennium.' In Norman K. Denzin and Yvonna S. Lincoln, eds., *Handbook of Qualitative Research*, 2nd ed., 215–56. Thousand Oaks, Calif.: Sage.

O'Neill, Patrick. 1998. 'Communities, Collectivities, and the Ethics of Research.' *Canadian Journal of Community Mental Health* 17: 67–78.

Palys, Ted. 1997. *Research Decisions: Quantitative and Qualitative Perspectives.* 2nd ed. Toronto: Harcourt Brace.

Parsons, Talcott. 1951. *The Social System.* New York: Free Press.

Phtiaka, Helen. 1994. 'What's In It for Us?' *Qualitative Studies in Education* 7: 155–64.

Pilnick, Alison, Robert Dingwall, Elaine Spencer, and Rachael Finn. 2000. *Genetic Counselling: A Review of the Literature.* Sheffield, England: Trent Institute for Health Research.

Pollack, Shoshana. 1999. 'Conducting Qualitative Research with Women in Prison: Ethical Issues and Challenges.' Paper presented at the 16th Qualitative Analysis Conference, Fredericton, NB, May.

Polsky, Ned. 1969. *Hustlers, Beats, and Others.* Chicago: Aldine.

Potter, Jonathan, and Margaret Wetherall. 1987. *Discourse as Social Psychology.* London: Sage.

Powdermaker, Hortense. 1966. *Stranger and Friend: The Way of an Anthropologist.* New York: W.W. Norton.

Pring, George, and Penelope Canan. 1996. *SLAPPS: Getting Sued for Speaking Out.* Philadelphia: Temple University Press.

Punch, Maurice. 1986. *The Politics and Ethics of Fieldwork.* Beverly Hills, Calif.: Sage.

– 1989. 'Researching Police Deviance: A Personal Encounter with the Limitations and Liabilities of Fieldwork.' *British Journal of Sociology* 40: 177–204.

– 1994. 'Politics and Ethics in Qualitative Research.' In Norman K. Denzin and Yvonna S. Lincoln, eds., *Handbook of Qualitative Research,* 83–97. Thousand Oaks, Calif.: Sage.

Reamer, Frederic G. 1994. 'Social Work Values and Ethics.' In Frederic G. Reamer, ed., *The Foundations of Social Work Knowledge,* 195–229. New York: Columbia University Press.

Reason, Peter, ed. 1994. *Participation in Human Inquiry.* London: Sage.

Regehr, Cheryl, M. Edward, and J. Bradford. 2000. 'Research Ethics with Forensic Patients.' *Canadian Journal of Psychiatry* 45 (10): 23–9.

Regina v. Gruenke. 1991. 3 S.C.R. 263.

Regional Residential Services Society and Nova Scotia Department of Health. 1998. *Relationships and Sexuality: A Guide for Individuals with Intellectual Disabilities and Their Residential Service Providers.* Halifax: Province of Nova Scotia

Reid, Síân. 1999. '"Witch Wars": The Tensions between Ideology and Practice in Neopagan Communities.' Paper presented at the 16th Annual Qualitative Analysis Conference, Fredericton, NB, May.

Reinharz, Shulamit. 1992. *Feminist Methods in Social Research*. New York: Oxford University Press.

– 1993. *On Becoming a Social Scientist*. 4th ed. New Brunswick, NJ: Transaction.

Ristock, Janice L., and Joan Pennell. 1996. *Community Research as Empowerment: Feminist Links, Postmodern Interruptions*. Toronto: Oxford University Press.

Robertson, Gerald. 1994. *Mental Disability and the Law in Canada*. Scarborough, Ont.: Carswell.

Rodwell, Mary K. 1998. *Social Work Constructivist Research*. New York: Garland.

Royal College of Physicians. 1990. *Guidelines on the Practice of Ethics Committees in Medical Research Involving Human Subjects*. Oxford: Oxprint.

Rozovsky, Lorne Elkin. 1997. *The Canadian Law of Consent to Treatment*. Vancouver: Butterworths.

Ryan, Joanna, (with) Frank Thomas. 1987. *The Politics of Mental Handicap*. London: Free Association Books.

Sands, R.G., and K. Nuccio. 1992. 'Postmodern Feminist Theory and Social Work.' *Social Work* 37 (6): 489–94.

Scarce, Rik. 1994. '(No) Trial (But) Tribulations: When Courts and Ethnography Conflict.' *Journal of Contemporary Ethnography* 23 (2): 123–49.

– 1995. 'Scholarly Ethics and Courtroom Antics: Where Researchers Stand in the Eyes of the Law.' *American Sociologist* 26 (1): 87–112.

– 1999. 'Good Faith, Bad Ethics: When Scholars Go the Distance and Scholarly Associations Do Not.' *Law and Social Inquiry* 24 (4): 1301–10.

Schensul, Jean J., Margaret D. LeCompte, R.T. Trotter, E.K. Cromley, and M. Singer. 1999. *Mapping Social Networks, Spatial Data, and Hidden Populations*. Walnut Creek, Calif.: AltaMira Press.

Schneider, Steven. 1996. 'Creating a Democratic Public Sphere through Political Discussion.' *Social Science Computer Review* 14 (4): 373–93.

Schrum, Lynne. 1995. 'Framing the Debate': *Ethical Research in the Information Age*. *Qualitative Inquiry* 1 (3): 311–26.

Schwartz, M. 1964. 'The Mental Hospital: The Researched Person in the Disturbed World.' In Arthur J. Vidich, J. Bensman, and Maurice. R. Stein, eds., *Reflections on Community Studies*, 85–117. New York: Harper and Row.

Schwimmer, Brian. 1996. 'Anthropology on the Internet: A Review and Evaluation of Networked Resources.' *Current Anthropology* 37 (3): 561–8.

Scott, Dorothy. 1989. 'Meaning Construction and Social Work Practice.' *Social Service Review* (March): 39–51.

Seale, Clive. 1999. *The Quality of Qualitative Research*. London: Sage.

Shaddock, Anthony, L. Dowse, H. Richards, and A. Spinks. 1998. 'Communicating with People with an Intellectual Disability in Guardianship Board Hearings: An Exploratory Study.' *Journal of Intellectual and Developmental Disability* 23: 279–93.

Sharf, Barbara. 1999. 'Beyond Netiquette: The Ethics of Doing Naturalistic Discourse Research on the Internet.' In Steve Jones, ed., *Doing Internet Research: Critical Issues and Methods for Examining the Net*, 243–56. Thousand Oaks, Calif.: Sage.

Sigelman, Carol, Edward Budd, C. Spenhel, and C. Schoenrock. 1981. 'When in Doubt, Say Yes: Acquiescence in Interviews with Mentally Retarded Persons.' *Mental Retardation* 19: 53–8.

Sigelman, Carol, Edward Budd, G. Winer, and P. Martin. 1982. 'Evaluating Alternative Techniques of Questioning Mentally Retarded Persons.' *American Journal of Mental Deficiency* 86: 511–18.

Smith, Dorothy E. 1987. *The Everyday World as Problematic.* Toronto: University of Toronto Press.

– 1996. 'The Relations of Ruling: A Feminist Inquiry.' *Studies in Cultures, Organizations, and Societies* 2: 171–90.

Snyder, Linda. 1999. 'Women's Employment Initiatives as a Means of Address-ing Poverty: A Comparative Study of Canadian and Chilean Examples.' PhD dissertation, Faculty of Social Work, Wilfrid Laurier University, Waterloo, Ont.

Sobsey, Dick, Ssharmine Gray, Don Wells, Diane Pyper, and Beth Reimer-Heck. 1991. *Disability, Sexuality and Abuse: An Annotated Bibliography.* Baltimore: Brookes.

Sorenson, Andrew. 1978. 'A Sociological Study of Informed Consent in a University Hospital: Problems with the Institutional Review Board.' *Clinical Research* 26 (1) (Jan.): 1–5.

Stacey, Judith. 1991. 'Can There Be a Feminist Ethnography?' In Sherna B. Gluck and Daphne Patai, eds., *Women's Words: The Feminist Practice of Oral History*, 111–19. New York: Routledge.

Stalker, Kirsten. 1998. 'Some Ethical and Methodological Issues in Research with People with Learning Difficulties.' *Disability and Society* 13: 5–19.

Stanley, Liz. 1992. *The Auto/biographical I.* Manchester, England: Manchester University Press.

Stanley, Liz, and Sue Wise. 1990. 'Method, Methodology, and Epistemology in Feminist Research Processes.' In Liz Stanley, ed., *Feminist Praxis. Research, Theory and Epistemology in Feminist Sociology*, 20–60. London: Routledge.

Stebbins, Robert A. 2000. 'Exploration: A Modern Social Science Enigma.' Paper presented at the 17th Qualitative Analysis Conference, University of New Brunswick and St Thomas University, Fredericton, NB, May.

Stratton, Mary. 1994. 'Choosing Science: The Social Construction of Students'

Course Selection Decisions.' Master's thesis, Laurentian University, Sudbury, Ont.

– 2001. 'Getting an Education: Students' Views on Entering and Exiting High School.' PhD dissertation, in progress. Department of Sociology and Anthropology, Carleton University, Ottawa.

Strauss, Anselm. L. 1987. *Qualitative Analysis for Social Scientists.* Cambridge: Cambridge University Press.

Swain, John, Bob Heyman, and Maureen Gillman. 1998. 'Public Research, Private Concerns: Ethical Issues in the Use of Open-ended Interviews with People Who Have Learning Difficulties.' *Disability and Society* 13: 21–36.

Tesson, Geoffrey, John Lewko, and Brian J. Bigelow. 1987. 'The Social Rules Children Use in Their Interpersonal Relations.' In J.A. Macadam, ed., *Interpersonal Relations: Family, Peers, and Friends*, 36–57. New York: Karger.

– 1990. 'Adolescent Social Rule Usage in Family, Peer and Adult Relationships.' *Sociological Studies of Child Development* 3: 175–99.

Thompson, Hunter S. 1967. *The Hell's Angels: A Strange and Terrible Saga.* New York: Ballantine.

Thorne, Barry. 1980. 'You Still Takin' Notes?: Fieldwork and Problems of Informed Consent.' *Social Problems* 27 (3): 272–83.

Tom, Allison. 1996. 'Building Collaborative Research: Living the Commitment to Emergent Design.' *Qualitative Studies in Education* 9: 347–59.

– 1997. 'The Deliberate Relationship: A Frame for Talking about Faculty–Student Relationships.' *Alberta Journal of Educational Research* 43: 3–21.

Tri-Council Policy Statement. See MRC, NSERC, and SSHRC, 1998d.

Turnbull, Rutherford, Douglas Biklen, Elizabeth Boggs, James Ellis, Charles Keeran, and Greig Siedor. 1977. *The Consent Handbook.* Special Publication No. 3. American Association on Mental Deficiency.

Tymchuk, Alexander. 1997. 'Informing for Consent: Concepts and Methods.' *Canadian Psychology* 38 (2): 55–75.

United States Public Health Service. 1973. *Final Report of the Tuskegee Syphilis Study Ad-hoc Advisory Panel.* Washington, D.C.: Service.

University of Toronto. 1979. 'Guidelines for the Use of Human Subjects.' Unpublished. Toronto: University of Toronto, Office of Research Administration.

van den Hoonaard, Will C. n.d. *The Dark Side of the Moon: Gender in Historical and Contemporary Cartography* (book ms. in progress).

– 1996. *The Origins of the Bahá'í Community of Canada, 1898–1948.* Waterloo, Ont.: Wilfrid Laurier University Press.

– 1997. *Working with Sensitizing Concepts: Analytical Field Research.* Thousand Oaks, Calif.: Sage.

– 2001. 'Is Ethical Review of Research a Moral Panic?' *Canadian Journal of Sociology and Anthropology* 38 (1) (Feb.): 19–36.

Van Maanen, John. 1983. 'The Moral Fix: On the Ethics of Fieldwork.' In Robert Emerson, ed., *Contemporary Field Research*, 269–87. Boston: Little, Brown.

Vega-López, Mariá, and Guilleromo Gonzalez-Perez. 1999. 'Domestic Violence or Exercising Male Authority?' Paper presented at the 16th Annual Qualitative Analysis Conference, Fredericton, NB, May.

Vidich, Arthur J., and Joseph Bensman. 1968. *Small Town in Mass Society.* Princeton, NJ: Princeton University Press.

Vidich, Arthur J., and Stanford M. Lyman. 1985. *American Sociology: Worldly Rejections of Religion and Their Directions.* New Haven, Conn.: Yale University Press.

Von Hoffman, Nicholas. 1970. 'Sociological Snoopers.' *Washington Post* (30 Jan.).

Wallis, Roy. 1977. 'The Moral Career of a Research Sociologist.' In Colin Bell, and H. Newby, eds., *Doing Sociological Research*, 149–69. London: Allen and Unwin.

Walton, Gerald. 1999. 'Between a Rock and a Hard Place: Gay and Christian Identity Integration.' Paper presented at the 16th Annual Qualitative Analysis Conference, Fredericton, NB, May.

Waskul, Dennis, and Mark Douglass. 1996. 'Considering the Electronic Participant: Some Polemical Observations on the Ethics of On-Line Research.' *Information Society* 12 (2): 129–39.

Wax, Murray. 1983. 'On Fieldworkers and Those Exposed to Fieldwork: Federal Regulations and Moral Issues.' In Robert Emerson, ed., *Contemporary Field Research*, 288–99. Boston: Little, Brown.

Wax, Rosalie H. 1971. *Doing Fieldwork: Warnings and Advice.* Chicago: University of Chicago Press.

Weis, Lois, and Michelle Fine, eds. 1993. *Beyond Silenced Voices: Class, Race, and Gender in United States Schools.* New York: State University of New York Press.

Weisstub, David, and Julio Arboleda-Florez. 1997. 'Ethical Research with the Developmentally Disabled.' *Canadian Journal of Psychiatry* 42: 492–6.

Welsome, Eileen. 1999. *The Plutonium Files: America's Secret Medical Experiments in the Cold War.* New York: Dial Press.

While, Alison. 1995. 'Ethics Committees: Impediments to Research or Guardians of Ethical Standards?' *British Medical Journal* 311: 661

Whyte, William H. 1996. *Street Corner Society: The Social Structure of an Italian Slum.* Chicago: University of Chicago Press.

Wigmore, John Henry. 1983. *Evidence in Trials at Common Law.* Boston: Little, Brown and Co.

Wise, Sue. 1990. 'Becoming a Feminist Social Worker.' In Liz Stanley, ed., *Feminist Praxis. Research, Theory and Epistemology in Feminist Sociology,* 236–49. London: Routledge.

Wolf, Diane. 1996. 'Situating Feminist Dilemmas in Fieldwork.' In Diane Wolf, ed., *Feminist Dilemmas in Fieldwork,* 1–55. Boulder, Colo.: Westview.

Wood, Katherine. 1990. 'Epistemological Issues in the Development of Social Work Practice Knowledge.' In L. Videka-Sherman and W.J. Reid, eds., *Advances in Clinical Social Work Research,* 373–90. Silver Spring, Md.: National Association of Social Workers.

Woodrow, Helen, and Innes, Frances. 1994. *Women of the Fishery.* St John's, Nfld.: Educational Planning and Design Associates.

Woodward, David, and G. Malcolm Lewis, eds. 1998. *The History of Cartography: Cartography in the Traditional African, American, Arctic, Australian, and Pacific Societies.* Vol. 2, book 3. Chicago: University of Chicago Press.

Worrell, Bill. 1988. *People First: Advice for Advisors.* Downsview, Ont.: Health and Welfare Canada and Disabled Persons Participation Program.

Yablonsky, Lewis. 1968. *The Hippy Trip.* New York: Ballantine.

Yates, Lyn. 1995. 'Education, Research Methodology and Fashionable Theory: Constructing a Methodology Course in an Age of Deconstruction.' Mimeographed. School of Education, La Trobe University, Australia.

Yin, Robert K. 1994. *Case Study Research: Design and Methods.* 2nd ed. Thousand Oaks, Calif.: Sage.

Young Adult Institute (YAI). n.d. *The YAI Policy for Determining Sexual Consent.* New York. Author.

Index

Date Due